Return to the Silk Routes

Return to the Silk Routes

Current Scandinavian Research
on Central Asia

EDITED BY

Mirja Juntunen & Birgit N. Schlyter

KEGAN PAUL INTERNATIONAL
LONDON AND NEW YORK

First published in 1999 by
Kegan Paul International
UK: P.O. Box 256, London WC1B 3SW, England
Tel: (0171) 580 5511 Fax: (0171) 436 0899
E-mail: books@keganpau.demon.co.uk
Internet: http://www.demon.co.uk/keganpaul/
USA: 562 West 113th Street, New York, NY, 10025, USA
Tel: (212) 666 1000 Fax: (212) 316 3100

Distributed by
John Wiley & Sons Ltd
Southern Cross Trading Estate
1 Oldlands Way, Bognor Regis
West Sussex, PO22 9SA, England
Tel: (01243) 779 777 Fax: (01243) 820 250

Columbia University Press
562 West 113th Street
New York, NY 10025, USA
Tel: (212) 666 1000 Fax: (212) 316 3100

© Institute of Oriental Languages, Stockholm University, 1999

Printed in Great Britain by Short Run Press Ltd, Exeter, Devon

All rights reserved. No part of this book may be reprinted or reproduced or utilized in any form or by any electronic, mechanical or other means, now known or hereafter invented, including photocopying and recording, or in any information storage or retrieval system, without permission in writing from the publishers.

ISBN: 0-7103-0608-3

British Library Cataloguing in Publication Data
Return to the silk routes: current Scandinavian research on Central Asia
1. Asia, Central - History 2. Asia, Central - Civilization
I. Schlyter, Birgit N. II. Juntunen, Mirja
958

ISBN: 0-7103-0608-3

Library of Congress Cataloging-in-Publication Data
Return to the silk routes: current Scandinavian research on
Central Asia / edited by Birgit N. Schlyter and Mirja Juntunen.
p. cm.
Includes bibliographical references.
ISBN 0-7103-0608-3 (alk. Paper)
1. Asia, Central. J I. Schlyter, Birgit N. II. Juntunen, Mirja.
DS327.5.R47   1998
958--dc21   97-50188
                    CIP

*To Gunnar Jarring,
for his great knowledge and
generous attitude towards
fellow researchers*

Contents

Preface *ix*

Remarks on Transcription and Spelling *x*

CENTRAL ASIA RESEARCH – A BACKGROUND

Nordic Research on Central Asia: Past, Present and Future *3*
Mirja Juntunen & Birgit N. Schlyter

Marginal Centrality: Central Asian Studies on the Eve of a New Millennium *23*
John Schoeberlein

ARCHAEOLOGY

Chinese Excavations at Turfan *47*
Susanne Juhl

The Sino-Swedish Expedition to Yar-tonguz in 1994 *59*
Staffan Rosén

RELIGION

Superscribing the Hegemonic Image of Chinggis Khan in the *Erdeni Tunumal Sudur* *75*
Johan Elverskog

'They only weep ...': Stories about Tibetan Travellers to the Other Worlds *87*
Per-Arne Berglie

LANGUAGE

Regional Aspects of the Turkic Influence on Mongolian *99*
Maria Magdolna Tatár

Remarks on the Mongolian Vowel System *109*
Vivan Franzén & Jan-Olof Svantesson

Towards a Sociolinguistic History of Sinkiang *119*
Joakim Enwall

POLITICAL ASPECTS

Russia and Post-Soviet Central Asia: Reintegration Ahead? *135*
Bo Petersson

Democracy versus Stability in Kazakstan *149*
Marianne Øhlers

War and Change in Afghanistan: Reflections on Research Priorities *167*
Kristian Berg Harpviken

Biographical Notes on the Contributors *187*

Preface

As will be further explained in our introductory chapter, the rest of the contributions to this volume have their origin in a symposium which was held in Stockholm on 27–29 September 1996 under the Swedish title of *Nordisk Centralasienforskning: språk – kultur – samhälle*, i.e. 'Nordic Central Asia Research: Language – Culture – Society'. The main purpose of this meeting was to obtain a general view of current research activities and study programmes in this field and to help establish contact between Central Asia researchers in the Nordic countries. Therefore, by designating a general theme for the symposium we hoped to attract most Nordic scholars and graduate students involved in Central Asia research to the Stockholm symposium.

This symposium was prepared by a working committee from the Institute of Oriental Languages at Stockholm University consisting of Joakim Enwall, Mirja Juntunen, Staffan Rosén and Birgit N. Schlyter. The symposium and the present volume were sponsored by generous grants from the Nordic Academy of Advanced Study, Oslo, and the Swedish Council for Research in the Humanities and Social Sciences, Stockholm. A travel grant was obtained from the Wenner-Gren Center, Stockholm.

Participants in each of the fields represented at the symposium were invited to submit their papers for publication. Our first chapter, which gives a brief historical background to the ensuing articles, was written with the aid of information received from several persons in different parts of the Nordic countries: Christel Braae, Bernt Brendemoen, Ole Bruun, Gerd Carling, Ester Fihl, Anette Jensen, Folke Josephson, Pål Kolstø, Ida Nicolaisen, Staffan Rosén, Volker Rybatzki, Erik Skaaning, Ingvar Svanberg, Per Sørensen and Bo Utas. The Nordic Institute of Asian Studies, Copenhagen, made its contribution by offering one of the present editors an opportunity to use its library and benefit from the good services of its librarians. The renowned Swedish scholar and ambassador, Professor Gunnar Jarring, to whom this book is dedicated, has also been engaged in our work. His long experience and excellent memory as well as his keen interest in present-day research on Central Asia render his comments and advice an extraordinary status.

Consultants for questions on the English language were Judith Monk, William Smith and Michael Stevens.

Kräftriket, Stockholm
June 1998
The Editors

Remarks on Transcription and Spelling

It has been our ambition to keep as coherent a spelling as possible throughout the book, with certain exceptions; for example, the two American contributors were permitted to retain their American spelling where it differs from British spelling (as in *neighbor, center* etc.). Quoted titles in English, including translations from other languages, were everywhere spelt with capital initial letters in prominent words.

Quotations, lexical items and references to publications originally in non-Latin scripts were transliterated according to international scientific standards; for example, for Chinese we followed the Pinyin scheme convention. Names appearing in the main text (not references), on the other hand, were treated in a somewhat different manner. Geographical names and the names of languages and dialects, both transcribed ones and names originally in the Latin script, were rendered in a common English spelling, as long as there was one (e.g. *Peking,* not *Beijing*, and *Sinkiang*, not *Xinjiang*, *Aarhus*, instead of Danish *Århus*, and *Gothenburg*, instead of Swedish *Göteborg*). Where there were alternatives, each more or less as frequent as the other, either of them was chosen for all articles. For example, *Tajikistan* was preferred to *Tadzhikistan* under the motivation that the affricate sound [dz] is represented by the letter *j* in most other transcribed names (e.g. *Jigda-bulung* and *Jungaria*). As to personal and institutional names in the Latin script, these were spelt as we have most often seen them written in the country of their origin (e.g. Norwegian *Kværne* and Danish *Grønbech, Moesgård*). Proper names originally spelt in other alphabets were rewritten in accordance with conventions adhered to in the English mass media; e.g. *Yeltsin* and *Turkmenbashi*, not *Elcin* and *Turkmenbašy*, which would be standard scientific transliterations of the Russian Cyrillic and Turkmen Cyrillic versions of these two names, respectively. In a small number of cases, for example, less common Mongolian names, the aforementioned transliteration standards were followed (e.g. Xürëlbaatar).

Central Asia Research - A Background

Nordic Research on Central Asia
Past, Present and Future

MIRJA JUNTUNEN AND BIRGIT N. SCHLYTER

After decades of political seclusion, the vast region of Central Asia – from the Caspian Sea to the Khingan Mountains and from the Iranian Plateau and the Himalayas to the Siberian Steppes – is in a process of profound sociocultural metamorphosis and reassertion. This state of affairs challenges present-day and future Central Asia research by making demands for new knowledge and perhaps even a new outlook on the organization of the research itself; a new era has started in Central Asian studies.

Central Asia research in Scandinavia and more generally, the Nordic countries, has a long and rich tradition to fall back on but is today entering a new state of development and expansion, in a fashion similar to Central Asia research elsewhere in the international community. The following chapters, most of which are reports from ongoing projects on contemporary Central Asian settings and based on papers read at a symposium held in Stockholm in 1996, further elucidate the course of development and future perspectives in this field of research.[1]

Nordic scientific contacts with the Central Asian region started in the early 18th century, after the defeat of the Swedish King Charles XII at Poltava and the capture of his army by the Russian enemy. Some of these prisoners of war were sent to the woodlands and steppes in the eastern parts of the Russian empire, where they became interested in and acquainted with the people and languages as well as the geography of the area. When

---

[1] For this chapter an attempt was made to cover Central Asia research in all the Nordic countries of Denmark, Finland, Iceland, Norway and Sweden. The reason for referring to Scandinavia in the title of the whole volume is that the account of current research projects in the present chapter and the symposium from which the manuscripts of the book originated were confined to persons and institutions in Denmark, Norway and Sweden (cf. the comment on p. 16).

they were finally released by the tsar and returned to Sweden, these early explorers of North-East and Central Asia brought back with them valuable future research material including Tibetan and Mongolian manuscripts.[2]

The Governor General of Siberia, Prince Gagarin, realized the importance and ability of the Swedes and allowed them to travel without hindrance in this vast area. The most famous of them, Philipp Johann von Strahlenberg (1676–1747), travelled extensively in Siberia during his captivity, which lasted some sixteen years. His book published in Stockholm in 1730 and entitled *Das nord- und ostliche Theil von Europa und Asien*[3] was one of the first accounts of the region beyond the Ural Mountains. Another Swede, Ambjörn Molin (d. 1731), a cavalry captain, who was on an expedition organized by Prince Gagarin to the shores of the Pacific Ocean, wrote a book about the people in North-East Asia.[4] The journey of Johann Christopher Schnitscher resulted in a book about the Kalmucks and their folklore, traditions and religion.[5] Johan Gustaf Renat (1682–1744), an artillery-sergeant, who took part in an expedition sent to Central Asia to look for gold sand, was even more closely acquainted with the Kalmucks, as he and his first wife, Brita Scherzenfeldt, were held prisoner by them for several years. Before Renat's release, the Kalmuck khan presented him with two maps of Jungaria. Renat made a Swedish version, a copy of which, drawn in 1738, was published after almost 150 years of oblivion along with an introduction, comments and an index in French.[6]

---

[2] The manuscripts are preserved at the university libraries of Uppsala and Lund; see Helmut Eimer, *Tibetica Upsaliensia: Handliste der tibetischen Handschriften in der Universitätsbibliothek zu Uppsala* (Bibliotheca Ekmaniana 66), Uppsala 1975.

[3] A facsimile of the original work was published in *Studia Uralo-Altaica* 8, Szeged 1975, with an introduction by J. K. Krueger.

[4] Ambjörn Molin, *Berättelse om de i Stora Tartariet boende Tartarer som träffats längst nordost i Asien*, Stockholm 1880.

[5] Johann Christopher Schnitscher, *Berättelse om Ajuckiniska Calmuckiet, eller om detta folks ursprung, huru de kommit under Ryssarnas lydno, deras gudar, gudsdyrkan och prester, huru de skiftas uti 4 Ulusser eller folkhopar, deras politique och philosophie, med flera deras lefwernes sätt och seder så wid bröllop som begrafningar*, Stockholm 1744.

[6] John Gustaf Renat, *Carte de la Dzoungarie dressée par le suédois Renat pendant sa captivité chez les Kalmouks de 1716-1733. Édition de la Société impériale russe de géographie*, St. Péterbourg 1881. All of the Renat maps have been thoroughly commented on in John F. Baddeley, *Russia, Mongolia, China*, vol. 1, London 1919, pp. clxvi-ccxvi. The person mainly instrumental in the rediscovery, at the end of the last century, of the Central Asian adventures of Renat and his fellow Carolingian officers was August Strindberg, who then worked as an assistant at the Royal Library in Stockholm and who later became one of Sweden's best-known writers; cf. Gunnar Jarring, 'Swedish Relations

Scandinavian explorers in Central Asia

After more than a century with hardly any contacts at all, a new Scandinavian interest focused on Central Asia when a large number of expeditions to the region were undertaken towards the end of the 19th century and in the first few decades of the 20th. Between 1890 and 1935 the Swedish explorer Sven Hedin (1865–1952) went out on six long expeditions, which took him on different routes through the western parts of Central Asia and the terrifying Takla-makan desert as far as Lake Lop-nor and Tibet. His renowned *Central Asia Atlas* and other maps by his hand are still excellent sources of information as regards Central Asian toponomy[7] – a field of research of the utmost importance to our understanding of extinct languages along the Silk Routes in Central Asia. Furthermore, Sven Hedin brought back to Sweden important archaeological material from Khotan and it was he who discovered the desert town of Loulan in the vicinity of Lop-nor. The most extensive and important Hedin expedition was the last, made between 1927 and 1935. Hedin travelled with a large multidisciplinary team of more than 40 specialists of different nationalities including archaeologists, geologists, ethnographers and many others. The aim of the expedition was to explore, among other areas, Inner Mongolia, the Tarim basin, Tianshan and the north-western part of Tibet. The extensive Hedin collection – maps, drawings, photos, scientific notations etc. and Hedin's own writings – is kept at the National Museum of Ethnography, Stockholm.[8]

The Mongolian texts in the Hedin Collection containing material from various fields of Central Asian studies have been carefully catalogued by Pentti Aalto[9], the productive Finnish scholar, who himself has published a

---

with Central Asia and Swedish Central Asian Research', *Asian Affairs. Journal of the Royal Central Asian Society* 61 (1974), pp. 257–266.

[7] See e.g. D. M. Farquhar, G. Jarring and E. Norin, *Sven Hedin Central Asia Atlas: Memoir on Maps, Vol. II: Index of Geographical Names* (Reports from the Scientific Expedition to the North-Western Provinces of China under the Leadership of Dr. Sven Hedin, I:3 Geography, Publication 49), Stockholm 1967.

[8] In 1992 an international symposium on 'Central Asian Studies in the 20th Century and the Legacy of Sven Hedin' was held in Urumchi in Sinkiang. There were some 70 participants from six different countries including members of the board of the Sven Hedin Foundation in Sweden (Staffan Rosén, Håkan Wahlquist, Bertil Nordenstam); see the symposium volume Ma Dazheng, Wang Rong and Yang Lian (eds), *Xiyu kaocha yu yanjiu* [Studies and Research on the Western Region], Ulumuqi [Urumchi] 1994.

[9] Pentti Aalto, 'A Catalogue of the Hedin Collection of Mongolian Literature', in *Contributions to Ethnography, Linguistics and History of Religion* (Reports from the Scientific Expedition to the North-Western Provinces of China under the Leadership of

great number of works on Mongolian philology and ethnography as well as on topics relating to Indo-European cultural traits in the eastern part of Central Asia.[10]

Explorers and adventurers from other Nordic countries also deserve mention. Two Danish Pamir expeditions headed by Lieutenant Ole Olufsen (1865–1929) set out in the late 1890s.[11] The Finnish geographer Johannes Gabriel Granö (1882–1956) toured the southern parts of Siberia, Mongolia and the Altay Mountains.[12] The Finnish Colonel, later Field-Marshal, Carl Gustaf Mannerheim (1867–1951), travelled on horseback from the Caspian Sea to Peking passing among other places the Swedish missionary station in Kashghar (see below).[13] Henning Haslund-Christensen (1896–1948) from Denmark had participated in Sven Hedin's 1927–1930 expedition as a caravan leader.[14] Inspired by the experiences gained during this journey he organized expeditions of his own to Mongolia[15] and Afghanistan. He died in Kabul in 1948, just as he had started his third expedition. His companions went on with the work and remained in Afghanistan until 1954, studying various

---

Dr. Sven Hedin, Publication 38), Stockholm 1953, pp. 69–108. A useful bibliography on Mongolian studies in Sweden is Ingvar Svanberg and Eva-Charlotte Ekström, *Mongolica Suecana: Bibliography of Swedish Books and Articles on Mongolia* (Uppsala Multiethnic Papers 3), 2nd edition, Uppsala 1988.

[10] For a bibliography of publications by Pentti Aalto, see *Studia Orientalia* 47 (1977), pp. 287–311.

[11] See e.g. O. Olufsen, *Through the Unknown Pamirs: The Second Danish Pamir Expedition, 1898–99* (with maps and numerous illustrations), New York 1969 (reprint of the 1904 edition, published by William Heinemann, London). Olufsen and his colleagues not only explored the Pamir region but travelled extensively in Western Turkestan and spent some time in both the Khanate of Khiva and the Emirate of Bukhara as well as in Merv in present-day Turkestan; see id., *The Emir of Bokhara and his Country*, Copenhagen and London 1911, and notice the reference to a forthcoming volume in footnote 33.

[12] Johannes Gabriel Granö, *Altai: Upplevelser och iakttagelser under mina vandringsår*, 1–2, Helsingfors 1919–1921.

[13] Mannerheim's diaries were published in id., *Across Asia from West to East in 1906–1908* (Travaux éthnographiques de la Société finno-ougrienne 8), Helsinki 1940.

[14] Thanks to Haslund-Christensen's love of Mongolian music we have today a unique and large collection of Mongolian folk songs, the greater part of which he recorded during the first Sino-Swedish Expedition. The recordings are now in the possession of the Swedish Broadcasting Corporation. The musical material, including a translation of the texts by Kaare Grønbech, was published in *The Music of the Mongols. Part 1. Eastern Mongolia* (Reports from the Scientific Expedition to the North-Western Provinces of China under the Leadership of Dr. Sven Hedin, Publication 21) Stockholm 1943. See also footnote 33 on p. 11.

[15] Henning Haslund-Christensen's Mongolian adventures are related in his *Asiatiske strejftog. Med tegninger af Lodai Lama fra Khalka-Mongoliet*, København 1945.

aspects of Afghan geography and Afghan nomadism.[16] One member of this team, Klaus Ferdinand from Aarhus, later headed a number of Danish Scientific Missions to Afghanistan in the 1960s and 1970s. Collections made by the Danish expeditions are kept at the National Museum and the Royal Library in Copenhagen and at the Moesgård Museum in Aarhus.

The Scandinavian participants of the 1927 Hedin expedition. From left to right: Georg Söderbom, Folke Bergman, David Hummel, Erik Norin, Henning Haslund-Christensen, Frans August Larsson and Sven Hedin. A picture from YMER (Tidskrift utgiven av Svenska sällskapet för antropologi och geografi) 71:3 (1951), p. 163 (Photo: Lieberenz)

---

[16] See e.g. Johannes Humlum, *La géographie de l'Afghanistan: étude d'un pays aride avec des chapitres de M. Køie et K. Ferdinand,* Copenhague–Oslo–Helsinki 1959, and Klaus Ferdinand, 'Preliminary Notes on Hazāra Culture (The Danish Scientific Mission to Afghanistan 1953–55)', *Det Kgl. Danske Videnskabernes Selskab. Historisk–filologiske meddelelser* 37:5 (1959).

Previous research on Central Asian topics

In addition to what had been collected by King Charles' officers, material acquired and experience gained by participants in various Scandinavian expeditions and by single Nordic explorers constituted the basis for later scholarly works in general history, philology, archaeology, ethnography, religion, cartography, geology and other disciplines.[17]

The turn of the century was a period of comparative philology, and several scholars from Scandinavia and Finland were engaged in Central Asian linguistic research. Runic inscriptions on the shores of the Yenisey River had been discovered by the above-mentioned von Strahlenberg already in the 18th century, and more material was collected by, among others, Charles Schulman (1721), Johan Reinhold Aspelin (1889) and Axel Olai Heikel (1890). With access to these findings the Danish Professor of Comparative Philology in Copenhagen, Vilhelm Thomsen (1842–1927), succeeded in deciphering the Old Turkic Orkhon inscriptions from the 8th century,[18] which are the oldest Turkic texts known. Thomsen's achievement gave a very substantial impetus to Turkological and Altaic research, which was continued in his own country by Vilhelm Grønbech (1873–1948) and his son Kaare Grønbech (1901–1957)[19] as well as Kaare Thomsen Hansen (1924–1997). An outstanding representative of Altaic philology in Finland was Professor Gustaf John Ramstedt (1873–1950), who carried out extensive fieldwork of his own in Central Asia.[20] The first Finnish Turkologist of

---

[17] The scientific outcome of the Swedish Carolingian research was documented by Sven Hedin in the first volume of his *Southern Tibet: Discoveries in Former Times Compared with my own Researches in 1906–1908*, Vol. 1–9, Atlas, Maps 1–2. Stockholm 1917–1922. A bibliography of Swedish publications on Central Asia up to the 1990s compiled by Ingvar Svanberg appeared in Staffan Rosén and Bo Utas (eds), *Det okända Centralasien – en utmaning för svensk forskning*, Uppsala 1994. Other accounts of the history of Central Asia research in the North are found in e.g. Pentti Aalto, *Oriental Studies in Finland 1828–1918* (The History of Learning and Science in Finland 1828–1918), Helsinki 1971, Klaus Karttunen, *Itää etsimässä: Eurooppalaisen Aasiantutkimuksen vaiheita*, Helsinki 1992, and K. V. Jensen (ed.), *Dannebrog på stepperne*, Institut for Orientalsk Filologi, Københavns Universitet, København 1988.

[18] Vilhelm Thomsen, 'Déchiffrement des inscriptions de l'Orkhon et de l'Iénisséi, notice préliminaire', *Oversigt over Det Kgl. Danske Videnskabernes Selskaps Forhandlinger...*, København 1893, pp. 285–299.

[19] Among the best-known works by the latter are K. Grönbech, *Der türkische Sprachbau*, Kopenhagen 1936, and id., *Komanisches Wörterbuch: Türkischer Wortindex*, Kopenhagen 1942.

[20] Besides the handbook G. J. Ramstedt, *Einführung in die altaische Sprachwissenschaft* (Société finno-ougrienne. Mém. 104), 3 vols, Helsinki 1952–1966, which appeared after

great prominence was Martti Räsänen (1893–1976) with comprehensive works on Turkic historical phonology, morphology and etymologies.[21]

A special source of inspiration for Swedish philological studies on Central Asia, besides the Hedin expeditions, was the Swedish mission to Eastern Turkestan, present-day Sinkiang, 1892–1938.[22] The first missionary station was set up in Kashghar in 1892 by the Rev. N. F. Höjer. In addition to their ordinary religious duties, the missionaries devoted much time to humanitarian work as well as to scholarly and cultural activities, such as publishing and printing books. One of them, Gustaf Raquette, who was also a doctor of tropical medicine and a linguist, compiled a grammar of Eastern Turki.[23] His scientific work at Lund was continued by Gunnar Jarring (b. 1907), who had been in Kashghar in his twenties to study the Uighur language and collect material. The months spent in Kashghar were the beginning of Jarring's long and successful career as a Turkologist.[24] Part of his own collection of Turkological literature was donated to the University Library in Lund, where Gunnar Jarring was Associate Professor of Turkic languages for a short period before he started his eminent career as a Swedish diplomat. Still active at the age of 90, Ambassador Jarring has completed a huge work on the Central Asian Turkic place names that appear in Sven Hedin's

---

his death, Ramstedt also published works on Kalmuck, Korean and Pashto. A list of publications by G. J. Ramstedt can be found in *Studia Orientalia* 14:12 (1950).

[21] See e.g. Martti Räsänen, *Versuch eines etymologischen Wörterbuchs der Türksprachen*, Helsinki 1969. Bibliographies of Räsänen's works were published in *Studia Orientalia* 19:13 (1954) and *Studia Orientalia* 28:17 (1964).

[22] See, for example, John Hultvall, *Mission och revolution i Centralasien: Svenska Missionsförbundets mission i Östturkestan 1892–1938*, Stockholm 1981.

[23] Gustaf Raquette, *Eastern Turki Grammar: Practical and Theoretical with Vocabulary (I–III)*, Berlin 1912–1914.

[24] Gunnar Jarring's doctoral thesis was *Studien zu einer osttürkischen Lautlehre*, Lund 1933. This pioneering work was later followed up by *An Eastern Turki-English Dialect Dictionary*, Lund 1964. His *opus magnum*, with presentations and analyses of philological and ethnological material from his own fieldwork in Eastern Turkestan, is id., *Materials to the Knowledge of Eastern Turki: Tales, Poetry, Proverbs, Riddles, Ethnological and Historical Texts from the Southern Parts of Eastern Turkestan. With Translations and Notes*, 4 vols, Lund 1946–1951. Recently, this work appeared in an Uighur translation (Beijing 1997). Publications by Gunnar Jarring have been listed in Christopher Toll and Ulla Ehrensvärd, *Gunnar Jarring: En bibliografi*, Stockholm 1977, Ulla Ehrensvärd (ed.), *Turcica et Orientalia: Studies in Honour of Gunnar Jarring on his Eightieth Birthday 12 October 1987*, Swedish Research Institute in Istanbul, Transactions 1, Stockholm 1988, pp. 192–204, and Ulla Ehrensvärd, *Gunnar Jarring: En bibliografi 1988–1997*, Stockholm 1997.

of a Central Asian section at the Asia Library that was recently opened at the Institute of Oriental Languages in Stockholm by donating an impressive collection of books on the ethnography, languages and history of Central Asia, especially Eastern Turkestan.[26]

Recent works on Central Asian Turkic languages in other Nordic countries have been published by, *inter alia*, Even Hovdhaugen (Norway), Juha Janhunen (Finland) and Volker Rybatzki (Finland).[27]

As to Indo-European languages, the Norwegian indologist Sten Konow (1867–1948) distinguished himself through studies on Khotanese Saka and became a leading scholar in the field of north-eastern Iranian languages.[28] One of his students, Georg von Munthe af Morgenstierne (1892–1978), became an expert on Indo-Iranian frontier languages.[29] Prods O. Skjærvø continued the Oslo tradition of Khotanese studies before leaving Norway for Harvard University. Iranian studies in Sweden, which owe their solid foundation to the legendary scholar of Semitic and Iranian languages, Professor H. S. Nyberg (1889–1974) at Uppsala University, also comprise specific works focusing on the Central Asian region or areas bordering on this region.[30] Nordic contributions to research on Tokharian were made first

---

Attempt at Classification and Explanation Based on Sven Hedin's Diaries and Published Works (Reports from the Scientific Expedition to the North-Western Provinces of China under the Leadership of Dr. Sven Hedin, VII:11 Ethnography, Publication 56), Stockholm 1997.

[26] This donation was made possible by financial support from the Swedish Royal Academy of Letters History and Antiquities.

[27] Before entering the broader field of general linguistics Even Hovdhaugen wrote on various Turkic languages, among them Old Turkic from the 8th century Turkic inscriptions in his article 'The Relationship between the Two Orkhon Inscriptions', *Acta Orientalia* 36 (1974), pp. 55–82. Juha Janhunen is conducting research on an Altaic basis. His publications include articles on eastern Turkic languages, such as Sayan Turkic, Khakas and Shor. Besides ethnological studies on Turkic as well as Mongolian documents, Volker Rybatzki has recently published an extensive work on 'Die Inschrift des Toñuquq', *Studia Uralo-Altaica* 40, Szeged 1997.

[28] See e.g. *Zwei Handschriftenblätter der alten arischen Sprache aus Chinesisch-Turkestan*, Oslo 1912, and *Khotansakische Grammatik*, Oslo 1941. A list of Konow's works was published in *Norsk Bibliografisk Bibliotek* 3:5 (1942), pp. 92–103. See also R. E. Emmerick, *A Guide to the Literature of Khotan* (Studia Philologica Buddhica: Occasional Paper Series III), 2nd rev. ed., Tokyo 1982, p. 8, for later publications by Konow concerning Khotanese. One of the most important collections of Khotanese documents is included in the Hedin collection at the National Museum of Ethnography in Stockholm.

[29] Georg von Munthe af Morgenstierne, *Indo-Iranian Frontier Languages*, 2nd rev. ed. and with new material, 4 vols, Oslo 1973.

[30] For example, Bo Utas, 'The Jewish-Persian Fragment from Dandan-Uiliq', *Orientalia Suecana* 17 (1968/1969), pp. 123–136, and Carina Jahani, *Standardization and*

and foremost by the Icelander Jörundur Hilmarsson (1946–1992).[31] In 1987, Hilmarsson founded the scholarly journal *Tocharian and Indo-European Studies*. After his far too early death in 1992, the editorship of this journal was handed over to Jens Elmegård Rasmussen, lecturer of Indo-European languages at Copenhagen. In Sweden, studies and research on Tokharian were supported and encouraged by Folke Josephson, Professor of Indo-European Comparative Philology and Sanskrit at Gothenburg.

The collections and publications resulting from Nordic expeditions as well as those coming from the Swedish Missionary Board have also provided a rich source of material for studies in religion, ethnology and ethnography.[32] In Finland, Harry Halén has worked on materials collected by such explorers and fieldworkers as the aforementioned A. O. Heikel, C. G. Mannerheim and G. J. Ramstedt. The broadest Scandinavian programme in this field at present is perhaps that of the Danish Nomad Research Project funded by the Carlsberg Foundation, which publishes a series of books both on materials from previous Danish expeditions and on more recent Danish fieldwork in the Central Asian region including Tibet, Mongolia and Afghanistan. Head and Editor-in-Chief of the project is the ethnographer Ida Nicolaisen, presently at the Nordic Institute of Asian Studies, Copenhagen. In the years to come volumes will be published on the legacies of the two previously mentioned Danish explorers, Ole Olufsen and Henning Haslund-Christensen.[33] Nordic university institutes with at least some continuous lecturing or publication on Central Asia from an ethnological and anthropological point of view are the Institute of Anthropology at Copenhagen (Ole Bruun), the Institute of Ethnography and the Department of Slavic languages at Aarhus (Esther

---

Orthography in the Balochi Language, Uppsala 1989.

[31] Jörundur Hilmarsson's doctoral thesis bears the title *Studies in Tocharian Phonology, Morphology and Etymology*, Reykjavík 1986. See also, id., *Materials for a Tocharian Historical and Etymological Dictionary*, Reykjavík 1996. A list of Hilmarsson's publications will be found in *Tocharian and Indo-European Studies* 6 (1993), pp. 11–14.

[32] The chief organizer and analyst of the ethnographic discoveries during the last Hedin expedition was Gösta Montell (1899–1975). See, for example, Gösta Montell, 'As Ethnographer in China and Mongolia 1929–1932', *History of the Expedition in Asia 1927–1935, Part IV: General Reports of Travels and Field-Work* (Reports from the Scientific Expedition to the North-Western Provinces of China under the Leadership of Dr. Sven Hedin, Publication 26), Stockholm 1945, pp. 329–449. Two collections of photographs from the Swedish missionary stations in Sinkiang, the so-called Fränne and Moen collections, are to be found at the Swedish National Archives in Stockholm.

[33] A book about Ole Olufsen by Esther Fihl, *Exploring Central Asia*, is due in 1999. Three book projects have been started on Haslund-Christensen's collections from Mongolia in the 1930s focusing on pastoralism (Christel Braae), folk music (Annette Erler) and Shaman costumes (Rolf Gilberg).

Fihl and Anette Jensen, respectively) and the Centre of Multiethnic Research at Uppsala.

Tibetan studies in Scandinavia have to a large extent been conducted within the sphere of religion. On the basis of Tibetan manuscripts from the Hedin collection Nils Simonsson (1920–1994) has demonstrated the significance of Tibetan translations in the interpretation of Sanskrit Buddhist texts.[34] Toni Schmid (1897–1972) also turned to the Hedin collection in her pioneering studies on Tibetan Buddhist scrolls.[35] Per-Arne Berglie, Professor of Comparative Religion at Stockholm University, has conducted research on ritual possession among the Tibetans, at the same time as the Gesar epic in Central Asia has caught his attention.[36] The Norwegian scholars Jens Braarvig[37] and Per Kværne,[38] have contributed to our understanding of Tibetan Buddhism. Tibetology in Denmark was firmly established through works by Erik Haarh (1929–1993).[39] Before he was appointed Professor of

---

[34] See, for example, his doctoral dissertation *Indo-tibetische Studien. Die Methoden der tibetischen Übersetzer, untersucht im Hinblick auf die Bedeutung ihrer Übersetzungen für die Sanskritphilologie*, Uppsala 1957, and numerous articles published later. A bibliography of Nils Simonsson is to be found in the volume Eivind Kahrs (ed.), *Kalyāṇamitrārāgaṇam: Essays in Honour of Nils Simonsson*, Oxford 1986. A complete list of Tibetan manuscripts in the Hedin Collection has not yet been published. See, however, the preliminary handlist of Helmut Eimer, 'Tibetica Stockholmiensia I–VII: Handliste der tibetischen Texte der Sven Hedin-Stiftung und des Etnographischen Museums zu Stockholm', *Zentralasiatische Studien* 6–12 (1972–1978).

[35] Tibetan Buddhist scrolls (*thankas*) and plates from the Sven Hedin collections were published in Toni Schmid, *The Eighty-Five Siddhas*, id., *Saviours of Mankind [I]: Dalai Lamas and Former Incarnations of Avalokiteśvara*, and id. *Saviours of Mankind II: Panchen Lamas and Former Incarnations of Amitāyus*, which were Reports from the Scientific Expedition to the North-Western Provinces of China under the Leadership of Dr. Sven Hedin, Publications 42, 45 and 46, Stockholm 1958, 1961 and 1964, respectively.

[36] For spirit-possession, cf. his doctoral dissertation, Per-Arne Berglie, *Gudarna stiger ned: Rituell besatthet hos sherpas och tibetaner*, Stockholm 1983, as well as his contribution to this volume. For the Gesar epic, see id., 'Spirit-Mediums and the Epic: Remarks on Gesar and the Epic Among Spirit-Mediums in Tibet and Ladakh', *Shaman* 4:1–2 (1996), pp. 17–26.

[37] Cf. his doctoral thesis on a Buddhist text in Tibetan, critically edited and translated: Jens Braarvig, *Akṣayamatirnirdeśasūtra: Edition of Extant Manuscripts with an Index*, Oslo 1988, and id., *The Akṣayamatirnirdeśasūtra and the Tradition of Imperishability in Buddhist Thought*, Oslo 1989.

[38] One main work is Per Kværne, *An Anthology of Buddhist Tantric Songs: A Study of the Caryāgīti*, Oslo–Bergen–Tromsø 1977, with extensive comments on Tibetan connections. He has also written on the Tibetan Bon religion; one short paper is Per Kværne, 'Religious Change and Syncretism: The Case of the Bon Religion of Tibet', in *Bon, Buddhism and Democracy: The Building of a Tibetan National Identity* (NIAS Report no. 12), København 1993, pp. 9–26.

[39] His doctoral dissertation bears the title *The Yar-luṅ Dynasty: A Study with Particular Regard to the Contribution by Myths and Legends to the History of Ancient Tibet and*

the History of Religion at Aarhus, Haarh worked as Head of Department at the Danish Royal Library in Copenhagen, which houses one of the largest book collections of Tibetan and Mongolian studies in Europe. The Danish traditions of Tibetan studies have been carried on by Per Sørensen,[40] who is now working at Leipzig as Head of the Department of Central Asian Languages.

Furthermore, in the field of Central Asian religions, the Swedish scholar Geo Widengren (1907–1997), the former Professor at the Department of the History of Religion at Uppsala, touched upon Eastern Manichaeism,[41] as did Peter Bryder from Lund a quarter of the century later.[42]

Less Nordic research has been carried out on Central Asian Islam. Survey articles on Islam in former Soviet Central Asia, Afghanistan and Sinkiang were published in a volume about Islam outside the Arab world.[43] Another contribution is a recent investigation into the political role of Islam in Afghanistan.[44]

Present-day projects on contemporary Central Asia

In dealing with all the various facets of present-day sociocultural reidentification in the Central Asian region, future Central Asia research will require much interdisciplinary work. One field gaining great attention at present is the process of forming and consolidating new states in the former Soviet Central Asia.[45] This process calls for coordinated analyses by

---

the Origin and Nature of its Kings, København 1969.

[40] Per K. Sørensen, *The Mirror Illuminating the Royal Genealogies: Tibetan Buddhist Historiography: An Annotated Translation of the XIVth Century Tibetan Chronicle: rGyal-rabs gsal-ba'i me-long*, Wiesbaden 1994.

[41] Geo Widengren, *Mani und Manicheismus*, Stuttgart 1961. Also in English translation: *Mani and Manichaeism*, London 1965.

[42] Peter Bryder, *The Chinese Transformation of Manichaeism: A Study of Chinese Manichaean Terminology*, Lund 1985.

[43] Ingvar Svanberg and David Westerlund (eds), *Majoritetens Islam: Om muslimer utanför arabvärlden*, Stockholm 1994.

[44] Asta Olesen, *Islam and Politics in Afghanistan*, Richmond 1995.

[45] A recent Swedish publication in this field is Bo Petersson and Ingvar Svanberg (eds), *Det nya Centralasien: Fem forna sovjetrepubliker i omvandling*, Lund 1996. A book on similar transformation to a new economic and political order in the former Soviet satellite state of Mongolia is Ole Bruun and Ole Odgaard (eds), *Mongolia in Transition: Old Patterns, New Challenges*, Nordic Institute of Asian Studies, London 1996. As to the complexity of ethnicity and nationalism, see Alf Grannes and Daniel

political scientists, socioanthropologists, linguists and philologists as well as researchers into the history of religions and others. A number of Scandinavian research projects of this character already exist.

Studies on nation-building are being carried out at the Norwegian Institute of Urban and Regional Research (NIBR), Oslo. Two projects headed by Arne Tesli and Pål Kolstø are entitled 'Political Mobilization, Rhetoric and Social Differentiation in Kazakhstan, Uzbekistan and the Horn of Africa' and 'Integration and Nation-Building in Bifurcated Post-Soviet Societies: the Cases of Latvia and Kazakhstan'. In one report related to these two projects, 'Territorial and Ethno-Cultural Self-Government in Nation-Building Kazakhstan',[46] the author, Jørn Holm-Hansen, discusses the nation-building strategies practised in Kazakstan and their ties to both the Russian-Soviet heritage and to ethnic and/or tribal loyalties. The russification of Kazakhstan is far-reaching and the so-called ethnic Kazaks are furthermore divided among three territorially but also culturally distinct super-tribes. Successful nation-building in Kazakstan must, according to the author, be a balance act between practices of territorial self-government aiming at state unity and self-government permitting ethno-cultural diversity. Local self-government is stronger in Kazakstan than elsewhere in the former Soviet Central Asia, although the central regime is careful to maintain its ability to overrule local decisions and prevent tendencies towards federalization and secession.

Sociolinguistic projects on language development and language policy in Central Asia have been started at the Institute of Oriental Languages, Stockholm, with the aid of grants from the Swedish Council for Research in the Humanities and Social Sciences. In a report on the project 'Language Renewal in Uzbekistan: From Russified Standard Uzbek to a New National Language', Birgit N. Schlyter examines the language laws which were passed by the Uzbek Parliament shortly before and after the disintegration of the Soviet Union.[47] Uzbek language planning, which is an important part

---

Heradstveit, *Etnisk Nasjonalisme: Folkegrupper og konflikter i Kaukasia og Sentral-Asia*, Oslo 1994.

[46] NIBR Report 1997:7, Oslo. Both of the projects mentioned are sponsored by the Research Council of Norway.

[47] *Language Policy in Independent Uzbekistan* (FoCAS Working Paper 1. Forum for Central Asian Studies), Stockholm 1997. Another report on this project was published in Swedish seminar proceedings on Central Asia, Farid Abbaszadegan and Bo Utas (eds), *Centralasien – gamla folk söker ny väg* (Skrifter utgivna av Sällskapet för asienstudier 6), Uppsala 1995.

of Uzbek nation-building, provides an example of centralized language planning as regards decision making as well as the implementation and assessment of language reform. To give an illustration of this the author comments on the notion of *millij til*, 'nationality/national language'. In the former Soviet republic of Uzbekistan, this notion stood for 'nationality language', i.e., in connection with Uzbekistan, one of the ethnic languages spoken in the republic (Uzbek, Tajik etc.). In the post-independency Uzbek language debate, on the other hand, there is a tendency to use *millij til* to refer to Uzbek as the language of the whole state of Uzbekistan in the sense of 'nation-state language'.

Another sociolinguistic project at the Institute of Oriental Languages, Stockholm, is headed by Joakim Enwall and bears the title 'The Role of Language in a Regional Power Structure: The Case of Sinkiang'. The main point of departure is Uighur and the role of this minority language as a uniting factor among different movements in Sinkiang for greater cultural and political autonomy in this province. Linguistic aspects to be studied in connection with this are such activities as language standardization and the creation of a new vocabulary. The position of Uighur in relation to other languages spoken in Sinkiang as well as the sociolinguistic history of the region are also under investigation in order to make possible a general analysis of the linguistic situation in this kind of transit area for languages, religions and cultures.

A third language project, on the phonology and phonetics of modern Mongolian, a report of which will be given later in this volume, is being conducted by Jan-Olof Svantesson and colleagues at the Department of Linguistics at Lund.[48]

One important feature shared by all of the above-mentioned projects is that they are based on extensive fieldwork in the Central Asian region and scientific contacts with Central Asian institutions and scholars. Research work is thus conducted on continuously renewed and updated material. Another type of cooperation between the Scandinavian countries and Central Asian societies on contemporary issues is to be seen in projects aiming at consultations on and engagement in development programmes, for example,

---

[48] Mongolian linguistics is a discipline in special need of future support at Nordic universities. Mongolian language courses are rare and hardly ever offered on a regular basis anywhere. Pioneers in this respect are Maria Magdolna Tatár, who teaches Mongolian at Oslo, and Professor James Bosson, Berkeley, who is of Swedish descent and who by his repeated scholarly visits to Sweden has become an advocate of the advancement of Mongolian studies in this country.

in teaching, humanitarian aid and technical improvement. One example is the participation of researchers from the Stockholm Institute of International Education in a UNESCO workshop on Citizenship Education in Central Asia held in Ashgabat, Turkmenistan, April 1996.[49]

The 1996 Stockholm Symposium on Central Asia

The integration of Scandinavian Central Asia research in the international community has so far been canalized mainly through the Nordic Institute of Asian Studies (NIAS) in Copenhagen. A Nordic Central Asia network was initiated by a NIAS workshop in October 1993. Two years later NIAS and representatives from different research institutes in Scandinavia and Finland helped to arrange the Fifth European Seminar on Central Asia (ESCAS V), which was held in Copenhagen on 21–26 August 1995 under the title of 'Central Asia in Transition'.[50] During the Copenhagen conference, the Nordic participants arranged a non-scheduled meeting to discuss the situation of Central Asian studies in the Nordic countries. The discussion concentrated on the problem of providing interim facilities for graduate students to specialize in research on Central Asian topics, until an institutional base and formal graduate programmes for Central Asian studies have been established. To promote this question and to further the development of a Nordic community of Central Asian scholarship, a decision was taken to start a new workshop in Stockholm in the autumn of 1996.

This workshop – or symposium, as we chose to call it – was given the title 'Nordic Central Asia Research: Language – Culture – Society' and it was organized by a working committee from the Institute of Oriental Languages at the University of Stockholm. Ultimately, participation was limited to the three Scandinavian countries Denmark, Norway and Sweden. The present volume, which contains material from the symposium, has consequently been renamed 'Scandinavian Central Asia Research', as it deals with a narrower sphere.

---

[49] See Alexander N. Kanaev and Ingemar Fägerlind, *Citizenship Education in Central Asia: Status and Possibilities for Cooperation. Final Report of a UNESCO Sub-Regional Workshop in Ashgabat, Turkmenistan, April 23–27, 1996*, Institute of International Education, Stockholm 1996.

[50] At this conference, ESCAS was transformed from being a series of seminars into an organization and renamed as European Society for Central Asian Studies. Ewa Chylinski from Esbjerg, Denmark, was elected the first chairman of ESCAS.

Young researchers in particular were encouraged to come to this meeting and give a presentation of their work. As a result, several new members were added to the Nordic Central Asia network – young scholars whose fieldwork and analyses we will undoubtedly hear more about in the years to come. One of these young scholars, Joakim Enwall, who was also one of the original organizers, could not participate in the final meeting, because he had to leave for an appointment in Peking shortly before the symposium. Instead he was invited to submit his paper for publication – a paper relating to his research project on minority languages in Sinkiang mentioned above.

The programme for the symposium proceeded from historical and archaeological aspects to atemporal cultural issues and present-day topics. A brief summary is rendered below including papers that were not intended for publication.[51] The following fields of research were highlighted at the meeting in Stockholm:

Archaeology

Recent changes in the political climate of the Central Asian region seem to be opening up new horizons favourable to a continuation of the archaeological tradition initiated by Sven Hedin and his chief archaeologist, Folke Bergman. The Swedish Council for Research in the Humanities and Social Sciences has sponsored a programme for a joint Swedish–Chinese investigation of ruin sites in the Takla-makan desert with the aim of promoting future archaeological and philological research. At the symposium, Staffan Rosén and Håkan Wahlquist, Stockholm, gave a report of the work done on this project and their own participation in the Swedish–Chinese 1994 excursion to Yar-tonguz-darya in the south-eastern part of Takla-makan. Good contacts with Chinese authorities and scientists are crucial for foreign research teams interested in working in this still rather inaccessible region. On the other hand, the Chinese appreciate Western technical know-how and possibilities to benefit from it in their own extensive archaeological activities in Sinkiang. An account of previous Chinese excavations at Turfan was presented at the Stockholm symposium by Susanne Juhl, Aarhus.

---

[51] The summaries given below are a modified version of a report by the present authors published soon after the symposium in the NIAS newsletter *NIASnytt,* No. 4 1996, pp. 20–22.

Religion

Central Asia is in many respects the meeting point of South Asian Buddhism and North Asian Shamanic conceptions. Per-Arne Berglie, Stockholm, presented a paper about Tibetan travellers in the worlds beyond. Stories about people, who after their death return to this worlds to share their experiences from the other side are well-known motifs in Tibetan literature and religion. Mirja Juntunen, Stockholm, gave a report on her trip to Buryatia in the spring of 1996 to study the revitalization of Buddhism in the region.[52] Johan Elverskog, a scholar of Swedish descent from Bloomington, USA, shed new light on Mongolian religion during the 16th century. His presentation was based upon a newly discovered manuscript from Inner Mongolia – important source material for the elucidation of the second conversion of Mongols to Buddhism. Tina Hamrin, Stockholm, read a paper on the Bar-do and its influence on Aum Shinrikyo in Japan.

Social anthropology

In the field of social anthropology, Anneli Augustsson, Gothenburg, discussed the concepts of place and identity among Mongolian nomads and their ways of expressing them in ritual and cosmology as well as in everyday speech and activities. After the collapse of the Soviet socialist system and the disintegration of collective farms in Mongolia, such practices have gained new importance, as old family pasture lands have once again become homelands and symbolic anchors at a time when great social changes are taking place in the country. De-russification in Kirghizstan was elucidated by Erlend H. Hvoslef, Oslo, who gave some examples from his own field notes of the resuscitation of tráditional name forms in this republic after independence.

---

[52] The field-trip was undertaken together with Joakim Enwall; see Joakim Enwall and Mirja Juntunen, 'Hos lamor och shamaner i Burjatien', *Orientaliska Studier* 90–91 (1996), pp. 15–31.

Language and literature

Linguistic diversity and language contact are two other intriguing fields in Central Asia research. Birgit N. Schlyter, Stockholm, commented on the possible future effects of Uzbek language policy on Tajik in Uzbekistan.[53] Roberta Micallef, Uppsala, presented the Uzbek poet Erkin Vahidov, examining his role as a 'people's poet' in Uzbekistan. Vivan Franzén, Lund, reported on a computerized formant analysis of vowels in modern Mongolian, and Maria Magdolna Tatár, Oslo, presented a paper dealing with the much-debated and still controversial question of the relationship between the so-called Altaic languages.

Political science

Afghanistan, on which, due to the capture of Kabul by the Talibans on 27 September 1996, world news was once again focused on the very day our symposium opened, was the subject of a paper by Kristian Berg Harpviken, Oslo. He pointed out the need for a more insightful knowledge of the changes in Afghanistan brought about by the war and the necessity of realizing that responsibility must be broad and international if a lasting solution to the Afghan crisis is to be achieved. The remaining papers at this session were devoted to the former Soviet Central Asia. Marianne Øhlers, Roskilde, discussed the political development in the largest country in the region, Kazakstan, under Nazarbayev's government. Anette Jensen, Aarhus, sought to clarify the political factors governing the 'national delimitation' of the Central Asian Soviet republics in the 1920s, especially that of the Uzbek Republic. Araz M. Fanni, Gothenburg, elaborated on the problem of creating a formula for regional cooperation between the newly born Central Asian states, which are at the same time preoccupied with the intricate and sensitive task of nation-building. Bo Petersson, Uppsala (presently at Lund), viewed the former Soviet Central Asian republics from a Russian perspective pointing out problems as well as possible Russian ambitions in her approach to these republics.

---

[53] This paper was included in the above-mentioned Stockholm FoCAS Working Paper 1, *Language Policy in Independent Uzbekistan*, footnote 47 on p. 14.

New perspectives

The above-mentioned speeches were set in the framework of two introductory lectures presented at the opening session of the Stockholm symposium. Bo Utas, Uppsala, had been asked to give a retrospective survey of Central Asian studies in the Nordic countries. John Schoeberlein from the Harvard University Forum for Central Asian Studies, USA, had been invited to comment on 'Central Asian Studies in a New International Context'.[54] In his contribution to the present volume he elaborates further on this theme and draws attention to the need for new types of scholarly training, not least in linguistic research and other humanities disciplines.

Future achievements in shaping these new types of scholarly training will be dependent on much collaboration both in terms of institutional resources and by means of researchers' networks. As could be seen from the preceding account, an impressive amount of Central Asia research is being carried out in the Nordic countries today. However, the endeavours to pave the way for broader Central Asia study and research programmes at the university level need to be fuelled by still stronger support – morally as well as financially. The networks of Central Asia researchers that already exist will have an important role to play in the years to come.

The Central Asia network at NIAS, Copenhagen, was mentioned in the preceding section. Another newly founded association for inderdisciplinary dialogues between scholars is Forum for Central Asian Studies, FoCAS, at Stockholm University.[55] The establishment of this forum was one of the direct consequences of the 1996 Nordic Central Asia Symposium, the final document from which is the present volume. The main research framework of the Stockholm FoCAS at present is entitled 'Central Asian Languages as Transmitters of Culture From a Religio-Ethnological and Sociopolitical Perspective'. It has been prepared for research on language contact and language policy as well as the spread and adaptation of script systems among Indo-European and Turko-Mongolic languages, which are to be

---

[54] In this connection he has made his own substantial contribution by compiling a *Guide to Scholars of the History and Culture of Central Asia* (Publications of Harvard Central Asia Forum 1), Cambridge (Mass.) 1995, which will be updated during 1998. Another forthcoming compilation in this vein is John Schoeberlein et al., *Guide to Scholarly Resources for the Study of Central Asia* (Publications of Harvard Central Asia Forum 2), Cambridge (Mass.), due in 1998 or 1999.

[55] The NIAS and FoCAS Homepages are *http://nias.ku.dk* and *http://www.orient.su.se/scas/FoCAS/FoCAS.htm*, respectively.

studied parallel with analyses of belief systems, mainly in the sphere of Buddhist and Shamanic religious patterns. Hopefully, networks and research initiatives such as these will eventually lead not only to continued scholarly work but also to introductory courses and graduate programmes in the field of Central Asian studies.

Marginal Centrality
Central Asian Studies on the Eve of a New Millennium

JOHN SCHOEBERLEIN

It is a peculiar irony that what is called 'Central' in geography is often in fact marginal. Like Central Africa, Central America and Central Europe, the central part of Asia is on the edge of world areas which are generally considered to be more important. Central Asia had achieved a state of unsurpassed remoteness following the rise of maritime trade routes and a concomitant decline of the mediaeval 'Silk Road'. In the 19th century, Asia became a continent inhabited by empires and Central Asia sat on the periphery between them. If in the days of the 'Great Game' – the imperial rivalry between Russia and England in Central Asia – the region claimed some international interest as a contested domain, in the 20th century, the marginality of Central Asia was firmly fixed when the contests were ended with the consolidation of Soviet and Chinese Communist rule. Some flicker of interest was maintained by the struggle over Afghanistan and the unfounded supposition that Muslim Asia would challenge Communist rule.[1]

In the world of scholarship, Central Asia's marginality was guaranteed by the post-war formation of area studies domains combined with utter physical separation of Western scholarship from the subject of study. While around the turn of the century a handful of Western scholars were visiting the region, after the 1920s in the USSR and the 1940s in China the Communist

---

[1] Works in this vein include Michael Rywkin's *Moscow's Muslim Challenge*, Armonk (N.Y.) 1982, a re-edition of his *Russia in Central Asia* (1963), which provided little in the way of new information to warrant the more sensational title. The appearance of Alexandre Bennigsen and Marie Broxup's *The Islamic Threat to the Soviet State*, New York 1983, can also undoubtedly be correlated with the Soviet invasion of Afghanistan a few years earlier.

governments closed virtually all opportunity to carry out research in the field or in historical archives. With these physical and political barriers to research, there was little impetus for scholars to overcome the other practical hurdles encumbering entry into this field. Among such daunting obstacles was the need to master multiple unrelated and difficult languages and to gain background knowledge in a field where much foundation scholarship is simply absent. The combination of these factors virtually closed all doors.

It must be stressed, however, that the neglect of Central Asian studies has resulted not only from practical difficulties. Intellectual and academic agendas situated Central Asia out of view of mainstream scholarship. In the social science and humanities disciplines, Central Asia occupied no noticeable place whatsoever. The difficulty is that the importance of a region for a discipline is measured by the role that theoretical and substantive contributions to the discipline have been made by scholars working in the particular region. This may be illustrated by the admittedly rather extreme example of my own field of anthropology. It matters little that many of the key issues which have occupied anthropology in this century are very present and could be richly studied in the Central Asian context. The fact is that virtually no anthropology was done in Soviet and Chinese Central Asia in the period of anthropology's contemporary development as a discipline. Anthropology requires fieldwork – something that was essentially impossible until recently. Consequently, the major schools and contributors in anthropology have been based on work in Africa, Latin America, South-East Asia and a few other areas. This also determines the future of the field because, regardless of the stress on theoretical and thematic issues in the field and the secondary significance assigned to regional considerations, departments of anthropology consider coverage of Latin America, Africa and the other cradles of anthropological theory to be essential and a region like Central Asia to be much more difficult to justify.

Similar circumstances obtain in the other disciplines. Sadly, it is probably true to say that no theoretical or substantive contribution of major importance to any discipline has ever been made drawing on case material from Central Asia, with the possible exception of H. J. Mackinder's Eurasian 'heartland' concept from 1904.[2]

In this article, I examine the difficult straits of Central Asian studies and what will be required to put the field on a better footing. My main focus

---

[2] Halford John Mackinder, 'The Geographical Pivot in History', *Geographic Journal* 33 (1904), pp. 421–444.

will be on the problems of study of the region in the contemporary period, though some attention will be given to studies of the past as well, as these fields have often dominated the key Central Asian studies institutions. The focus will be not on substantive issues of research, but on the institutional and 'sociological' problems of scholarship. The main focus will be on the situation in the United States, giving only passing attention to scholarship in the former Soviet Union, Europe and other places where important research traditions have also developed.[3]

On the margins of area studies

In post-war area studies, Central Asia was the poor cousin in relation to several neighboring fields. Middle Eastern and Islamic studies virtually ignored the existence of this major Islamic domain following the establishment of the Soviet Union, in spite of Central Asia's centrality in the Islamic world during pre-modern times. Even in those countries which were most proximal and historically related, politics compelled scholarship to put on blinders which obscured the Soviet domain. In Iran and Turkey, scholarship on Soviet Central Asia was even more severely neglected than in Europe and America. Prior to Soviet times, Oriental studies had treated Islam as an integrated domain, and indeed Russian was one of the primary languages of scholarship of Eastern Islam. By the mid-century it became truly extraordinary for a scholar of Eastern Islam – particularly in contemporary studies – to know Russian or the literature on Central Asia.

In East Asian studies, the field has been dominated by the study of China, Japan and Korea. Though Mongolia, Tibet and Eastern Turkestan nominally also fall into this domain according to accepted practice, these areas receive an insignificant fraction of the field's resources, such as fellowships, professorships and publications. As is often the case in marginal fields of study, those scholars who have entered the field often base their commitment to it on their own origin from the region or on a romantic

---

[3] In particular, missing from the picture presented here is discussion of the largest tradition of Central Asian studies – that developed in Russia and the Soviet Union – and one of the strongest schools for the contemporary study of the region in England, which featured the establishment of the Central Asian Research Centre at Oxford in the early 1950s, the most prominent journal for contemporary studies, *Central Asian Survey*, and one of the most active programs in Central Asian studies at the School of Oriental and African Studies (University of London).

stance toward an exotic domain, sometimes bound up with religion, such as is the case with many of those who take an interest in Tibet. Such fundamentally parochial orientations toward the area of study have worked against the integration of these studies into the wider area studies domain, not to speak of areas outside the East Asian area or scholarship more broadly.

During Soviet times the most concentrated focus on contemporary Central Asia was maintained within the field of Soviet studies. In this context, the portion of Central Asia which falls into the territory of present-day Kazakstan, Kirghizstan, Tajikistan, Turkmenistan and Uzbekistan was treated as an entity unto itself, and sometimes Kazakstan was even isolated as a separate domain.[4] Further, this was a field that was considered ancillary to the study of Russia. The greater proportion of scholars who dealt with Central Asia within Soviet studies relied overwhelmingly or exclusively on Russian language sources and had very limited training in the history and society of Central Asia itself and its connections with neighboring parts of the region outside of the Soviet borders.

The pre-Soviet period was studied largely by scholars operating in different intellectual domains from those studying the present. With few exceptions, the period from the Russian conquest and especially from the advent of Soviet rule was studied by people who honored the luminaries of the Russian field, such as E. H. Carr, Merle Fainsod and Leonard Schapiro, and who gave scant attention to scholars of history and politics in the Islamic world. A separate intellectual domain was maintained for the study of the region prior to Russian rule – a domain shared with scholars of south and south-west Asian Islamic societies.

This peculiar division produced an odd disconnect between history and culture on the one hand and politics and the contemporary world on the other. This disconnect was very characteristically expressed when, in the late Soviet period, the Hoover Institution Press began to publish a series of books which took on the history of various individual Soviet republics from ancient times to the present.[5] The point of departure was the contemporary administrative unit and its officially associated 'national' group. Azerbaijan

---

[4] See, for example, William Fierman, 'Introduction', in W. Fierman (ed.), *Soviet Central Asia: The Failed Transformation*, Boulder (Colorado) 1991, p. 3.

[5] This series included such titles as Martha Brill Olcott's *The Kazakhs*, Stanford 1987, Audrey L. Altstadt's *The Azerbaijani Turks: Power and Identity under Russian Rule*, Stanford 1992, and Edward A. Allworth's *The Modern Uzbeks*, Stanford 1990.

and the 'Azerbaijani Turks,' Kazakhstan and the 'Kazaks' were taken as units of analysis, and the authors, who were in most cases products of the Sovietological approach, were obliged to delve deeply into historical domains which they appeared little-prepared to explore. Yuri Bregel (b. 1925), an early modern historian of the Orientalist school (and one of the most respected and resented in his field), undertook a broad critique of this kind of scholarship in a long paper entitled 'Notes on the Study of Central Asia.'[6] In it, he takes on some of the products of the Hoover series, as well as other works by scholars of the contemporary period writing about history; in a scathing overview he dismisses these works through meticulous critique. Even if this attack were to be explained as resentment against 'interlopers,' it is indicative of the degree to which scholarship of past and present in Central Asia are bifurcated domains with very poor communication between them.

An area studies domain in Asia's interior

One should not overlook, meanwhile, the initiatives which were undertaken to establish a scholarly apparatus focused on Central Asia in its own right, alongside the major fields of area studies. In the United States, these efforts were focused in several universities. At the University of Washington, Seattle, in the immediate post-war period, Nicholas Poppe (1897–1991) was the founding figure of a program oriented primarily toward the study of language. Poppe, an *émigré* from the Soviet Union, was a Mongolist and a scholar of Uralo-Altaic linguistics. In his tradition, Ilse Laude-Cirtautas, a European-schooled philologist, has maintained perhaps the most outstanding program for the study of Central Asian languages anywhere in the world. At Indiana University, Bloomington, the founding figure was Denis Sinor (b. 1916), also a philologist and specialist in Altaic linguistics. Under his leadership, the Department of Uralic and Altaic Studies was established, as well as a government-funded research institute with the same profile. This program, more recently under the leadership of Yuri Bregel, has continued to flourish until the present.

Both of these – the largest and best-funded programs in the U.S. – were conceived according to linguistic criteria, and though the Indiana program has especially featured a strong emphasis on historical scholarship, there

---

[6] Yuri Bregel, 'Notes on the Study of Central Asia' (Papers on Inner Asia 28), Research Institute for Inner Asian Studies, Bloomington 1996.

has always been a tension between the principle of linguistic unity and the need for a coherent area studies domain. For example, the Uralic and Altaic program at Indiana (recently renamed with the post-Soviet euphemism the Department of Central Eurasian Studies), encompasses under one institutional umbrella studies of societies as diverse as Estonia, Hungary, Turkey, Turkmenistan, Eastern Turkestan and Mongolia, based on a disputed theory of their linguistic relatedness. The coherence of this domain is easier to posit for mediaeval times whilst the major migrations were in progress. In relation to contemporary times, its coherence rests exclusively in the broad domination of Eurasia by Soviet government, and as a rationale for a coherent domain of study, this principle was already claimed – and more plausibly so – by the field of Soviet studies.

The post-war era also saw the rise of area studies centers at some of the more influential universities, where the study of Central Asia was made part of these area centers but where the main core of Central Asian studies was in other departments. These include Harvard University, where prominent area centers were established, such as the Russian Research Center (recently renamed the Davis Center for Russian Studies), the Center for Middle Eastern Studies and the Fairbank Center for East Asian Research. While these centers supported the study of Central Asia in a relatively peripheral way, a strong faculty in this area developed in various teaching departments including especially area studies departments such as Near Eastern Languages and Civilizations and East Asian Languages and Civilizations. A program in Inner Asian and Altaic Studies was also established in the 1970s. In these teaching programs, the overwhelming emphasis was on the study of language, philology and historical texts. The prominent figures were such historian-philologists as Francis Cleaves (1911–1995; a Mongolist), Richard Frye (b. 1920; an Iranist), Omeljan Pritsak (b. 1919; a Turkologist) and, succumbing to an unfortunate death at the peak of his career, Joseph Fletcher (1934–1984; a historian of broad profile). However, due to the non-contemporary focus of the teaching programs and the peripheral treatment of Central Asia in the area research centers where the strength in contemporary studies was focused, the study of present-day Central Asia was relatively weakly developed.

A similar situation obtained at Columbia University, where strong research centers were established for the study of the Islamic world (the Middle East Institute) and the Soviet bloc (the Russian Institute, later renamed the Harriman Institute), yet the greater emphasis on Central Asia was located in teaching departments. Here the founding figures were Karl Menges (b. 1908) and Tibor Halasi-Kun (b. 1914) – again representing history and philology. Later, Edward Allworth (b. 1920) was the field's major proponent at Columbia, and he was a quite unique figure among the U.S. scholars mentioned in that he has bridged the gap between historical-philological and contemporary studies. While himself a literary historian, he encouraged his students to pursue contemporary topics as few of the other U.S. programs in Central Asian studies did.

While these four universities long had the strongest programs, there was always a low degree of concentration of talent in the field, and many of the most prominent scholars are not affiliated with any of these programs. Recent years have seen some changes in this configuration. University of Wisconsin, Madison, joined the first rank of departments in the late 1980s under the leadership of Kemal Karpat (a political historian of Turkey). Around the same time, Indiana became the first to break out of the historical-philological mould by hiring two social scientists – Nazif Shahrani (an anthropologist) and William Fierman (a political scientist). After Allworth's retirement at Columbia, that program fell into neglect, whereas the new interest in Central Asia on the part of foundations following the Soviet break-up furthered some new developments, such as an expansion of the program at Harvard and the establishment of a Central Asia Institute, featuring a major focus on policy questions under the leadership of S. Frederick Starr (a scholar of Russian history and politics), at Johns Hopkins University, School of Advanced International Studies.

The closer to the present, the more marginal

In the eyes of funds allocaters, the established historical-philological programs inspired little enthusiasm because they focused on remote times and places and esoteric topics. Operating with an insular area studies orientation, the Central Asianists in all of the early programs were continually confronted with the challenge that their contributions were not sufficiently relevant. They did not address pressing current issues. They did not systematically train practical specialists. Even within the academic domain itself, it is very difficult to name a historical-philological scholar in Central Asian studies who enjoyed more than a modicum of prominence outside of this narrow regional field.

Thus, a marked divide formed between the historical-philological and contemporary approaches. It is noteworthy that a large number of the founding figures mentioned above were *émigré* scholars trained in the European philological tradition, thus firmly placed in a separate intellectual world. A large percentage of those who wrote dissertations on contemporary Central Asian topics prior to the very last years of Soviet rule treated the region as a case for the 'nationalities' subfield of Sovietological analysis and often did not focus on this region any further in their careers. Richard Pipes, for example, who devoted a substantial portion of his dissertation to Central Asia and the Caucasus,[7] became very prominent in the field of modern history and policy – even a presidential advisor – but scarcely returned to focus study on Central Asia. One may cite a long series of essentially one-off contributions to this field in the post-war period which were written by scholars who subsequently devoted only a fraction of their attention to Central Asia, including those of Alexander Park,[8] Richard A. Pierce,[9] Teresa Rakowska-Harmstone[10] and Serge Zenkovsky.[11] This illustrates how the dominant treatment of the contemporary field was almost as an incidental adjunct to Soviet studies.

The allocation of contemporary Central Asia to the nationalities branch of Soviet studies had some important negative consequences for the development of the field. First, as a peripheral subfield of the study of Russia, young scholars saw it as superfluous and unpromising to invest too much in specializing in this subject. This accounts for the fact that many of the contributions were not from those who ultimately remained in Central Asian studies. In view of this, it is not surprising that local language knowledge was scarce among such scholars. A fiction was propagated that every source of any import in the modern period was written in Russian after all, and few scholars had the competence to test this assumption. Second, Soviet

---

[7] Richard Pipes, *The Genesis of Soviet National Policy*, Ph.D. thesis, Harvard University 1950.

[8] Alexander Garland Park, *Soviet Nationality Policy, 1917–1927: A Study of Bolshevik Doctrine and Practice with Special Reference to Central Asia*, Ph.D. dissertation, Columbia University 1954.

[9] Richard A. Pierce, *Russian Central Asia, 1867–1917: A Study of Colonial Rule*, Berkeley 1960.

[10] Teresa Rakowska-Harmstone, *Russia and Nationalism in Central Asia: The Case of Tadzhikistan*, Baltimore 1970.

[11] Serge Alexander Zenkovsky, *Pan-Turkism and Islam in Russia* (Russian Research Center Studies 36), Cambridge (Mass.) 1960.

studies had its own well-known shortcomings. Notably, social scientists in this field often did not participate actively in the discourse on theory and methodology which permeated the social sciences in general, and consequently did not meet the same standards of rigor and did not partake of the same process of intellectual growth. In this context, research on Central Asian subject matter suffered especially, as it was treated as novelty (as it continues to be), and being validated as novelty, did not have to be judged by the same standards of rigor, even in the Sovietological context.

In addition, being a subfield of Russian studies had a detrimental impact on the range of topics that were studied. During the Cold War, the chief focus on the Soviet Union was in its capacity as a threat to the West, and consequently, interest in Central Asia was concentrated almost solely around the question of how it might constitute a danger to Moscow and thus a boon to the West. This not only constricted the focus to questions relating to internal security, such as the 'Islamic threat,' but also put a premium on analyses that provided the 'good news' that the threats to stability were real. The less emotionally anti-Soviet scholars typically focused on the insidious ways that the Soviet system mistreated the population and failed to live up to its promises and propaganda. The more virulently anti-Soviet scholars were taken up with the massive misdeeds of Stalin and his successors. These approaches did touch upon a great many important issues in Central Asian history, society, culture and politics. The treatment of these issues, meanwhile, diverged sharply from approaches to similar issues in other parts of the world, and neglect was pervasive of issues which lacked a political edge.

The combination of a lack of rigor and an ideological orientation together with the inaccessibility of good data sources resulted in a field that was permeated with highly questionable 'conventional wisdom.' For example, innumerable authors have firmly declared that the division of Central Asia into national republics in 1924 can be fully explained by a policy in Moscow of divide and rule.[12] In fact, some evidence bearing on this question has recently begun to emerge, but the best that could be said for this oft-repeated view is that it was perhaps a plausible supposition based on scarce evidence,

---

[12] See, for example, Alexandre Bennigsen and Chantal Lemercier-Quelquejay, *Islam in the Soviet Union*, London 1968, pp. 130–134 (translated from *L'Islam en Union soviétique*, Paris 1967), Olaf Caroe, *Soviet Empire: The Turks of Central Asia and Stalinism*, London 1967, pp. 143–145, and Gavin Hambly et al., *Central Asia*, New York 1969, pp. 234–236.

as opposed to the firmly established fact that it was declared to be. It is perhaps more plausible that a complex interaction between local political actors and changing central policies must account for this process of political reorganization, but the bias against such explanations was sustained by a desire to see Moscow as a cynical force and Central Asians as powerless victims. Meanwhile, paradoxically, Central Asia's Muslims were figured as fundamentally subversive, mobilizing clandestinely under the banner of Islam against the Soviet state.[13] This false empowerment of the Central Asians toward Western strategic goals led to frequent predictions of their breaking away from Moscow – and this mindset has been so persistent that even after the fact of the Soviet Union's demise due to other causes, counterfactual statements are still common proclaiming the overthrow of Soviet power by Central Asian nationalism and Islamic assertiveness.[14]

In the wake of the Soviet collapse

Already in the last three years of Soviet rule (1989–1991), scholarship of Central Asia had begun to experience markedly different circumstances. First, it became possible for many scholars to conduct research in the region in a way that had previously been impossible. Second, the ideological opposition between Communism and the West and between the state ideology and the inclinations of the population had significantly declined. Thus, local authorities came to see the prospect of foreign scholars understanding Central Asia as less of a danger.

At the same time, the former Soviet Union lost much of its intrinsic interest in the eyes of funding organizations and the general public, having lost its status as arch-rival. This eliminated much of the special market for

---

[13] The prodigious works of Bennigsen and his various collaborators (e.g. Bennigsen and Broxup, op. cit., Bennigsen and Lemercier-Quelquejay, op. cit., and Alexandre Bennigsen and S. Enders Wimbush, *Mystics and Commissars: Sufism in the Soviet Union*, Berkeley 1985) and Hélène Carrére d'Encausse, *Decline of an Empire: The Soviet Socialist Republics in Revolt*, New York 1979 (translation of *L'Empire Éclaté*, Paris 1978), are prominent in this vein.

[14] For example, Hafeez Malik, a political analyst specializing in Pakistan and convener of one of the numerous recent conferences on Central Asia, claimed in 1994 that he had predicted the demise of the Soviet Union in 1989 based on his observation that 'Muslim nationalities in the Soviet Union have entered a new phase of self-assertion ... [which] would call for the restructuring of relations with Moscow...'; see Hafeez Malik, 'Preface', in H. Malik (ed.), *Central Asia: Its Strategic Importance and Future Prospects*, New York 1994, p. vii.

Soviet scholarship that had previously existed, and scholarly products had to enter the market of scholarship on the same disciplinary terms as those of other world regions. In fact, scholars of the Soviet domain found themselves at a significant disadvantage in the disciplinary context. In some fields, such as political science, there was a marked mismatch between supply and demand. Where previously scholars had built their careers, for example, on speculation about power relations based on scant information, such problems lost their currency and the methodologies did not answer to the requirements of the field more broadly. Political study of the region had also been a focus of the *émigré* community, and of anti-Soviet Turkish and other regional scholars, but once the 'enemy' status of the government of Central Asian states evaporated, so did the main orientation of this scholarship. In other fields, such as anthropology or sociology, there was simply no significant tradition of scholarship, and thus, a lack of individuals who could guide students well and serve in the role of patron which is so important in the development of a scholarly career.

In studies focused on language, there were well-established traditions of scholarship. However, most scholars were trained in Turkology or Iranian philology, and not in the theory and methodology of linguistics or literary studies. The field had found a niche for itself in training the small but steady stream of language readers required to digest sources from Central Asia for the U.S. Department of State and other intelligence gathering organizations. This built-in demand sustained university departments offering training in these languages, in part by special government funds. This tended to diminish the need to provide the quality of training that was required in other language departments. It is remarkable that in the nearly thirty-year history of government-funded Central Asian language training in U.S. universities before the collapse of the Soviet Union, not a single adequate textbook or descriptive grammar of any Central Asian language was published. I have noted that the majority of relevant departments were formed by comparative philologists, and their intellectual priority was in developing esoteric knowledge about historical languages and the relationships between them – typically focusing on languages which are of little practical significance, such as dead languages and languages spoken by tiny and dwindling populations. In the language field, following the Soviet collapse, the demand-side has changed markedly, as the need has arisen for diplomats, staff of international NGOs and people in business who have a command of the languages. However, the field has been slow to meet this demand, and it may be that the intellectual orientation of departments formed in other times are ill-suited to adjust to new needs.

The field of Central Asian history faces a different set of problems which in some ways is more analogous to the problems of history as a field in general. Historians of many parts of the world find their primary home in area studies fields, as opposed to a disciplinary approach to history. This is in part because, in the West, history has been conceptualized as a humanity rather than a social science, and consequently there is much less emphasis on theory and methodology, and more on particularist problems which are specific to a given region and time period. Meanwhile, there has been a substantial counter-trend in history in recent years toward greater intellectual integration between history and other fields such as anthropology and cultural studies. As a result, historians have increasingly focused on such non-regionally specific broad thematic issues as nationalism, state-formation, processes of economic integration, colonialism, cross-cultural encounters and gender. Historians of the 'old school' typically look on these new orientations with disdain and argue that these thematic orientations have merely detracted from the historian's fundamental job of elucidating textual sources.[15]

In determining the future direction of Central Asian studies, historians of the 'old school' are at a strategic disadvantage. In the past, their institutional base was often precisely in area studies, and area studies programs are in danger of moving towards extinction, having lost their cold-war *raison d'être*. If required to justify their textual studies before an audience which is not versed in the importance of their particular texts, they have less to go on than those who can offer work that is relevant to broader themes which scholars (and funders) who are not specialists in the region will recognize as important. The problem of relevance outside of the regional specialty is particularly acute in Central Asian studies, because while it can be argued that the history of France or Russia is intrinsically important to a liberal education, it is harder to argue this for Central Asia.

And yet, until now the 'old school' seems to predominate in Central

---

[15] A recently edited volume which includes contributions taking precisely such a new, thematic approach to the field, Daniel R. Brower and Edward J. Lazzerini (eds), *Russia's Orient: Imperial Borderlands and Peoples, 1700–1917*, Bloomington 1997, has already evoked this kind of response from historians with whom I have spoken. Also, Bregel's assertion that there are scarcely any historians of Central Asia in America seems to be based on such a notion of what counts as valid history (Yuri Bregel, 'Notes on the Study of Central Asia' [Papers on Inner Asia 28], Bloomington 1996, pp. 3–4).

Asian historical studies in the U.S. much more than in history generally. This is probably to be explained precisely by the fact that Central Asian studies has been a marginal field within the context of history and has been sustained not by intellectual imperatives generated internally within the discipline of history, but rather by the cold-war area studies imperative. This has generated a space where the 'normal science paradigm' in Thomas Kuhn's terminology[16] did not hold sway, even in the limited sense that it does in history otherwise. And for those working in the 'textological' paradigm, the field of Central Asian studies is condemned to work at an earlier stage in the development of scholarship, characterized by the production of scholarly editions of historical sources, as opposed to the broader analysis and generalization which they feel can only be done when the documentary groundwork has been completed. This close focus on sources, combined with the avoidance of broadly relevant themes, helps to ensure that scholarly products in this field will be of little interest to non-specialists.

It is reasonable to predict that a battle is brewing for the future of the historical study of Central Asia. Inasmuch as young scholars entering this field will necessarily be concerned about the prospects for grant support and employment, they will be inclined in the direction of thematic relevance over particularism and textology in a way that may not find the support of the 'old school' scholars. This could have the effect of producing a situation where the successful young scholars in the field are trained, not by historians of Central Asia but by others who are willing to support more innovative and relevant approaches. The potential danger is that such mentors will be inadequately familiar with the sources and the field to hold their students to an adequate standard of rigor. Clearly the field would be better off if it were not so divided.

Creating social science of Central Asia

The social sciences in certain respects are no less ill-poised for successful future development. One wonders if the sheer lack of pre-existing scholarship on this region in most of the social sciences will liberate the field from the problematic legacies that we see in other disciplines or if it will leave the

---

[16] Thomas S. Kuhn, *The Structure of Scientific Revolutions*, Chicago 1962.

field like a ship which is captainless and rudderless. If in history there is something of a divide between those who know the field best and those who can carry it into the future, the social sciences are simply severely short of experienced senior scholars. Only a small handful of those who are now producing the literature on contemporary Central Asian politics and society are scholars who were trained in the social science disciplines *and* have substantial research experience in Central Asia. There are extremely few disciplinary programs in the social sciences which have faculty with a major focus on Central Asia. The majority of recent graduates who are seeking careers in the contemporary study of this region are products of area studies programs and have sufficiently weak disciplinary training and little access to the scholarly networks in the social sciences that it will be virtually impossible for them to find positions in academia, particularly in disciplinary departments.

In the past, the existence of area studies programs, albeit focused not on Central Asia but on neighboring regions, as well as a funding priority given to contemporary studies, allowed for the development of some institutional momentum. As in philology and history, this created a fragmented area studies domain which was intellectually separated from disciplinary scholarship in the social sciences. With a severe shortage of social scientists, scholars trained in history, philology and area studies stepped forward to fill the need for current affairs expertise. To the extent that such scholars dominate the contemporary study of Central Asia, and may be unaware of – possibly even unsympathetic with – the theoretical and methodological standards of the social sciences, this can also pose a significant obstacle to the development of the field.

In many respects, the present moment is not propitious for expansion of a field of scholarship such as Central Asian studies. Academic budgets in general are shrinking substantially, which results in an ethos of retrenchment, where institutional momentum usually favors sustaining what is already strong over developing a new direction. In addition, area studies as an approach is under massive assault in American academia from both a fiscal and an intellectual point of view.[17] Universities are cutting back on

---

[17] See, for example, Christopher Shea, 'Political Scientists Clash over Value of Area Studies: Theorists Say that a Focus on Individual Regions Leads to Work that is Mushy', *The Cronicle of Higher Education*, 10 January, 1997, and Edward L. Keenan, 'Our Once and Future Life in Area Studies', in M. Matsubara and J. Campbell (eds), *Japan-USA Area Studies Conference* (JCAS Symposium Series 1), Osaka 1997, pp. 39–42.

international studies, and area studies in particular have been declared obsolete after the United States achieved the status of the sole superpower. Some of the problems of which I have identified in the context of Central Asian studies – problems of parochialism and isolation from disciplinary approaches – have also been criticized even in the much more developed and mainstream area studies fields. Thus, it might seem futile to hope that a new domain of area studies can now expand and flourish.

In the face of this inhospitable academic environment, Central Asian studies has recently experienced a limited sort of boom. In the period beginning in 1992, the number of articles and books published on Central Asian topics skyrocketed. With the breakup of the Soviet Union, Central Asia drew considerable attention as a region with new geopolitical actors, rich mineral resources and an apparent danger of ethnic strife and the spread of Islamic militancy. As a result, a number of those Soviet area specialists who saw a shrinking market for Russian expertise turned their attention to Central Asia. Similarly, the Islamic character of the region as well as the increasing involvement of Iran, Turkey and Pakistan there encouraged experts on the Middle East and Islam to apply themselves to Central Asia. The small and beleaguered Afghanistan studies community, having experienced more than a decade of chaos and inaccessibility to research in that country, welcomed the opportunity to study a neighboring region with much in common.

New blood has the potential of revitalizing a field, and to some extent this has indeed been the result. Scholars with far better linguistic skills in the local languages have listened to voices that were not previously heard. Much more nuanced approaches to Islam and questions of local society and culture have resulted from the arrival of scholars who derive their ability to enter more deeply into the culture from extensive experience in the closely related cultures of neighboring Afghanistan and Iran. In the context of the former Soviet Union, Central Asia has received much more sustained and serious attention by political analysts.

However, expertise in such a complicated and difficult-to-study region cannot develop overnight, and on the whole, amidst the small flood of new literature on the region, the percentage is very modest of scholarship which builds on a strong empirical base, draws on a solid general knowledge of the region and answers to the standards of disciplinary scholarship. Much of the literature consists of overviews of the scene which provide little new information, and speculative and sensational assessments of new geostrategic configurations.[18] Many scholars entering the field from Middle Eastern studies fail to grapple adequately with the problem that the vast majority of essential source material for the study of contemporary questions is in Russian. One of the more ironic new appearances in Central Asian studies is that a number of Russian experts who previously worked in the highly ideologized field of Soviet foreign relations with Islamic countries have now cast themselves into the study of 'Islam' within the former Soviet Union and have been drawn upon extensively in the West for expertise.[19] Not surprisingly, these new experts are producing highly ideologized work in this domain, too, but now with its anti-Islamic bent; it is an ideology which finds a ready market among Western political analysts.

The influx of new scholars into this field has introduced a new dimension of fragmentation. Such scholars are often too new to the field to know who is already working on the subject and what has already been written. The field in any case lacks the coherence that other fields gain from having a few solid journals, annual conferences and other established scholarly institutions. The networks which integrate a field are weakly developed, and most scholars are primarily engaged in networks which orient them outside Central Asian studies toward other scholarly domains. New scholars entering the field typically do not become integrated into networks focused

---

[18] But a few of the many examples which could be cited include R. Craig Nation, 'The Turkic and Other Muslim Peoples of Central Asia, the Caucasus, and the Balkans', in V. Mastny and R. C. Nation (eds), *Turkey between East and West: New Challenges for a Rising Regional Power*, Boulder (Colorado) 1996, pp. 97–130, the April 1994 issue of *Current History* devoted entirely to Central Asia, Ahmed Rashid, *The Resurgence of Central Asia: Islam or Nationalism?*, London 1994, and Daniel Pipes's sensationally titled 'The Event of Our Era: Former Soviet Muslim Republics Change the Middle East', in M. Mandelbaum (ed.), *Central Asia and the World: Kazakhstan, Uzbekistan, Tajikistan, Kyrgyzstan, and Turkmenistan*, New York 1994, pp. 47–93.

[19] Russian proponents of the new Islamic threat in the former Soviet domain who have found an eager audience in the West include Aleksei Malashenko, 'Islam and Politics in the Southern Zone of the Former USSR', in V. V. Naumkin (ed.), *Central Asia and Transcaucasia: Ethnicity and Conflict*, Westport (Connecticut) 1994, pp. 109–126, and ibid., 'Does Islamic Fundamentalism Exist in Russia', in Y. Ro'i (ed.), *Muslim Eurasia: Conflicting Legacies*, London 1995, pp. 41–51, Sergei A. Panarin, 'The Ethnohistorical Dynamics of Muslim Societies within Russia and the CIS', in M. Meshabi (ed.), *Central Asia and the Caucasus after the Soviet Union*, Gainesville (Florida) 1994, pp. 17–33, and Yuri Kul'chik, 'Central Asia after the Empire: Ethnic Groups, Communities and Problems', in R. Z. Sagdeev and S. Eisenhower (eds), *Central Asia: Conflict, Resolution, and Change*, Chevy Chase (Maryland) 1995, pp. 91–114, as well as Yuri Kul'chik et al., *Central Asia after the Empire*, London 1996. Incidentally, it is an unfortunate commentary on the state of the field that these two sources of Kul'chik are essentially duplicate publications with no reference to one another, and no references given for any of the assertions they contain.

on Central Asia but rather remain oriented toward the networks of the fields from which they have come.

Creating a scholarly critical mass

While there are many problems that can arise in scholarship as carried out in area studies enclaves, there is no question that the lack of a critical mass of scholarship in Central Asian studies results in many of the current shortcomings of scholarly work on the region. If an area studies domain serves to bring together scholars working within strong disciplinary contexts – as opposed to a domain where scholars shelter from the standards of the discipline – it can serve as an incubator or forge for good scholarship. It is of course not sufficient that scholarly research and training be in tune with theoretical issues of the discipline; it must also be solidly grounded in empirical work and the general knowledge which enables empirical observations to be adequately understood. For this, the knowledge generated by area studies is irreplaceable. Unfortunately, this is precisely what is lacking in much of the work on Central Asia.

In order to raise the standards of scholarship in Central Asian studies, it is essential that the scholarly-intellectual infrastructure of the field be improved. Scholars in general must know at least one Turkic or Iranian language of the region as well as Russian, in addition to other languages of the scholarly literature. If we are to expect that students will be able to master this considerable burden, we must have better language study programs for the key languages. There is some hope that current initiatives in this area can meet much of this need,[20] but it will require that efforts to build language study programs be conceptualized as efforts to build the field in general rather than to build a single institution's program.[21]

Similarly, there is a great need for basic texts which can serve the purpose of introducing Central Asia to students on various levels, as well as

---

[20] Uli Schamiloglu of University of Wisconsin, Madison, and colleagues at other universities are currently seeking to establish a consortium for Central Asian language instruction. The goal of greater collaboration is also being pursued by the U.S. Dept. of Education and the Social Science Research Council which have been major sources of funding for language programs.

[21] An indication of the contrary trend in previous initiatives is the fact that several of the major programs offering languages taught on the basis of textbooks which were neither published nor shared with other programs.

to scholars newly entering the field and indeed to non-specialists. Currently, there is no adequate introductory historical text. All the available works have a minimum shortcoming of being hopelessly out-of-date, and most have much more serious problems than this.[22] Similarly, there is but one introductory text on culture and society – Elizabeth Bacon's *Central Asians under Russian Rule*[23] – which was written on the basis only of secondary literature. Some of the available introductory texts on politics and economics have the problem of being superficial, spotty or tendentious, though this is one area where new contributions to the literature have been helpful.[24]

There is also a severe lack of reference works. There is no encyclopedia, for example, in which one can be assured of finding coverage even of many of the most basic concepts, individuals, places and events relating to the region. For most of the languages of the region, there is an almost complete lack of good quality bilingual dictionaries (other than in Russian). There is no atlas with good coverage of Central Asia. Only recently has one comprehensive bibliography of the region appeared, and it covers a limited time period, excluding recent history and the contemporary period altogether.[25]

Meanwhile, perhaps the most important lack in Central Asian studies is that of the institutions and habits of a community of scholars. The functions of such a community would include the exchange of ideas, sharing of constructive criticism, focused debate, building a corpus of literature which has been held to a high standard and construction of a scholarly consensus on issues relating to the full spectrum of Central Asian history, culture and society. This is not to suggest that the field should aspire to homogeneity and a unanimity of views – rather the goal must be to form a community of scholarship in which alternative views confront one another and are evaluated on the basis of theoretical, methodological and empirical considerations.

---

[22] General historical overviews are available in Geoffrey Wheeler's *The Modern History of Soviet Central Asia,* London 1964, and Olaf Caroe's, op. cit., both written at the height of the Cold War with ensuing implications for their content, and neither written by a trained historian with familiarity with the non-Russian sources.

[23] Elizabeth E. Bacon, *Central Asians under Russian Rule: A Study in Culture Change,* Ithaca (N.Y.) 1966.

[24] E.g. Mehrdad Haghayeghi, *Islam and Politics in Central Asia*, New York 1995.

[25] In three large volumes, Yuri Bregel's *Bibliography of Islamic Central Asia* (Uralic and Altaic Series 160), Bloomington 1995, covers from the Arab conquest to the Russian conquest. It should be noted that bibliography is one area where a great deal of valuable work has been done by Soviet scholars, though their coverage of Western literature is poor at best.

The fragmentation of Central Asian studies to which I have referred throughout this article has meant that there has been very little opportunity for such a community to develop.

On one level, the lack of a community may be traced to personal attitudes. For an extremely small field, Central Asian studies has had more than its share of rivalries, and among many of the key figures, in the United States at least, there has been a predominant attitude of disdain and competition rather than respect and cooperation. This may be understood in part as a product of competition over scarce resources. It may also be seen as a result of the fact that much of the scholarship in the field does have significant shortcomings, which has led to criticism that is unfortunately belligerent rather than constructive. As a marginalized field of scholarship, Central Asian studies falls victim to the double-edged sword which first discourages good quality students from entering the field, and then puts up such obstacles to career development that it is difficult for scholars to sustain a strong output of research products. There is most certainly something of a frontier mentality among many scholars in this field: each thinks of himself as the only one who has really ventured into this unexplored domain, and therefore there is no need to engage with others.

Thus, the most important step requirement for improving the quality of scholarship is improving the environment in which it is produced. It is crucial that mechanisms be developed and enhanced which can foster exchange of ideas and constructive criticism. I would argue that the most important reason why scholarship in this field has not been better is not because we lack the intellectual capacity, the energy or even the financial resources. The problem is a lack of mechanisms by which scholars are helped and encouraged to meet high standards.

First and foremost, this is a problem of outlets of scholarly production. A large number of recent publications have appeared as a consequence of the fact that funding organizations consider this region to be 'hot' and this 'heat' in itself has come to serve as a sufficient standard of quality. Much recent literature has appeared in publications where there is a low standard of documentation – where it is sufficient to state 'facts' and opinion without making a credible effort to engage the existing scholarship on the topic. A rather smaller portion of the new literature has appeared in refereed journals in the disciplines where the problem is that, though disciplinary standards are upheld, there may be a fundamental lack of knowledge about the empirical case material. In the short term, there is little that can be done about the shortage of suitable referees for such journals to evaluate contributions on Central Asia, but the lack of organization in the field undoubtedly results in a failure to identify those who are available.

While I think it would be ill-advised for the field to rely primarily on journals with a regional profile, since this would encourage the isolation of the field, it is nevertheless important that regionally oriented publications play a role in the development of a scholarly critical mass. The greatest problem now is the lack of specialist evaluations in the editorial process for those journals which exist in this field. The journals *Central Asian Survey* and *Central Asia Monitor*, for all the valuable material that they have printed, suffer from uneven quality of scholarly contributions. The refereeing process not only helps to establish a standard to which submitting authors aspire, but is also an interactive process which improves submissions before they are published. When the editorial process thereby sets credible standards, the publication achieves recognition and can attract the best quality submissions. None of the existing periodicals focusing on contemporary Central Asian topics appears to operate on this principle.

The problem of standards also has important impact in the allocation of grant support. There is a limited pool of disciplinary scholars who focus on this region, and there is insufficient coordination in the field for those who are available to be identified and drawn upon by grant-making organizations. Consequently, the allocation of support for projects in this area is not always well-targeted. In the case of some foundations, these decisions are made by program officers who are unlikely to be well-versed in Central Asian studies. This means that cutting-edge projects may not be recognized as such. It also means that grants may be given too easily, with the result that the salutary role which a demanding grant committee can play in improving a research design is lost. These problems can only be overcome by greater coordination between scholars in the field and the grant-making organizations.

On another level, the problem of a critical mass is a problem of basic communication. In Europe, the trend appears to be toward greater communication and cooperation, as exemplified by the recent formation of the European Society for Central Asian Studies (ESCAS). ESCAS has grown out of regular international conferences, has established a relationship with the Asia Committee of the European Science Foundation and has plans of producing a bulletin in addition to its existing series of conference proceedings. In the former Soviet Union, the trend has been one of dramatic disintegration. Formerly, the role of integration was served by the Soviet Academy of Sciences, the network of state universities, all-union scholarly societies and other centralized institutions. Since 1991, virtually all forms of integration dissolved, and the only significant force that is countering this trend is the involvement of international organizations such as the International Research and Exchanges Board (IREX), the Soros Foundation, and the Carnegie Endowment for International Peace, supporting conferences and collaborative programs across the former Soviet space. UNESCO has established an international Institute for Central Asian Studies (ICAS) which is to center its activities in Samarkand, but after several years of organizational initiatives which have had to contend with disunity among the new Central Asian states, the Institute has yet to demonstrate significant activity.

Regarding North American initiatives to promote coordination and collaboration in the field, the trend has also not been positive. Prior to the 1980s, there were no broad-based scholarly societies in this domain. Central Asianists were obliged to meet at the conferences of the Slavists, Middle East scholars and Asian studies scholars, each of which devoted scant attention to Central Asia.[26] Then in the late 1980s, two rival organizations appeared, the Association for Central Asian Studies (ACAS) and the Association for the Advancement of Central Asian Research (AACAR), and due to their rivalry, the two organizations have perhaps done more to foster fragmentation in the field than to promote collaboration. It would be wrong to be pessimistic, however, and I believe there is reason to hope that the divisiveness of the past can be overcome. There is considerable energy and new blood in the field. There has been increased foundation support. If the commitment to the field – as expressed in conferences, Ph.D. dissertations and publications – can be translated into the development of collaborative activity and the development of a community of scholarship, then there is hope that the field's current minor boom can be translated into enduring strength and momentum.

Nearly ten years ago I spent half a year in the Nordic countries working on scholarly materials which resulted from a tradition that received its major impetus nearly a century ago from the outstanding and prodigious achievements of such explorers as Hedin, Olufsen and Mannerheim. At that time, I also sought out current Nordic scholars who were studying Central

---

[26] The respective organizations are the American Association for the Advancement of Slavic Studies (AAASS), the Middle East Studies Association (MESA) and the Association for Asian Studies (AAS).

Asia and I found extremely few. It is tremendously heartening to note that the Nordic countries now have begun to build their own substantial critical mass in this field, as reflected by the symposium which produced the present volume and the young scholars from these countries who are pursuing ground-breaking research in the region. If the scholarly potential in other parts of the world can show similar growth, and if there is development of a strong international community of scholars, then there are grounds for great optimism.

ARCHAEOLOGY

Chinese Excavations at Turfan

SUSANNE JUHL

Since the turn of this century when large-scale, mainly European, expeditions set out to investigate the vast Central Asian continent, this region has been the focus of much Western scholarly attention. Already in the last decade of the 19th century and the first of the 20th there was a large-scale scramble by expeditions in Central Asia, including the Takla-makan desert which covers most of present-day Sinkiang and the northern part of China (see Figure 1).[1] Because of the dry climate of this region, large quantities of organic materials including artefacts of wood, paintings and documents had been preserved for thousands of years. Although some of the expeditions carried out scientific surveys, most resources were devoted to the finding of material remains with the object of transporting these, often in great quantities, back to Europe where most of them are still stored in libraries and museums.

The Turfan county is a large green depression in what is known today as Eastern Sinkiang. The depression is located on the northern branch of the so-called Silk Routes, which throughout most of Chinese history fringed the Takla-makan desert. If one travelled to China overland from the Near Orient, the Turfan oasis was one of the last stations before reaching the Jade Gate, the symbolic entrance to China proper. The area has a very low position and Lake Aiding in the Turfan county lies 156 metres below sea level. The Turfan depression is bounded to the north by a range of high mountains constituting the eastern part of the Tianshan range. To the south-east the area is bounded by the Gobi desert and to the south-west by the Takla-makan desert. The depression is extremely dry with averaging temperatures of 38°C in the three hot summer months. Although the

---

[1] Among the explorers and scientists who carried out excavations were Dmitri Klementz, Petr Koslov and Sergei Oldenburg from Russia, Sir Aurel Stein from Great Britain (Hungary), Albert Grünwedel from Germany, Albert von Le Coq from France, Count Kozui Otani from Japan and Sven Hedin from Sweden.

depression is practically rainless, the area is very fertile. Throughout its history the fertility of the depression has depended on irrigation, using an ingenious system of subterranean channels, the so-called *karez*, which lead melt water down from the Tianshan mountains to irrigate cultivated lands.

Sir Aurel Stein, one of the Europeans who participated in the race among explorers at the beginning of this century, brought large quantities of archaeological materials to Britain and to New Delhi. On his third expedition to Central Asia from 1913 to 1916 he also went to the Turfan area. Stein and his team worked at the cemeteries close to Turfan for two weeks, in which they opened some thirty tombs. During their work they recovered an impressive amount of remains most of which were taken to Britain.[2]

After the founding of the People's Republic of China in 1949, a number of Chinese archaeological surveys have been conducted in the Sinkiang province.[3] Within the last decade, Western teams of scientists have to a certain degree been allowed to participate in fieldwork in the region, which will most certainly provide us with much new knowledge in this field.[4] This article will focus on some of the Chinese archaeological investigations that have taken place after 1949 in Turfan, Sinkiang. The greatest attention will be given to burial sites assigned close to that period when the non-Chinese Juqu clan of the Lushui people ruled the state of Northern Liang (AD 397–439), from AD 420 also including the area of the Turfan depression, at that time named Gaochang Commandery. Northern Liang was one of a number of small short-lived states established in the north-western part of China in the historical period of the Southern and Northern Dynasties (*Nanbeichao*). For the northern territories of China a part of the period is known as the Sixteen Kingdoms (*Shiliuguo*) (AD 304–439). Most of these states were founded and ruled by non-Chinese tribes. Within the 4th and

---

[2] The third expedition is published in Sir Aurel Stein, *Innermost Asia: Detailed Report of Explorations in Central Asia, Kan-su and Eastern Iran*, 5 vols, Oxford 1928. Reprint New Delhi 1981.

[3] A brief English survey of Chinese archaeological investigations in Sinkiang (up to the eighties) is to be found in Mu Shunying, 'Development and Achievement of Archaeology in Sinkiang Since the Founding of New China', *Journal of Central Asia* 7:1 (1984), pp. 55–72. A detailed survey of Chinese archaeological investigations is collected in the Sinkiang Academy of Social Science, the Archaeological Research Institute (*Xinjiang shehui kexueyuan kaogu yanjiusuo*), *Xinjiang kaogu sanshi nian* [Thirty Years of Sinkiang Archaeology], Ulumuqi [Urumchi] 1983.

[4] Today it is almost impossible to keep up with the large bulk of new publications. However, the Newsletter *Circle of Inner Asian Art* (CIAA) published by the Department of Art and Archaeology, SOAS (University of London), provides a list of new publications including Western, Indian and Russian works.

5th centuries a total of five states, all with the name of Liang, were established in the north-western part of the region. According to historical sources, three of these Liang states (including Former Liang, Western Liang and Northern Liang) administered Gaochang Commandery during different periods.

A brief historical outline of the Turfan area

Being the gate to the 'Western Regions' (*xiyu*) the region of Turfan had since Early Han in the 2nd century BC occupied an important economic and strategic position. In the earliest documentary references, all written in Chinese, the area is referred to as *Cheshi*.[5] During the reign of Emperor Yuandi of Western Han (r. 48–32 BC), the Chinese empire extended the boundaries to include large territories to the west and north of the old frontier. For strategical reasons Chinese authorities established military control at Turfan and a number of Chinese military colonies were established. According to Chinese sources large numbers of Han Chinese households (according to some references more than 70,000 households) were transferred to resettle in the Turfan area. These families, mainly farmers from the densely populated areas of central China, were to execute part-time farming and part-time military service.

However, during the four hundred years of the Han Dynasty, the Chinese authorities were never able to maintain firm political control of the region. Several times they completely lost authority and the area came under the control of various warlords, chieftains etc. During the 4th century the Former Liang dynasty (AD 313–376) under the Chinese Zhang family controlled most of the Liang region in the north-western part of China. During this period the Turfan area was once more annexed by the Chinese of Former Liang and the designation of the Cheshi region was altered to Gaochang Commandery.[6] The political control and administrative divisions established during Former Liang were on the whole continued by the succeeding small states of the Sixteen Kingdoms. Gaochang Commandery came to an end in AD 460 when the Ruanruan tribes conquered the remnants of the Juqu clan

---

[5] *Hanshu* [History of the Han Dynasty] (204 BC–AD 24) by Ban Gu (AD 32–92). Ch. 96b, pp. 3921–3932. Reprint Beijing 1990.
[6] *Jinshu* [History of the Jin Dynasty] (AD 265–419) by Fan Xuanli (AD 578–648) et al., Ch. 86, p, 2238. Reprint Beijing 1991.

of the Lushui people. After their conquest by Northern Wei in AD 439, a part of the Juqu clan had managed to perpetuate the Northern Liang state in this region. Hereafter a succession of princes was established (*Gaochang wang*). The region was once more occupied by the Chinese empire in AD 640 during Early Tang and set up as the Western province (*Xizhou*) with the administrative centre for the Area Command (*dudu fu*) located in Gaochang City.

Chinese excavations

Between 1959 and 1975 a team from the Sinkiang Museum and members of the Turfan Cultural Relics Preservation Office undertook to excavate some thirteen sites in cemeteries north of Astana (*Asitana*) village and east of Karakhoja (*Halahezhuo*) village in the Turfan county. Further excavations were carried out in 1979 and the most recently reported one was conducted in 1983. More than 450 tombs dating from the Han (206 BC–AD 220) to the Tang (AD 618–905) period have been found during these excavations. Among their contents were more than 2,000 documents, of which 160 range within the period of the Sixteen Kingdoms. This large number of documents constitutes by far the most important of the discoveries at these sites.[7] The following survey provides a brief summary of Chinese archaeological excavations and studies of tombs dated from the period of the Sixteen Kingdoms.

The ancient city of Gaochang was situated south-east of the village of Astana and south-west of the village of Karakhoja. No detailed layout of the tombs is provided in the reports. The greatest importance is attached to the documents that were found, and the tombs are only described in broad outline. Only a small percentage of the tombs have remained unrobbed. Most of the ancient grave robbers paid little attention to the documents, which in most cases were left behind. On the other hand, when the Western explorers came to the sites, they quickly discovered the cultural values hidden in the documents and they removed as much as they had the strength

---

[7] In order to annotate and publish the documents the Administrative Bureau of National Cultural Relics (*Guojia wenwu shiye guanli ju*) in 1975 established a team under the editorship of Tang Changru. The series *Tulufan chutu wenshu* [Documents Excavated at Turfan] was published in one edition of ten volumes (Beijing 1981-1992). A large-size edition of four volumes was published by the Chinese Institute of Cultural Relics et al. (*Zhongguo wenwu yanjiusuo*), Beijing 1992.

to remove. At the same time, locals of the area began to sell written material from tombs on a large scale. The majority of the surviving documents contain written dates. The remainder have been roughly dated, most frequently by other datable evidence. Occasionally, mortuary artefacts from a number of tombs have been mixed up by the thieves so that fragments of one document have been found in various tombs. Some of the documents are official and were placed in the tombs as proper grave goods, but the majority of them, often found in fragments, are there because they were used as wrapping material for the belongings of the deceased or as parts of the tomb figures.

The first Chinese excavation was conducted in 1959 and published in the Chinese series *Wenwu* in 1960. Subsequent excavations have been reported in *Wenwu* in 1972, 1973, 1975 and 1983.

Large numbers of enclosed clan burials were found in the area to the north and north-east of the village of Astana. In 1959 three enclosed clan burials, each containing two tombs, were excavated one kilometre north of the village.[8] All tombs were previously robbed. One tomb, numbered TAM 305 (Figure 2), yielded a document dated AD 384 of Former Liang. The remainder of the documents were from the 6th and 7th centuries when Gaochang was ruled by the Qu family and by the Tang Empire, respectively. The tombs, none of which are reported individually, are all of the earth-chamber type and characterized by a sloping entrance passage and a single grave chamber. Tomb 305 was a joint burial of male and female. The remains of both occupants and of their clothing were intact. Both were dressed in silk garments with a slanting collar lining, under which they wore tight skirts. The female wore shoes of deep red patterned silk, and by the side of the male's feet were a pair of blue hemp shoes. The face of each was covered by a piece of silk. Documents were found inside the dress of both male and female. Best preserved of these were two documents, each 24 by 10 cm in size, found inside the collar lining of the dress of the female. One document has an era name corresponding to AD 384, the second has no date but was most likely written within the same period. The tomb yielded a total of 45 Chinese copper coins as well as a small number of cooking vessels, some of which still contained rice and black soya beans.

---

[8] The Museum of the Sinkiang Uighur Autonomous Region (*Xinjiang weiwu'er zizhiqu bowuguan*), 'Xinjiang, Tulufan, Asitana beiqu muzang fajue jianbao' [A Brief Report on the Excavation of the Cemetery in the Northern Area of Astana in Turfan, Sinkiang], *Wenwu* 1960:6, pp. 13–22.

A total of 105 tombs was examined in the course of four excavations conducted from 1966 to 1969.⁹ The tombs, excavated at the Astana and Karakhoja cemeteries, respectively, had all been previously opened. Twelve were completely emptied and the rest had been looted to some degree. As to the dates, a number of tombs belong to the period of the Sixteen Kingdoms. The large tombs comprised a sloping entrance passage and a single earthen chamber, occasionally with a small side-chamber. The mortuary objects in the larger tombs included earthenware and wooden artefacts such as figurines, horses, wagons and silk fabrics. The small graves contained only a few items such as some clothing and some objects of earthenware.

Between 1963 and 1965 another group of fifty-six tombs was excavated at the Astana and Karakhoja cemeteries.¹⁰ Even here earthen chamber tombs from the 4th and 5th centuries were found. The mortuary objects reported included a large variety of earthenware utensils, such as lamp stands, dishes and bowls. Some jars were inscribed with 'one jar yellow millet'. The wooden objects included figurines, dishes, cups, spoons and models of horses, wagons and camels, all rather crudely made. One tomb contained the remains of a young female. Her mortuary garment included a pair of brocade shoes, remnants of a silk robe, a silk-wadded quilt robe and the remains of an embroidered robe. The tombs yielded a number of documents. The contents of these are not discussed but some of the datings are mentioned; one is dated AD 367, another AD 370 and yet another AD 418.

In 1975 a group of fifty-one tombs was discovered near the village of Karakhoja.¹¹ The layout and construction of these tombs are very similar to those previously excavated at the cemeteries. No detailed description of the tombs is provided, but it is reported that all early dated tombs had a sloping passage entrance leading down to a square earthen chamber. The chambers

---

⁹ The Museum of the Sinkiang Uighur Autonomous Region, 'Tulufan xian Asitana-Halahezhuo gumuqun qingli jianbao' [A Brief Report on the Clearance of the Necropolis of Astana-Karakhoja in Turfan County], *Wenwu* 1972:1, pp. 8–19.

¹⁰ The Museum of the Sinkiang Uighur Autonomous Region, 'Tulufan xian Asitana-Halahezhuo gumuqun fajue jianbao (1963–1965)' [A Brief Report from the Excavations of the Necropolis of Astana-Karakhoja in Turfan County (1963–1965)], *Wenwu* 1973:10, pp. 7–20.

¹¹ The Sinkiang Museum Archaeology Team (*Xinjiang bowuguan kaogudui*), 'Tulufan Halahezhuo gumuqun fajue jianbao' [A Brief Report on the Excavations of the Necropolis of Karakhoja in Turfan], *Wenwu* 1978:6, pp. 1–14. A shorter version of the article has been published in English in *Chinese Archaeological Abstracts* 34 (Monumenta Archaeologica, vol. 9–11), vol. 4, edited by Albert Dien, Jeffrey Riegel and Nancy Price, Los Angeles 1985, pp. 1566–1569.

contained wooden coffins and a total of five tombs had murals painted on the back wall of the chamber (Figure 3). Most burial objects, only briefly noted, are made of wood including figurines, models of ox-carts, domestic animals, dishes and one wooden staff. The latter is 174 cm in length with a black shaft and a red handle carved in the shape of a bird. A number of wooden carved figurines, often in pairs of male and female, were found. Some figurines are carved with features such as deep-set eyes, prominent noses and square faces indicating that they were non-Chinese (Figure 4). Yet other figures are carved with features typically Chinese, such as thin eyebrows, narrow eyes and the hair in a bun. Often arms and legs are fitted to the torso with small wooden tabs indicating that they might have been moveable. The most detailed description of this excavation concerns the documents including 102 pieces, almost all written in Chinese characters. The documents dated from AD 408 include three answers given in reply to questions set for the imperial examination level *xiucai* ('flourishing talent'). The questions have not survived but the responses concern a famous battle during the Warring States period (403–221 BC) and, accordingly, within the Chinese cultural field of study. However, most of the documents deal with military affairs, such as the division of the army of Northern Liang into corpses, their designations and their duties. Some documents also concern the duties of military services and the payment of taxes, both obviously heavy burdens for the population of Gaochang.

The latest excavation to be mentioned took place in 1979.[12] In a shaft pit the well-preserved remains of a young adult female were discovered. The body was wrapped in hemp cloth and tied up with ropes of reed. The tomb had been previously looted but contained a few artefacts including fragments of embroidery silk textiles as well as a headblock covered in blue patterned silk (Figure 5). A pair of shoes, 21 by 9 cm in size, made of folded paper and covered in silk was also in the grave (Figure 6). They appeared to consist of eight pieces of inscribed papers, four of which have a text written on both sides. The documents, all dated from the 5th century of the Sixteen Kingdoms period, relate to disputes over official matters such as imprisonment, irrigation works and taxes. One inscription relates to a

---

[12] The Cultural Relics Office of the Sinkiang Turfan Area (*Xinjiang Tulufan diqu wenguansuo*), 'Tulufan chutu shiliuguo shiqi de wenshu – Tulufan Asitana 382 hao mu qingli jianbao' [Unearthed Documents from Turfan of the Sixteen Kingdoms Period – A Brief Report on the Clearance of Tomb 382 in Astana, Turfan], *Wenwu* 1983:1, pp. 19–25.

memorial sent by a person who had been imprisoned because he failed to levy some taxes. Another document relates to the military status of some soldiers who had to do forced labour and gather in the harvest. Earlier these soldiers had had the responsibility to look after the mulberry harvest in the Hall of Learning (*xue guan*). Two documents relate to a dispute concerning an irrigation problem. The farming depended on irrigation and the repair of the irrigation systems was very important. The duty of the inspectors of the waterways was to distribute irrigated water and keep the water channels in good repair. According to these two documents all problems concerning irrigation were handed by the labour section. Another document concerns the irrigation of vineyards indicating that at this time grapes were grown on a large scale in Gaochang.

Concluding remarks

From the Chinese excavation reports mentioned above, as well as from Stein's reports from the area,[13] it is notable that a distinct Chinese influence is found in burials from the Turfan area dated from the 4th to 6th centuries. According to the reports we must conclude that no non-Chinese influence appears to have affected the practices at this time. Around one hundred years later, on the other hand, a remarkable influence from the West rapidly affected various aspects of the burial habits.

Regarding the period in question, the layout and construction of tombs at the Turfan cemeteries are, except for minor differences, almost identical to those excavated from the Gansu province.[14] This kind of burial practice is by Chinese experts classified as a regional variation, i.e. very seldom found anywhere else in China. The style of the burials includes both independent tombs and what in Chinese archaeology is called 'enclosed clan burials'. Here members of the same clan or family were buried in

---

[13] Sir Aurel Stein, op. cit., vol. II, pp. 566–719.

[14] Compared to the attention given to archaeological investigations dated from the two great empires of China, the Han and the Tang, only a few studies of the period between those dynasties have been made. For brief descriptions of the burial practices of the Gansu province, see Zhang Xiaozhuang, 'Beifang diqu Wei Jin Shiliuguo muzang de fenqu yu fenqi' [Regional and Chronological Variation in the Burials of the Northern Region Dating from the Periods of Wei-Jin and the Sixteen Kingdoms], *Kaogu xuebao* 1987:1, pp. 19–43, and Wenwu Editorial Board (*Wenwu bianji weiyuanhui*), *Wenwu kaogu gongzuo shi nian 1979–89* [Ten Years of Cultural Relics and Archaeology], Beijing 1990, pp. 325–326.

tombs arranged side by side. The tombs were enclosed by an almost square embankment or wall of piled-up gravel. An opening, supposedly the entrance, was made in one of the walls and a tomb path was often constructed in front of the entrance opening. Some enclosures are of considerable size. For example, two enclosures at Jiayuguan in the northern part of Gansu, are arranged parallel to each other in a north–south alignment within an enclosure measuring almost 80 by 80 metres and still half a metre high. The entrance of the enclosure is 14 metres wide. Leading to the entrance is a tomb path 128 metres long flanked on each side by a wall of gravel. The tombs have a long sloping entrance passage leading down to one, two or occasionally three square or rectangular chambers, either constructed of earth or brick.

The tombs at Turfan are of the earth-chamber type and none are reported to have brick screen walls, decorated or plain, which is a significant feature of the tombs of Gansu. However, five tombs dated from the Northern Liang period were decorated with murals. These were painted on the back wall of the tomb chamber, four of them being very well preserved. Although much more primitive in artistic expression, the themes of the paintings are typically Chinese as we know them from murals in tombs from all over China since the Han period. Most often they show the tomb owner and his wife dressed in traditional Chinese style. In addition, venerated articles of Chinese civilization such as a table with a writing brush and an ink jar, sceneries of farming and motifs of heavenly symbols are painted. Regarding treatment of the dead and mortuary artefacts there are various points of significance. The dead were either buried in a wooden coffin or wrapped in a mat of straw, both being common Chinese burial practices. The large quantities of silk fabrics, both plain, coloured and patterned, are special features of the Turfan burials. Compared to the Gansu province and the rest of China the extraordinary large number of wooden artefacts are also of significance. However, it must be emphasized that it is not known whether a larger number of wooden objects were made at Turfan or whether they simply were better preserved in the dry climate. The large amount of well-preserved documents is of particular interest. Although no detailed study of their contents has been published yet, they do provide a great deal of information. Since the documents are written in Chinese, it is obvious that the Turfan area was under the influence of Chinese administration. The names of persons given in the documents are Chinese as well, yet it is not at all certain whether a person was actually Chinese or had adopted a Chinese name. The titles and posts are well-known Chinese ones and the duties of civil and military services are likewise of a typical Chinese character, all of which indicate an influence of Chinese administration.

From this brief description of the cemeteries of Turfan pertaining to the period of the Sixteen Kingdoms it is obvious that a large part of the upper stratum of the population either were Han Chinese or had adopted Han-Chinese cultural values, burial habits, art forms, mythology etc. If there were societies in the region adhering to other sets of cultural values, these are not to be found in the archaeological reports referred to in the survey presented above.

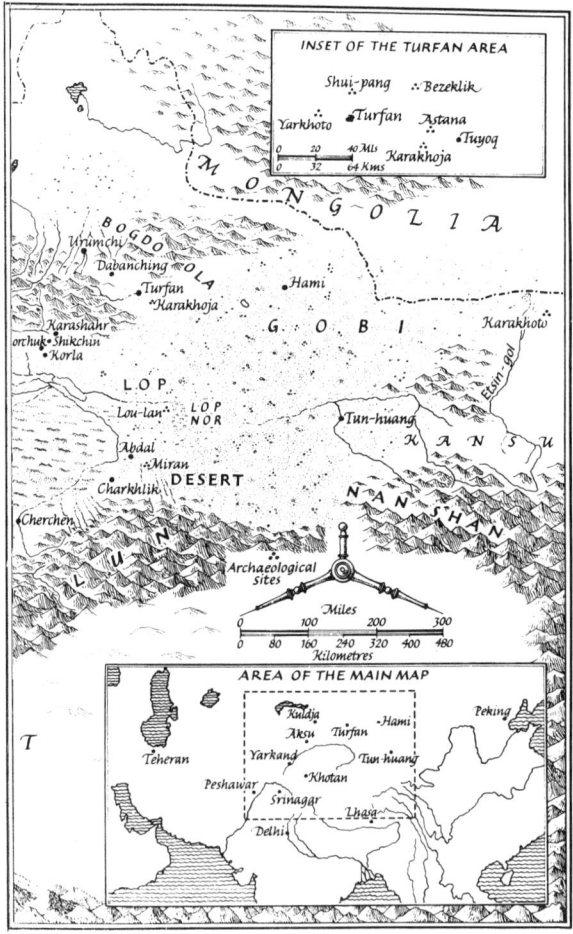

Figure 1. Chinese Turkestan
Source: Peter Hopkirk, *Foreign Devils on the Silk Road*, London 1980

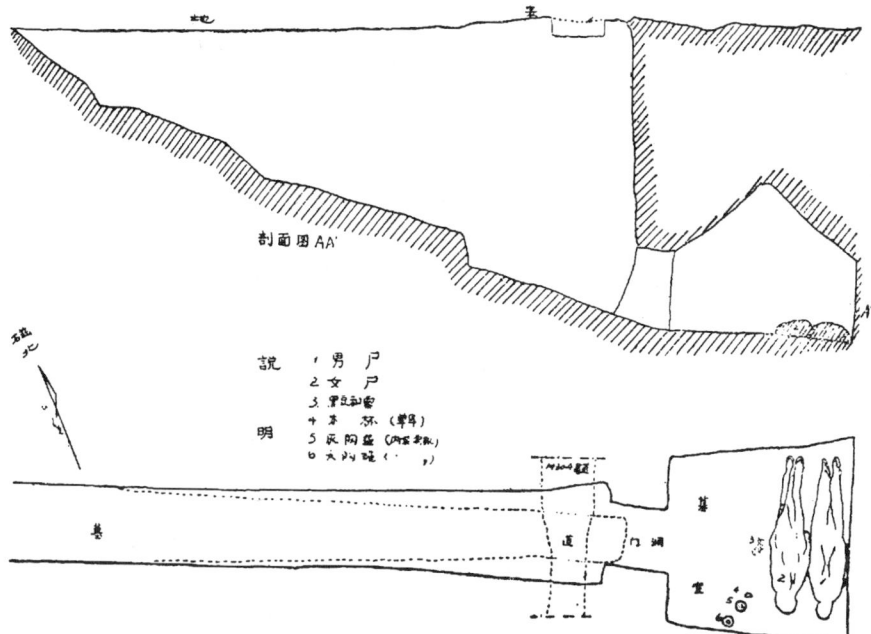

Figure 2. Drawing of Tomb TAM 305 at Astana, Turfan
Source: *Wenwu* 1960:6

Figure 3. Wall paintings from tombs excavated at Turfan
Source: *Wenwu* 1960:6

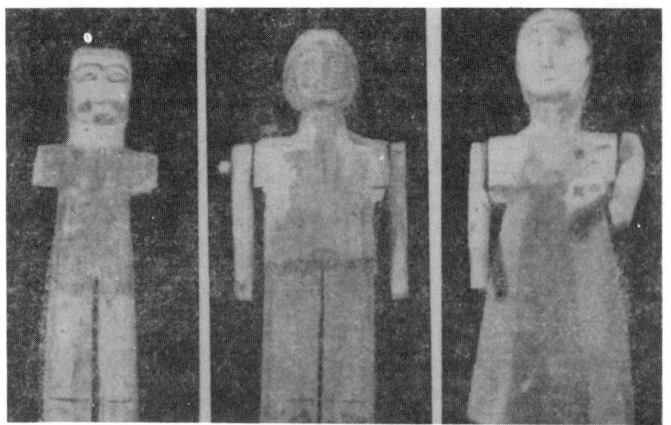

Figure 4. Wooden figurines
Source: *Wenwu* 1978:6

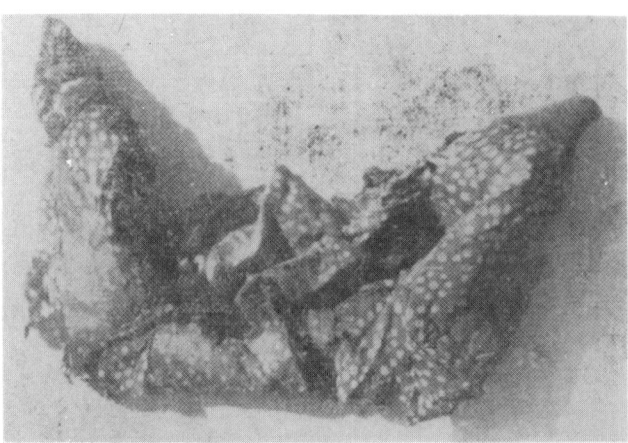

Figure 5. Headblock covered in blue silk
Source: *Wenwu* 1983:1

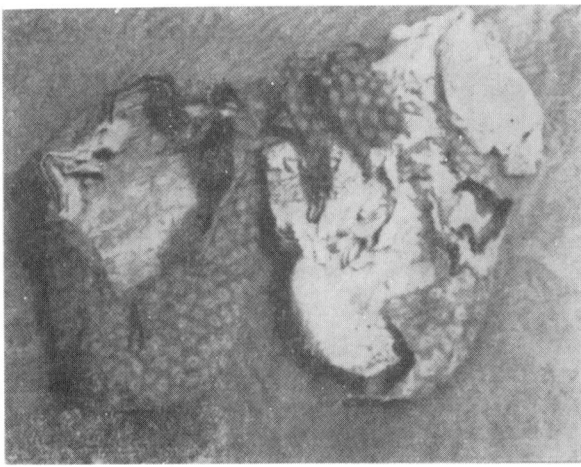

Figure 6. Pair of shoes in folded paper and covered in silk fabric
Source: *Wenwu* 1983:1

The Sino-Swedish Expedition to Yar-tonguz in 1994

STAFFAN ROSÉN

On a cold day in the middle of January 1994 the director of the Archaeological Research Institute in Urumchi, Professor Wang Binghua 王炳華 and his collaborator Dr. Zhang Ping 張平 arrived in Stockholm at the invitation of the Sven Hedin Foundation of the Royal Academy of Sciences. The purpose of their visit to the Swedish capital was to discuss the final plans for a proposed joint Chinese and Swedish archaeological survey expedition to the south-eastern area of the Takla-makan desert. Preparations for this moment had been going on for many years. In 1992 the Chinese and Swedish institutes had organized a seminar in Urumchi on 'The Study of the Western Regions', with the participation of some 30 scholars from China, Sweden, the United States, Great Britain, Japan and New Zealand. The seminar was followed by a weeklong survey expedition by car through the Takla-makan desert from Aqsu to Khotan along the river-bed of Khotan-darya. During the seminar and following field trip the scholars had ample opportunity to fulfil the main purpose of the meeting – to inform each other of what had been done in China and abroad, especially in Sweden, within the field of Sinkiang studies since the political turmoil of 1935 when the Sino-Swedish Expedition had ceased to operate.[1] The results of this seminar and field trip were published in Urumchi in 1994.[2]

During the discussions of 1992 between the Chinese and Swedish participants it had become clear that there was a common wish to revive, at

---

[1] Sven Hedin, *History of the Expedition in Asia I–IV* (Reports from the Scientific Expedition to the North-Western Provinces of China under the Leadership of Dr. Sven Hedin, Publications 23–26), Stockholm 1943–1945.

[2] Ma Dazheng 馬大正, Wang Rong 王嶸 and Yang Lian 楊鐮 (eds), *Xiyu kaocha yu yanjiu* 西域考察與研究, Ulumuqi 烏魯木齊 [Urumchi] 1994.

least to some degree, the great tradition of Sino-Swedish scientific cooperation in Sinkiang from the time of Sven Hedin and his collaborators, especially from his last expedition of 1927–1935. For obvious reasons it was also clear that any new project of this kind would have to be planned on a much smaller scale than its predecessors. As a first step it seemed most reasonable to focus our attention on one field of research. The decision that this field was to be archaeology is hardly surprising. Our counterpart in Urumchi was the Archaeological Research Institute and archaeology had been a very important and successful branch of Sven Hedin's last expedition through the epoch-making works of Folke Bergman.[3] Several unexplored areas on the archaeological map of Sinkiang still awaited investigation, and the Archaeological Research Laboratory at Stockholm University would constitute an important scientific asset to an archaeological project. The Swedish team could also offer philological and linguistic expertise as well as specialists in the history of art.

The final aim of the discussions in January 1994 was to decide upon the exact geographical area and the scope of the planned expedition. Several places along the southern Silk Road were considered, among them Dandan-öilik and Cherchen, but it was finally agreed to concentrate our efforts on the lower reaches of the Yar-tonguz-darya and its possibly abandoned riverbeds in the desert. The main reason for this decision was that the Yar-tonguz-darya constitutes a blank spot from an archaeological point of view, situated between two archaeologically more or less well-known sites, the Niya-darya and the Endere-darya. Ever since the days of Hedin, Stein and Huntington it has been clear that the Niya and Endere sites constitute remnants of important and fairly large settlements along the southern Silk Road, each of them supported by the water of their respective rivers. For unclear reasons no such settlement had been discovered along the Yar-tonguz-darya. The end station of the Yar-tonguz-darya, some 80 km north of the present Silk Road and today called Jigda-bulung, was visited twice by Aurel Stein (1901 and 1906)[4] and once by Huntington (1906).[5] Both

---

[3] Folke Bergman, *Archaeological Researches in Sinkiang: Especially the Lop-Nor Region* (Reports from the Scientific Expedition to the North-Western Provinces of China under the Leadership of Dr. Sven Hedin, VII:1 Archaeology), Stockholm 1939, id., 'Travels and Archaeological Field-Work in Mongolia and Sinkiang – A Diary of the Years 1927–1934', in Sven Hedin, *History of the Expedition in Asia,* vol. IV, Stockholm 1945.

[4] Cf. M. A. Stein, *Ancient Khotan,* Oxford 1907, pp. 417–419, id., *Serindia: Detailed Report of Explorations in Central Asia and Westernmost China,* Oxford 1921, pp. 270–272, and id., *Innermost Asia: Detailed Report of Explorations in Central Asia,*

travellers reported that nothing of archaeological interest was to be found in the area and no signs of any old settlements were reported. Both Stein and Huntington, however, found it worthwhile to mention the unpleasant taste of the borax saturated water in the river.[6]

Having a look at the archaeological map of south-eastern Takla-makan many questions pose themselves. Is it really true that no settlements ever existed along the Yar-tonguz-darya? If true, why was that so? Could it possibly have anything to do with the quality of the water in the river? Is the alleged absence of settlements true for neolithic and later periods? What do we know about the history of the area in general and the Yar-tonguz in particular?

Beginning with the first of these questions, our initiated task would be to conduct a survey of the present and former river-bed of the Yar-tonguz-darya in an effort to discover traces of settlements. It was specifically stated that the expedition would only survey the area and that no excavation should take place at this stage. It was also agreed that the expedition would set out from Urumchi and that the Archaeological Research Institute should provide it with suitable motor vehicles which, if necessary, could be supplemented by a local camel caravan.

These issues having been settled, the Swedish team through the help of the Sven Hedin Foundation of the Royal Academy of Sciences was able to secure the necessary funds. Substantial financial support was given by H.M. the King of Sweden, The Swedish Council for Research in the Humanities and Social Sciences and The Swedish Institute. In the meantime, our Chinese counterparts procured all the necessary documents from the Chinese and Uighur authorities. The date for the expedition was set for October–November 1994.

The historical background

The road stretching from Khotan via Keriya, Niya, Endere, Cherchen, Charkliq and Loulan was the first part of the system of roads which we today call the Silk Road(s) to fall into disuse. Around AD 641/642, at the

---

Kansu, and Eastern Iran, Oxford 1928, pp. 156–157.

[5] Ellsworth Huntington, *The Pulse of Asia: A Journey in Central Asia Illustrating the Geographic Basis of History,* Boston 1907, pp. 210ff., and Stein, *Serindia,* pp. 270ff.

[6] Huntington, op. cit., p. 212, and Stein, *Serindia,* p. 212.

time of the visit of the famous Chinese pilgrim Xuan Zhuang (Hsüan Ts'ang) 玄奘 to Endere, only a few kilometres east of Yar-tonguz, it had already been abandoned and the area was somewhat enigmatically referred to by the locals as the old 'Tuholo 都貨羅 country'.[7] The abandoning of this part of the Silk Road was most likely due to climatic and environmental changes. Unstable river-beds and the entailing draughts or floods[8] would have destroyed the sensitive irrigation systems of the oasis cities, finally making the agricultural and stock-farming sectors of the economy of the area impossible to sustain. Another important factor was an ever spreading desert – a process which is operative even today.

The relatively early disappearance of the southern route as one of the main commercial and intellectual arteries between the West and the Far East is most likely the main reason for the lack of reference to this area in Chinese and other non-local written sources. To the best of my knowledge, the Yar-tonguz-darya is not mentioned in any important Chinese source, chronicle or travelogue. This fact speaks in favour of the interpretation that the Yar-tonguz for some reason was perceived as a sterile land. In contrast to the neighbouring areas, the Yar-tonguz-darya is nowadays known only by its Uighur name ('The Ravine Boar River'), although two other names, Aqtash-darya and Tollan-khoja (or Tolanghuja) have been recorded.[9] The toponyms Khotan, Niya, Endere and Cherchen are all of pre-Muslim, non-Turkic origin and most likely of considerable age, while the purely Uighur toponym Yar-tonguz is obviously of a much later date.[10]

---

[7] Cf. Stein, *Serindia*, pp. 286ff.

[8] Cf. Stein, *Serindia*, pp. 274ff., and Stein, *Innermost Asia*, p. 157.

[9] Cf. D. M. Farquhar, G. Jarring and E. Nori, *Sven Hedin Central Asia Atlas: Memoir on Maps, Vol. II, Index of Geographical Names* (Reports from the Scientific Expedition to the North-Western Provinces of China under the Leadership of Dr. Sven Hedin, I:3 Geography, Publication 49), Stockholm 1967, p. 90, and Stein, *Ancient Khotan*, p. 418. For a comment on the toponym *Yar-tonguz;* cf. Gunnar Jarring, *Central Asian Turkic Place-Names. Lop Nor and Tarim Area: An Attempt at Classification and Explanation Based on Sven Hedin's Diaries and Published Works* (Reports from the Scientific Expedition to the North-Western Provinces of China under the Leadership of Dr. Sven Hedin, VIII:11 Ethnography, Publication 56), Stockholm 1997.

[10] Cf. Jarring, op. cit., pp. 470–471.

THE SINO-SWEDISH EXPEDITION TO YAR-TONGUZ IN 1994

The geopolitical location of Yar-tonguz

From the 1st century BC until the Tibetan conquest in the second half of the 8th century, the southern fringes of the Takla-makan desert were dominated by two political entities, Khotan in the West and Shanshan 鄯善 in the East. The political power centre of Khotan seems to have been very stable through the centuries, situated in Yotkan a few kilometres to the west of present-day Khotan.[11] In Shanshan, also known as Loulan 樓蘭 or Kroraina, the situation was less stable. The first capital may have been the city of Loulan, once situated on the western shore of Lake Lop-nor and for environmental reasons abandoned in the 4th century (and finally rediscovered in 1901 by Sven Hedin). The cities of Miran, Cherchen and Vash-shahri might also at various times have served as capitals of the kingdom.[12] This political, and to some extent cultural, division of the southern Silk Road between the two states was in effect from at least the first century BC until the Tibetan conquest of the whole area in the 8th century.

The populations of the two states were multiethnic and multilingual. Khotan was dominated by the Saka population speaking the Saka (or Khotan-Saka) language – a member of the Iranian language group – but several other languages like Prakrit, Sanskrit, Persian, Tibetan and Chinese were used by minorities and perhaps by bilingual representatives of the original Saka population living in the various oasis cities along the southern border of the desert. Loulan, or Shanshan, seems to have been even more multiethnic and multilingual than its competitor in the West. Documents found in the sand at various places in the former Loulan territory show that Chinese, Saka, Prakrit, Sanskrit, Tibetan, Tokharian and Turkic were in use among the obviously heterogeneous population of this transit state between East and West.[13]

---

[11] For further references to Yotkan and the old Khotan, cf. Stein, *Ancient Khotan*, chapter VII–VIII, Li Yinping 李吟屏, *Foguo Yutian* 佛國于闐, Ulumuqi 烏魯木齊 [Urumchi] 1991, and Zhang Guangda 張廣達 and Rong Xinjiang 榮新江, *Yutian shi congkao* 于闐史叢考 Shanghai 上海 1993.

[12] For a discussion about Shanshan and its various capitals, see Stein, *Serindia*, vol. 1, chapter IX, pp. 319–345. Cf. Meng Fanren 孟凡人, *Loulan xinshi* 樓蘭新史, Guangming Press Publishing House and B & T Holland Publications Ltd, s. l. 1990, and Kazutoshi Nagasawa, *Rōran ōkokushi no kenkyū*, Tokyo 1996.

[13] For an exposé of the various kinds of documents in different languages found on the territories of the former states of Khotan and Loulan, see Stein, *Ancient Khotan*, pp. 521–574, Stein, *Serindia*, vol. 3, pp. 1329–1339, Stein, *Innermost Asia*, vol. 4, A. Conrady, *Die chinesischen Handschriften- und sonstigen Kleinfunde Sven Hedins in*

The function of the Tarim basin oasis states as a melting pot and shunting yard for the great religious, intellectual and artistic currents of the world is well known. Buddhism, Zoroastrianism, Nestorianism, Manichaeism, Islam, Confucianism and Taoism with their roots in Greece, Rome, Byzantium, Persia, Gandhara, India and China coexisted, influencing the form and content of local artistic manifestations. However, recent research has shown that within the framework of these main sources of artistic influence it is possible to identify local artistic schools which clearly contrast with each other. For example, the French archaeological team working in Qara-dung has been able to show that the Qara-dung school of Buddhist painting was basically influenced by Indian artistic traditions in contrast to Buddhist paintings from Miran, where the Graeco-Roman influence was more prevalent.[14] A similar analysis still remains to be done on the material from the Japanese excavations at Niya.[15] However, the facts which we already have at our disposal raise the question as to whether national borders also served as borders between the different spheres of artistic influence. Only additional material from the border areas and further research can give answers to these questions. Considering the fact that the border between the Khotan and Shanshan states is considered to have existed somewhere between Niya and Keriya,[16] any material relevant to the history of art that might be found along the Yar-tonguz-darya would naturally be of prime importance.

The 1994 Sino-Swedish expedition

Early in the morning of the 10th of October 1994, the expedition set out from the Archaeological Research Institute in Urumchi. There were three Swedish members: Staffan Rosén (Professor of Korean at the Institute of Oriental Languages of the University of Stockholm and Secretary of the

---

Lou Lan, Stockholm 1920, and B. A. Litvinskij (ed.), *Vostočnyj Turkestan v drevnosti i rannem srednevekov'e: Étnos, jazyki, religii,* Moskva 1992.

[14] Corinne Debaine-Francfort and Henri-Paul Francfort, 'Oasis irriguée et art bouddhique ancien à Karadong: Premier résultats de l'éxploration franco-chinoise de la Keriya', *Académie des inscriptions & belles-lettres: Compte rendus des séances de l'année 1993 novembre-décembre,* Paris 1993.

[15] *Chūnichi nitchū kyōdo Niya yuiseki gakujutsu chōsa hōkokusho. Dai ikkan.* 中日日中共同尼雅跡學術調查報告書，第一卷, Bukkyo University, Kyoto 1996.

[16] For Niya as dependant on Shanshan, cf. Stein, *Serindia,* pp. 328–329.

THE SINO-SWEDISH EXPEDITION TO YAR-TONGUZ IN 1994

Sven Hedin Foundation), Håkan Wahlquist (Curator at the National Museum of Ethnography in Stockholm and Keeper of the Sven Hedin Foundation) and Joakim Enwall (Doctor of Sinology, specialist in Chinese minority languages; served as official interpreter for the Swedish team). The Chinese members were: Wang Mingzhe 王明哲 (Professor of Archaeology and the official leader of the team), Zhang Ping 張平 (archaeologist with extensive experience of this area of the desert), Zhang Chuan 張川 (geologist), Akbar (archaeologist and interpreter of Uighur and Chinese) and three drivers, Mr. Du, Mr. Shu and Mr. Muhammed. The expedition had at its disposal two Japanese Landrovers and one small Chinese truck for the heavy equipment. It had been agreed to make Niya our base camp and to proceed from there with the two jeeps, a desert truck to be rented on a daily basis at Yarkend and/or camels if the terrain so demanded. Due to difficult conditions on the eastern road from Korla to Niya via Charkliq and Cherchen, it was decided that all three vehicles should travel the much longer but safer road via Aqsu, Kashghar and Khotan. This is not the place to relate all the sights and events of scientific and other interest that the expedition met with on its way; suffice it to say that this long detour gave the Swedish members of the expedition ample opportunity to become aquainted with both the heads of the various cultural and archaeological authorities in the whole province of Sinkiang and the way in which the local Chinese and Uighur authorities operate.[17] This experience certainly will be of vital importance in connection with any future work in the province.

The designated base camp, Niya-bazar (Chinese name Minfeng 民豐), was reached in the evening of the 17th and later the same evening the desert truck, a brand new Mercedes, which had been rented in Yarkend, arrived. Most of that evening and the following morning we were busy repacking the equipment from the smaller truck onto the big Mercedes. Our personal equipment, maps and some of the food were stored in the two Landrovers, one of which was to carry the Chinese-Uighur team and the other the Swedish team. As soon as the packing was completed, the vehicles set off for Yar-tonguz-langar some 40 km further east, at the junction of the present Silk Road and the river Yar-tonguz-darya. The director of the Bureau of Culture in Niya, Mr. Khoja Abdullah, accompanied us as the local guide. The *langar* ('inn') consisted of only two desolate brick houses close

---

[17] For a detailed relation of the Sino-Swedish Expedition in Swedish, cf. Joakim Enwall, 'Mot Yar-tonguz – Den svensk-kinesiska Taklamakan-expeditionen 1994', *Orientaliska Studier* 86–87 (1995), pp. 3–34.

to the road, but we soon found an old man who was able to give us some information about the driving conditions along the river. It quickly became clear that only the western side with its fairly even sand plains was suitable for our vehicles, the eastern side having high dunes which reached almost onto the road. The river held little water and was comparatively shallow, with large areas along the banks covered by white saline deposits. The 80 kilometres from the *langar* to the furthermost settlement along the river, Jigda-bulung, were covered with great difficulty in one day. We were very cordially received by the inhabitants of the little village and offered the use of the village elder's house as our headquarters. Contrary to what we had been told in Niya and elsewhere, there were no camels available in Jigda-bulung for the moment, a fact which caused great concern among the members of the expedition, since an early morning test tour with the new desert truck had shown only too clearly that the truck was useless in the wild dune landscape, which began but a few hundred metres from the edge of the village. We were relieved from our worries in a most unexpected way. In the afternoon of the 20th, a small camel caravan consisting of 12 animals suddenly arrived from Endere-maydan carrying a load of wheat to be delivered to the village of Jigda-bulung. Through the good efforts of Khoja Abdullah, the whole caravan and its two leaders were hired for about a week. The village elder ordered a man from the village, Muhammed Tokhti, to bring his own camel and join the caravan as a guide. Thus, early in the morning of the 21st of October, a caravan of 13 animals (one of which was a baby camel without any load) and 10 human beings set out for the long awaited survey of the old river-beds of the Yar-tonguz. The day before our departure three elderly gentlemen of Jigda-bulung had been interviewed in an effort to gather information about any possible ruins or other signs of earlier settlements in the desert. Our informants all agreed that they had heard about the remnants of a *Kone-shahr* or 'Old City' somewhere out there in a north-westerly direction from Jigda-bulung. In the 1960s, a wooden plough of considerable age had been found not far from the *Kone-shahr,* and sent to the museum in Niya. Such was the vague information that would lead us through this vast, beautiful and frightening ocean of sand.

THE SINO-SWEDISH EXPEDITION TO YAR-TONGUZ IN 1994

Kone-shahr

The vegetation, consisting mainly of tamarisks and a few yellow poplars, quickly became very scarce and finally gave way completely to sterile sand. Towards the early afternoon we reached the first of the dry river-beds at a place called Hizma-lihun and very soon afterwards came across three small rivulets. The third and largest of them was called, according to our guides from Endere-maydan, Chitlik-darya. After a short break we continued in a westerly direction and by late afternoon reached a 2 km wide belt overgrown with qamish and tamarisks – a definite sign of a former water-course. Through the binoculars, a small grove of poplars on the opposite side of the *sai* ('sand plain') was observed and after about half an hour's ride we were standing in the middle of yet another old river-bed about 50 metres wide. The luxuriance of the poplars disclosed the fact that deep under the dry surface of the old river-bed water was still present and sustaining these tough deep-rooted trees. Further west on the horizon was a high sandy ridge amid enormous dunes. Our first camp was set up here and its position was defined by our satellite compass as 37°53'96"N, 83°07'68"E. The temperature had risen to +25° in the early afternoon and around midnight it had sunk to –7°. On the following morning it was decided to survey this westernmost and largest of the abandoned river-beds. It seemed reasonable to believe that this river, once 50–100 metres wide, must have been able to support a fairly large settlement. Hence, if any 'ruined city' really existed, it should be somewhere here. Since the old river-bed was so thickly overgrown with trunks of long dead poplars and high sand cones covered with tamarisk it was very difficult to survey both banks of the former river. Therefore, we decided to split the caravan into two sections, each surveying its own bank as we now proceeded in a northerly direction. After a while, however, the danger of the two small caravans losing sight of each other became apparent and a few hours later the two halves were united again. The gradually decreasing vegetation and the narrowing of the river-bed made a fairly efficient survey of both banks easier than before. So far no signs of any human activities could be detected. Our continued search brought us out into a completely sterile dune landscape and towards evening we had reached the top of a high sand-ridge where we could look down into the valley through which we had travelled. On the other side of the ridge a few yellow poplars indicated a suitable camp site, which we reached just in time to arrange the camp before darkness. According to our information

Route of the Sino-Swedish Expedition to Yar-tonguz in October 1994

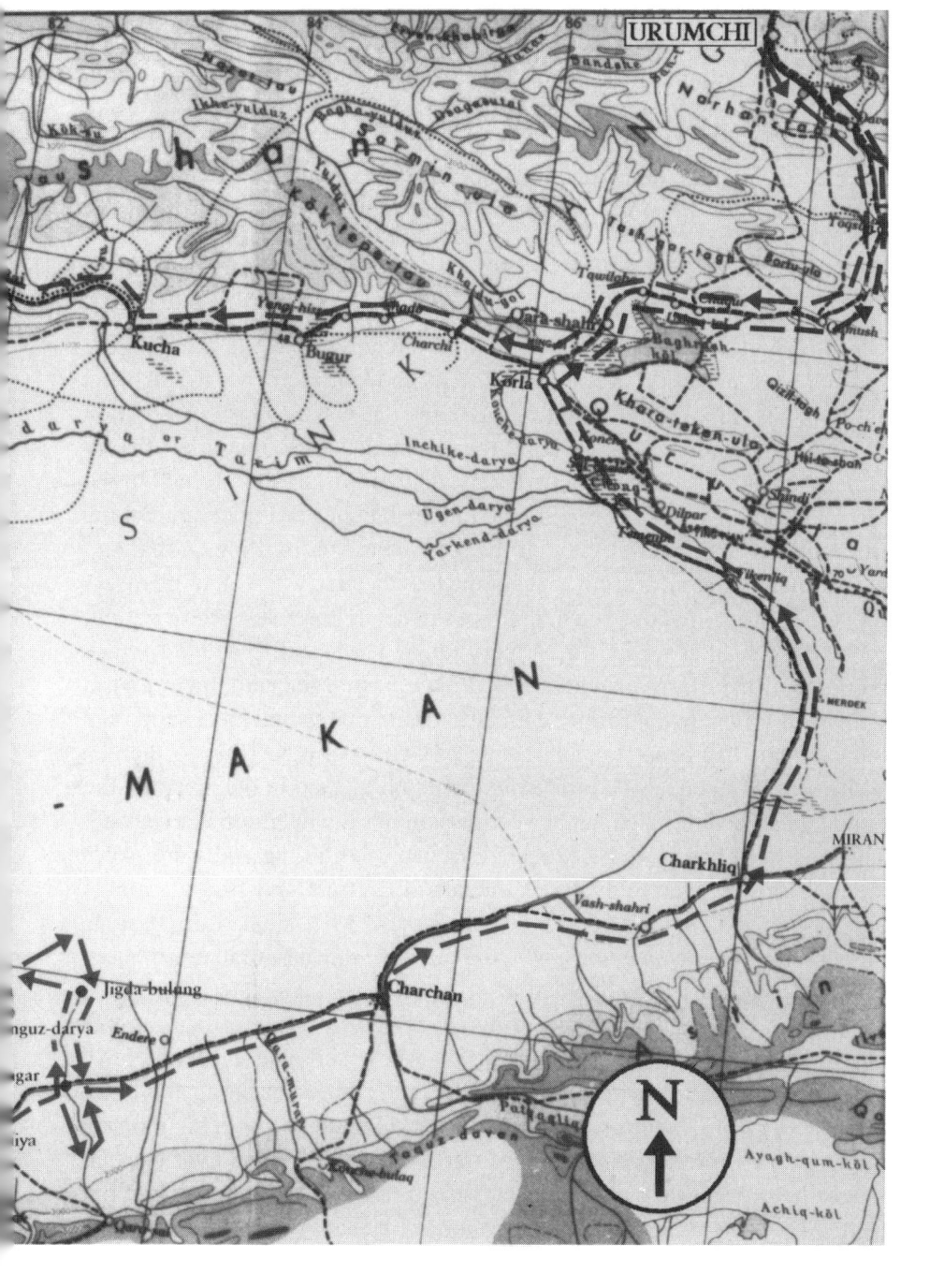

from the old gentlemen in Jigda-bulung, we were now approaching the area where the alleged *Kone-shahr* was said to be found, and the general vigilance increased. We did not have to wait long. As we were setting up our camp, Khoja Abdullah discovered a wooden pole, about 3 metres long, lying in the sand and with clear traces of having been worked by human hands. Before long another pole of the same type was found, an event which greatly enhanced our morale. The following morning a sample of one of the poles was taken for C_{14} analysis and the caravan continued its march towards the north and the evasive *Kone-shahr*. The terrain became more and more undulating and enormous tamarisk cones made it impossible to proceed along a straight course. Suddenly Muhammed Tokhti cried out the words so long awaited: 'Kone-shahr!' And indeed, there it was! In what was obviously the centre of a settlement could be seen the roof construction of a simple hut and scattered around it the remnants of foundations, barely visible under the sand but immediately discernible to the archaeologist Zhang Ping's trained eye. Even though tamarisk cones had piled up making it difficult to get an overall view of the settlement, Zhang Ping, Akbar and Zhang Chuan began measuring some of the foundations, while other members of the expedition set about documenting as much as possible of the location. Despite deep sand covering the former village, it was still possible to trace the course of the old river where it had once passed the settlement and to speculate as to where the former cultivation area, that would have supported its inhabitants, had been situated. No sherds, coins or other signs of human activity were sighted, and considering the depth of sand in the area and the fact that the expedition had neither permission nor the intention to excavate, such finds were hardly to be expected. Because both time and water were becoming scarce, we were forced to start our retreat and find a suitable place for the next camp in good time before dark. After lengthy discussions with our Uighur caravan guides, who did not have much faith in our modern satellite technique, it was decided to proceed in a south-eastern direction, i.e. to take a bearing that would bring us, hopefully, straight back to our camp in Jigda-bulung. The problem was that the desert landscape which we would have to cross was extremely wild, with dunes reaching towering heights of 150–175 metres, making it very difficult to progress along a straight course. Furthermore, none of our Uighur guides had ever been in this area before and they all had a very sound respect for the majesty of the desert. According to the calculations made by Håkan Wahlquist, navigator of the expedition, it should be possible to reach the northernmost tip of

Chitlik-darya before dark and pitch our tents there for the night. Of course, it was impossible to tell whether this small branch of the old Yar-tonguz-darya would still be carrying water so far north, but it would certainly be worth trying – especially for the camels who needed both food and water. The return journey to Jigda-bulung turned out to be eventful and troublesome, but successful. The Chitlik-darya held plenty of brackish water, much to the joy of the camels, who also found plenty of poplar leaves around the banks of the stream, and the following day our caravan navigated straight into Jigda-bulung – much to the delighted surprise of some of its members.

In connection with our journey to Yar-tonguz-langar, the upper reaches of the river north of the *langar* were surveyed and defined by means of our satellite compass, since the military maps with which the expedition had been equipped by the Chinese authorities were far from clear regarding the river and its various branches.

Helya-beg

Before returning to Urumchi one more mission had to be fulfilled. From various local informants we had heard about a site called Helya-beg situated approximately 20–30 km to the south of the *langar*. An old man living in the vicinity of the *langar*, Sadiq Rezge, related that he had visited the place some forty years earlier and was convinced that he could still find it. As far as he could remember, there were ruins of houses and perhaps even a Buddhist stupa. As in the case of the northern route, only the western side of the river seemed suitable for our vehicles. However, before long the Landrovers got stuck in the flour-like sand and had to be abandoned. It was decided that only the Swedish members together with Professor Wang, Akbar and Sadiq Rezge should proceed with the desert truck, while the rest of the party would try to get the jeeps back to the *langar*. After a few hours journeying over ever increasing dunes, which at one point almost caused the truck to overturn, we finally reached the bed of an old river. The truck could go no further due to a steep ravine and we were forced to proceed on foot following Sadiq Rezge who, barefoot and with impressive speed, disappeared towards the horizon. While walking along this old river-bed the first sherd finds were made. They were of a rather coarse type, ranging in colour from red-brown to black without any decorations. Professor Wang Mingzhe was of the opinion that they belonged to a type of ceramics commonly found along the southern Silk Road during the first centuries BC and AD.[18] After a while our local guide returned with a disappointed look saying that he could not find the ruins he had seen forty years ago – probably they had been covered by sand and were no longer visible. It was already late afternoon and since we had to return before dark, a number of sherds were collected and handed over to Professor Wang for further analysis at the Archaeological Research Institute in Urumchi. Like Stein before us, we had not been able to find any Buddhist ruins as we had hoped, but the sherds we found clearly indicate that the area was once inhabited and that further investigation of this tract could contribute to our understanding of the late neolithic history of southern Sinkiang.

The two Sino-Swedish Expeditions of 1992 and 1994 constitute a small but important step towards resuming the tradition of Swedish and Chinese scientific collaboration in Sinkiang. Negotiations to continue this research are in progress and an extended Swedish party consisting of archaeologists and linguists stands ready to meet the challenge. Irrespective of whether our target is the *Kone-shahr* at Yar-tonguz-darya or some other location, the continuation of this work so successfully begun will contribute to further clarification of the history of one of the most fascinating areas in Asia.

---

[18] Both Huntington and Stein had heard about the 'ruins' at Helya-beg. In *Serindia* Stein gives the following comment: 'It will be convenient to record here that I was unable to visit the alleged "ruins" of which Prof. Huntington heard as situated upstream about fifty or sixty miles from the terminal settlement, and which he mentions as "Haiyabeg, the large agricultural village of ancient times" (p. 212). But I took care to enjoin a search for them on Naik Rām Singh, my ill-fated assistant, when, in March, 1908, I let him start on that visit to Mīrān from which he was doomed to return blind (cf. *Desert Cathay*, ii. pp. 432sqq.). He duly visited the place on his way from Niya to Charchan and found it to be situated close to the river-bed, about six miles to the south of the caravan track. He described it to me as a small "Tati" with patches of eroded ground showing fragments of broken pottery of rough make, without a trace of structural remains. The seven specimens brought back by him are all of coarse hand-made pottery of ill-levigated clay fired in an open hearth. The clay is generally red on the outside, blackish-grey within. Coarse pottery of this kind appears to have been made for local use in the eastern parts of the Tārīm Basin through widely distant periods down to modern times. In the present state of our knowledge such débris can furnish no reliable indication as to the age when that "Tati" was occupied.' (Stein, *Serindia*, p. 271, footnote 5.)

RELIGION

Superscribing the Hegemonic Image of Chinggis Khan in the *Erdeni Tunumal Sudur**

JOHAN ELVERSKOG

The most enduring and powerful historical and national symbol among the Mongols has always been that of Chinggis Khan. Throughout history, the significance and nature of this initial founder of the Mongol Empire has been transformed in the minds of various peoples. For the Arabs and Persians, he represented their greatest fears, while for the Mongols themselves, Chinggis Khan has been transformed from the historical figure who initially united the Mongols into his later apotheosis as culture hero and bodhisattva incarnation.[1] His impact has continued into modernity, as evidenced in the carefully orchestrated Soviet and Chinese manipulations of his representation.

The focus of this study is not to present a historical semiological analysis of Chinggis Khan, however much such a study is needed, but to explore the 'superscribing' of the symbol of Chinggis Khan by the Mongols in the 16th century,[2] according to the rather recently discovered biography of Altan Khan, the *Erdeni Tunumal Sudur* ('The Jewel Translucent Sūtra').[3] In

---

* I would like to thank Christopher Atwood, Larry Clark and György Kara for reading drafts of this paper and giving many valuable criticisms and suggestions.

[1] Herbert Franke, *From Tribal Chieftain to Universal Emperor and God: The Legitimation of the Yüan Dynasty* (Bayrische Akademie der Wissenschaften. Philosophisch-Historische Klasse. Sitzungsberichte. Jahrgang 1978, Heft 2), München 1978, and Walther Heissig, *The Religions of Mongolia*, London 1980, pp. 59–69.

[2] The idea of 'superscribing' is used according to Prasenjit Duara's study of Guandi worship in China; cf. id., 'Superscribing Symbols: The Myth of Guandi, Chinese God of War', *The Journal of Asian Studies* 47:4 (1988), pp. 778–795.

[3] This work was found in the Royal Palace of the Prince of Üjümüchin, West Banner in Inner Mongolia. It contains an extensive and detailed history of Altan Khan written by an unknown clerical author in traditional Mongolian verse. Upon its discovery,

particular, this study will focus on how the cult of Chinggis Khan and its semantic resonances were used as a legitimizing rhetoric for Altan Khan.

Legitimation

Ever since the time of Khubilai Khan, successive Mongolian rulers have had access to two dominant symbolic elements of legitimacy: direct descent within the Borjigid clan, and following the example of Khubilai Khan and 'Phags-pa Lama, the unification of the State with Religion (invariably implying a school of Tibetan Buddhism). The first element pertaining to succession within the proper lineage has periodically been a problem in Mongolian politics ever since the time of Chinggis Khan and his four sons. The controversial impact of this restriction of imperial legitimacy to the Borjigid line was most evident in the Oirat-Mongolian wars of the 15th century, which were resolved with the victory of the Borjigids under Queen Mandukhai Sechen and Dayan Khan.[4] After Dayan Khan the title of Great Khan of the Great Yuan (*Dai Yuwan Yeke Qaɣan*) descended only in primogeniture to the Chakhar rulers of the Three Eastern Tümens.[5] The second element also played a large role in the semantic and scholastic formation of Yuan and post-Yuan legitimacy.[6] The most eloquent statement for this religio-political theory is the *Arban Buyan-tu Nom-un Chaɣan Teüke* ('White History Chronicle of the Ten Meritorious Laws'), attributed to Khubilai Khan, wherein he expounds upon the unification of the two spheres

---

Jürungy-a, an Inner Mongolian scholar, published an edition of the manuscript with a commentary, based primarily on Mongolian and Chinese sources: *Erdeni Tunumal Neretü Sudur Orosiba*, Beijing 1984. He postulated in his edition that the original version of the work was composed in the spring of 1607 by an unknown author at the court of Altan Khan's grandson, Namudai Sechen Khan. However, since the manuscript concludes with a genealogy of the Üjümüchin princely line from 1658 to 1690, Jürungy-a considered that the extant version is probably a copy from the 1690s.

[4] 'By recognizing the infallible Dayan Khan, thus it was that she lit [again] the Borjigid hearth fire', Jürungy-a, op. cit., p. 20.

[5] It is important to note that even though the eastern Chakhar rulers maintained the title of Yuan Khan, they had to receive this title in front of the Chinggis Khan shrine in the Ordos territory, which necessitated either control of or acquiescence of the Three Western Tümens; cf. Jürungy-a, op. cit., pp. 44–45.

[6] This discussion of legitimation is based on the theory of Jeremy Adams, who postulates that there are five dimensions in the legitimation process: procedural, coercive, semantic, scholastic and popular. For an outline of these elements, see Hok-lam Chan, *Legitimation in Imperial China: Discussions under the Jurchen-Chin Dynasty (1115–1234)*, Seattle 1984, pp. 16–17.

(*qoyar yosun*) of State (*törö*) and Religion (*shasin*) as fundamental to proper rule and legitimacy. On the basis of this document, and its reiteration by Khutugtu Sechen Khong Taiji in the famous 17th century Mongolian chronicle *Erdeni-yin Tobči* and other Tibetan sources,[7] scholars have developed the idea that this religio-political construction replicated a form of 'Lamaist caesaropapism'.[8] According to this theoretical system, the two syncretic spheres are mutually dichotomous, one being secular and the other religious, though each one provides legitimation to the other through a specific discourse:

> According to these ideas, secular and spiritual salvation are something that all living beings try to obtain. Spiritual salvation consists in complete deliverance from suffering, and worldly welfare is secular salvation. Both depend on a dual order, the order of religion (*nom-un yosun*) and the order of the state, or worldly rule (*törö-yin yosun*). Just as the religious order is based on the sūtras and magic formulae (*dhāraṇī*), the secular order rests on peace and quietness. The order of religion is presided over by the Lama, and the Ruler has to guarantee a rule which enables everyone to live in peace. Religion and state are thus mutually dependent. The heads of religion and state are equal, although each has different functions. The Lama corresponds to the Buddha, and the Ruler to the *cakravartin*.[9]

Of course, this was an ideal theoretical system and various other factors invariably played a role in reality. It nevertheless provided a foundation upon which later Mongol rulers could emulate and thereby obtain legitimacy. As the *Jewel Translucent Sūtra* explains, however, this union of Religion and State was lost with the fall of Daidu (Peking) in 1368 and not revived until the time of Altan Khan of the Twelve Tümeds.[10] The question naturally arises, given the gap of more than two centuries until this system of legitimation was readopted, most notably by Altan Khan, was the discourse the same? In particular, since Altan Khan genealogically had an inferior position to the Chakhar Great Yuan khans, was this unification of the two

---

[7] I. J. Schmidt, *Geschichte der Ost-Mongolen und ihres Fürstenhauses, verfaßt von Ssanang Ssetsen Chungtaidschi der Ordus*, The Hague 1961 (first edition St. Petersburg 1829), and Tsepon Shakaba, *A Political History of Tibet*, New Haven 1967, pp. 96–97.

[8] Herbert Franke, 'Tibetans in Yüan China', in John Langlois Jr. (ed.), *China Under Mongol Rule*, Princeton 1981, pp. 308–309. For a longer discussion of this caesaropapist theory, see Klaus Sagaster, *Die Weisse Geschichte: Eine mongolische Quelle zur Lehre von den Beiden Ordnungen Religion und Staat in Tibet und der Mongolei* (Asiatische Forschungen 41), Wiesbaden 1976, pp. 9–49.

[9] Herbert Franke, op. cit., p. 308.

[10] Jürungγ-a, op. cit., p. 14.

spheres, State and Religion, energized by his meeting the Dalai Lama, sufficient enough to legitimize his rule?

If one looks at the introduction to the *Jewel Translucent Sūtra*, where a brief history of Mongol rulers and their legitimacy is outlined, it would seem as if this were the case. The text reads as follows:

> Born by the fate of the Supreme Tengri,
> From its beginning creating the supreme State,
> [Temüjin] caused all those of the world to enter his power.
> Temüjin became famous as the Great Chinggis Khan.
>
> [He] brought the Five-colored Nations into his power,
> Set into order the State of the pleasant world,
> Invited Kun-dga' snying-po, the Supreme Sa-skya Lama,
> And was the first to propagate the religion of the Buddha.
>
> The third son of Chinggis Khan, Ögedei Khan,
> Invited the Vanquishing and Powerful Sa-skya Paṇḍita to come,
> Led the state of this world and the religion of the Buddha,
> And thus [Ögedei] caused the realm to rejoice with abundant peace and order.
>
> Afterwards, his grandson, born as an incarnate,
> The holy one, became famous as Khubilai Sechen Khan,
> [He] invited the Holy 'Phags-pa Lama to come,
> More importantly [he had] the sūtras and tantras translated into Uighur.
>
> [He] richly established the Three Foundations of Buddhism,
> Greatly and immensely spread to all, the world of religion,
> And made all that is in the universe to rejoice in peace and stability.
> He became famous as a Holy Cakravartin Khan of yore.
>
> Born to [Khubilai Khan's] family was Incomparable Khaisan, named Külüg Khan,
> [Who] commissioned the Omniscient monk, Chos-kyi Od-zer Lama
> To translate the Supreme Dharma into Mongolian,
> And extensively spread the powerful society.
>
> From the Great Chinggis Khan,
> Up through the reign of the fourteen noted Khans,
> During that time Religion and State were universal.
> By means of mutually supporting the educated and wise officials,
> Thus it was that the scriptural Dharma and the State were both held together.[11]

---

[11] Jürungγ-a, op. cit., pp. 8–13.

After seeing this pithy description of legitimacy, it seems that, for the author of the work and the implied reader, Altan Khan's legitimacy was to be subsequently based on the reunification of the two spheres, as the previous great khans had done, and on his being a descendant of Chinggis Khan and Dayan Khan. However, there is another element that becomes incorporated within this seemingly hermetically sealed system, and that is the role of the Supreme Tengri.

Tengri

As seen above in the *Jewel Translucent Sūtra*, the rule of Chinggis Khan was initiated under the auspices of the Supreme Tengri, an event that is well known from the *Secret History*. It is therefore not surprising that the collapse of the Mongol Empire during the reign of Toγan Temür Khan is attributed to two separate elements. One of them was the collapse of the Buddhist-Imperial relationship, which occurred because 'former evil deeds ripened, and they [the khans] became foolish'.[12] The second factor in the collapse of the Yuan dynasty was that the Supreme Tengri's blessing for rule was not forthcoming, and it was Toγan Temür Khan's fate to lose the Empire.[13] Therefore, in this early 17th century chronicle there were two parallel systems of legitimation, the relationship with the Buddhist institutions and another that involved the blessing of a Tengri. Yet, how did the blessing of the Supreme Tengri fit into the system of the two realms (*qoyar yosun*), and more importantly, how was this blessing maintained?

From an analysis of the legitimation structure incorporated in the *Jewel Translucent Sūtra*, it becomes apparent that the realm of State (*törö*) was not purely secular as maintained in the caesaropapist interpretation. Instead, the functioning of the State did not solely involve the application of laws, taxes etc. that allowed for peace and stability, but it was a sphere equally as sacred as the Religion, though in a different way. This sphere required the

---

[12] Jürungγ-a, op. cit., p. 14. There are also other Mongol interpretations for the demise of the Yuan dynasty; cf. Hirosato Iwai, 'The Buddhist Priest and the Ceremony of Attaining Womanhood during the Yüan Dynasty', *Memoirs of the Toyo Bunko* 7 (1937), pp. 105–161, Hidehiro Okada, 'An Analysis of the Lament of Toγon Temür', *Zentralasiatische Studien* 1 (1967), pp. 55–78, and Henry Serruys, 'A Manuscript Version of the Legend of the Mongol Ancestry of the Yung-Lo Emperor', in John G. Hangin and Urgunge Onon (eds), *Analecta Mongolica*, Bloomington 1972, pp. 19–61.

[13] Jürungγ-a, op. cit., p. 15.

blessing of the Supreme Tengri. This blessing, according to the *Secret History of the Mongols*, was initially bestowed on Chinggis Khan at Burkhan Khaldun, whereupon he unified the State and created the secular laws (*jasag*) that were to be used in the functioning of the State. Subsequently, it became imperative for a ruling khan to maintain this blessing of the Supreme Tengri in order to rule the State properly, and only by performing the appropriate rites to Chinggis Khan, who received the initial blessing of rule, was the legitimation of Tengri within a semantic chain recreated. Thereby the *ongɣon* of Chinggis Khan maintained at the Eight White Yurts (*Naiman chaɣan ger*) functioned as a relic, providing a 'transcendent immanence' of *praesentia*,[14] that empowered the controller and recipient of the relic/*ongɣon*'s blessing. Therefore, as noted above, in order to obtain legitimacy even within the esteemed hierarchy of Chinggis, Ögedei and Khubilai, a ruler within the proper lineage had to both receive the *potentia* of Tengri, which was done through the rituals towards Chinggis Khan at the Eight White Yurts in Ordos, and to have incorporated, parallel to this system, adherence to Buddhism.

The importance for a khan's legitimacy of recreating the Supreme Tengri's blessing through the rituals done at the Chinggis Khan shrine is amply evident in the *Jewel Translucent Sūtra*, where it is continually represented. The importance of its inclusion in the narrative is even more pertinent when we realize that the work was written by a Tibetan-trained Buddhist cleric, who is fundamentally proselytizing the wonders of the Buddhist religion and the glory of Altan Khan and his lineage who brought it back to the Mongols. Thus, within this Buddhist conversion narrative, the author incorporated the legitimacy of a ruler and his exercise of power, created through ritualization at the Chinggis Khan shrine.

The ritual's power, in a Geertzian sense,[15] is evident from the two narrative elements that highlight the importance of worshipping at the Chinggis Khan shrine. The first is that the bestowal of the ranks of Khan and Jinong (the khan's deputy or viceroy, who rules over the Three Western Tümens[16]), are

---

[14] Peter Brown, *The Cult of the Saints: Its Rise and Function in Latin Christianity*, Chicago 1981.

[15] Clifford Geertz's argument as developed in his work *Negara: The Theatre State in Nineteenth Century Bali*, Princeton 1980, is succinctly summarized in Catherine Bell's *Ritual Theory, Ritual Practice*, New York 1992, pp. 194–196.

[16] The true origin and meaning of this term has been extensively debated. For the most recent analysis with a bibliography of the preceding scholarly arguments, see Gombojab Hangin, 'The Mongolian Titles *Jinong and Sigejun*', *Journal of the American Oriental*

done in front of the Eight White Yurts. The second is the continued manifestation of the Supreme Tengri's blessing and its consequences for the Mongol rulers of the 16th century. The initial mention of the Eight White Yurts occurs as Dayan Khan sends his son to the Western Tümens to be enthroned as Jinong, whereupon he is immediately assassinated.[17] Afterwards, Bodi Khan, the successor of Dayan Khan as ruler of the Three Eastern Tümens, is given his title in front of the Eight White Yurts in the presence of all six Tümens, and later Bodi Khan gives Altan Khan his title in front of Chinggis Khan's shrine.[18] And finally, after Altan Khan's death, when the state is hypothetically an Imperial Buddhist state, since Altan Khan has met the Dalai Lama and unified the State and Religion, Altan Khan's son Sengge Dügüreng receives the title of Khan in front of the Eight White Yurts.[19] Invariably, as a result of these activities, Tengri's blessing is forthcoming and is repeatedly confirmed in the language of the narrative. This is most evident in the repeated claims of Altan Khan as being born by the will of the Supreme Tengri,[20] and not a Buddhist deity, as would be found in later legitimation structures.[21] As a result of this blessing, two important events in Altan Khan's career are interpreted as resulting from the fate of the Supreme Tengri: defeating the troublesome Uriyangqan and making them slaves,[22] and the great peace accord of 1571 between Altan Khan and the Ming dynasty.[23] From the elements presented within this Buddhist history, it becomes apparent that the cult of Chinggis Khan played a fundamental role in the construction of Altan Khan's legitimacy. For only by uniting the two spheres of political legitimation, the Supreme Tengri's blessing of the State through the Chinggis Khan cult and the

---

Society 100:3 (1980), pp. 255–266.

[17] Jürungy-a, op. cit., pp. 29–30, and Hidehiro Okada, 'The Khan as the Sun, the Jinong as the Moon', in Barbara Kellner-Heinkele (ed.), *Altaica Berolinensia* (Asiatische Forschungen 126), Wiesbaden 1993, p. 188.

[18] Jürungy-a, op. cit., pp. 44–45.

[19] Jürungy-a, op. cit., pp. 147–148.

[20] Jürungy-a, op. cit., pp. 60, 83.

[21] See in particular the opening passages of the addresses directed towards the Banner princes published by Henry Serruys, 'A Genre of Oral Literature in Mongolia: The Addresses', *Monumenta Serica* 31 (1977), pp. 555–613.

[22] Jürungy-a, op. cit., p. 43, and Hidehiro Okada, 'The Fall of the Uriyangqan Mongols', *Mongolian Studies* 10 (1986–1987), p. 52.

[23] Jürungy-a, op. cit., p. 71.

adoption of Buddhism as the imperial Religion, could Altan Khan claim affinity with Chinggis Khan and Khubilai Khan.

Buddhism

Even though Altan Khan is repeatedly referred to as being blessed by the Supreme Tengri, the author is not unaware of the importance of simultaneously portraying him as a Buddhist. This identification is therefore presented during the first appearance of Altan Khan in the text, where Mergen Jinong is said to have ruled the Ordos Tümen due to his 'administration' of the Eight White Yurts, while Altan Khan rules by the power of merit acquired from the 'two assemblies' (*qoyar chigulgan*).[24] Also when Altan Khan is born, as a fraternal twin of a girl to the Empress Bodon, he is invariably identified as a bodhisattva.[25] This identification is also evident in an incident where Altan Khan's 'striped calf' is wounded in battle, referring to one of the 32 marks of a Buddha or Cakravartin.[26] And finally, there is the longest section of the work which describes Altan Khan's meeting with the Tibetan Ashing Lama, who teaches him the fundamentals of Buddhism and advises him to invite the Dalai Lama. Altan Khan follows the suggestion, whereupon the two representatives of State and Religion meet and Altan Khan incorporates Buddhism once again into the Mongolian religio-political system.

From this brief overview of the legitimation structure presented in the *Jewel Translucent Sūtra*, it becomes apparent that the simple two-sphere system inherent in the caesaropapist model is insufficient to describe the legitimation process, since it ignores entirely the sacred element of the State that is manifested through the cult of Chinggis Khan.[27] However, it should be asked whether the rituals directed towards Chinggis Khan always

---

[24] Jürungγ-a, op. cit., p. 27. The 'two assemblies' refer to the Buddhist accumulation of merit and knowledge of the Dharma.

[25] Jürungγ-a, op. cit., p. 28.

[26] Jürungγ-a, op. cit., p. 49.

[27] Another problem with the caesaropapist model that needs further study elsewhere is the complete oversight of the importance of lineage. Since the Byzantine empire had no one ruling lineage, while the Mongols did, in this regard a more appropriate 'model' imperial system, as opposed to the Byzantine one, might be the Japanese imperial system. I would like to thank Christopher P. Atwood for pointing out this problem in the caesaropapist model.

were employed in this manner? Unfortunately, the true nature of the Chinggis Khan cult during the Yuan dynasty is far from certain. It may be a 'Shamanic' ancestor rite as noted by Rashīd al-Dīn and maintained by Walther Heissig and Klaus Sagaster,[28] or hark back to some primordial seasonal nomadic ritual as noted by Henry Serruys.[29] Nevertheless, the Yuan period ritualization does not seem to have an inherent continuity with rituals described in the modern ethnographical and philological studies of the Chinggis Khan cult as maintained at Ejen Khoroo in Ordos.[30] Nor do either of these two seem to have much resemblance to the apparent 16th century functional balance of power between the Chinggis Khan shrine and the Queen Eshi shrine, where the secularly weaker Western Tümen controlled the spiritually dominant Chinggis Khan shrine, and the more powerful Eastern Tümen controlled the spiritually inferior Queen Eshi shrine.[31] Even newer developments of the Chinggis Khan cult, such as his transformation into a protector deity of Buddhism in a tantric visualization text,[32] confirm the discontinuous nature of myth, a change that 'takes place in a way that sustains and is sustained by a dense historical context. In this way cultural symbols are able to lend continuity at one level to changing social groups and interests even as the symbols themselves undergo transformations. This particular modality of symbolic evolution is one I call the superscription of symbols.'[33] In this regard, within the interpretive arena of Chinggis Khan,

---

[28] John Andrew Boyle, *The Successors of Genghis Khan: Translated from the Persian of Rashīd al-Dīn*, New York 1971, p. 31, Walther Heissig, op. cit., pp. 59–60, and Klaus Sagaster, op. cit., pp. 204–206.

[29] Henry Serruys, *Kumiss Ceremonies and Horse Races*, Wiesbaden 1974, pp. 1–18. For more information on the Chinggis Khan cult during the Yuan dynasty, see Paul Ratchnevsky, 'Über den mongolischen Kult am Hofe der Grosskhane in China', in Louis Ligeti (ed.), *Mongolian Studies* (Bibliotheca Orientalis Hungarica 14), Budapest 1970, pp. 417–444, Sechin Jagchid, 'Chinggis Khan in Mongolian Folklore', in *Essays in Mongolian Studies*, Provo 1988, pp. 302–303, and Hidehiro Okada, 'The Chinggis Khan Shrine and the *Secret History of the Mongols*', in Klaus Sagaster (ed.), *Religious and Lay Symbolism in the Altaic World and Other Papers* (Asiatische Forschungen 105), Wiesbaden 1989, pp. 284–292.

[30] For a bibliography of the modern study of the Chinggis Khan cult, see Wonsoo Yu, *The* Five Hundred Shir-a Darqat Families *in Ordos: 'People in Eternal Mourning for Chinggis Khan'*, Unpublished Master's Thesis, Indiana University 1989.

[31] Hidehiro Okada, 'The Chakhar Shrine of Eshi Khatun', in Denis Sinor (ed.), *Aspects of Altaic Civilization III* (Indiana University Publications: Uralic and Altaic Series 145), Bloomington 1990, pp. 176–186.

[32] Henry Serruys, 'A Prayer to Cinggis-Qan', *Études mongoles et sibériennes* 16 (1985), pp. 17–36.

[33] Prasenjit Duara, op. cit., p. 780.

the question becomes: what were some of the underlying reasons for the author(s) of the *Jewel Translucent Sūtra* to superscribe Chinggis Khan as the legitimizer of State within a Buddhist symbolic narrative?

The choice of Chinggis Khan in this regard is obvious, as was noted above, since Chinggis Khan is the most powerful symbol within the Mongolian world, a construction that is premised on him initially creating the Mongol state – a symbolic power within the interpretive arena that has been maintained throughout the tumultuous history of the Mongols, even in the face of the horrors unleashed by fanatic Buddhists in the 16th and 17th centuries,[34] and more recently by Chinese Communist cadres. It is therefore understandable as to why the author of the *Jewel Translucent Sūtra* has chosen to highlight Altan Khan's performance of the cult of Chinggis Khan, since 'ritualization is first and foremost a strategy for the construction of certain types of power relationships effective within particular social organizations'.[35] Therefore, through the performance of the Chinggis Khan cult, Altan Khan was recreating the contemporary social order, whereby he attained the symbolic power as the most true legitimate heir of Chinggis Khan. Yet, in order to fully understand the implication of this superscription, and the reason for its adoption, the 'dense historical context' needs to be examined.

Mongol–Buddhist legitimation of the Yuan state

At the beginning of the 16th century, Dayan Khan (ca. 1465–1520), the re-establisher of true Borjigids supremacy, ruled over the Eastern Tümen and was instrumental in trying to unite the fractious Mongols of the Eastern and Western Tümens on the Mongolian plateau.[36] Upon his death, his role as Khan of the Three Western Tümens and the Three Eastern Tümens passed to his grandson, Bodi Khan. However, during his life, he had appointed

---

[34] Walther Heissig, 'A Mongolian Source to the Lamaist Suppression of Shamanism in the 17th century', *Anthropos* 48 (1953), pp. 1–29, 493–536.

[35] Catherine Bell, op. cit., p. 197.

[36] The historical information outlined here is drawn from several sources: Joseph van Hecken, 'Les princes Borjigid des Ordos depuis leur soumission aux Mandchoux en 1635 jusqu'à leur disparition en 1951', *Central Asiatic Journal* 16:2 (1972), pp. 132–155, Henry Serruys, *Genealogical Tables of the Descendants of Dayan-Qan* (Central Asiatic Studies 3), 's-Gravenhage 1958, and Antoine Mostaert, 'Introduction', in *Erdeni-yin Tobci*, Cambridge 1956.

his third son Barsubolod to be Jinong (the viceroy) of the Three Western Tümens. When Barsubolod died in 1531, his eldest son Gün Bilig became Jinong, and his second son Altan Khan became the head of the Twelve Tümeds, one of the Three Tümens comprising the Three Western Tümens (the other two being the Ordos and the Yüngshiyebü). These two brothers were extremely successful militarily, taking virtual control of the six Tümens and terrorizing many parts of northern China. However, since Mongol rule after Dayan Khan was based on primogeniture, they could never fully displace the authority of Bodi Khan who ruled the Three Eastern Tümens. In 1542 Gün Bilig died and his first son, Noyandara of the Ordos, became Jinong, while Altan Khan and his descendants only controlled the Twelve Tümeds.

It is thus within this structure of a contestation for power that Altan Khan became affiliated with the Dalai Lama and thereby recreated himself as the legitimate heir of the legacy of Chinggis Khan and Khubilai Khan. In the *Jewel Translucent Sūtra* it is emphasized that Altan Khan was the first khan to once again reunite the Great State (*yeke törö*) of Mongolia, China and Tibet, thus again recreating the geobody of the Yuan dynasty.[37] Thus by unifying the larger political 'Yuan' state with Buddhism as the earlier khans had done, Altan Khan attempted to override his genealogically subordinate position within the Mongolian imperial hierarchy. Yet, after Altan Khan initiated this Mongol-Buddhist legitimation structure, the uniqueness and symbolic power of this action was undermined as the Dalai Lama began to initiate every other Mongol ruler, such as Abatai Khan of the Khalkha, into a priest–patron relationship. Subsequently, for the author(s) of the *Jewel Translucent Sūtra*, which was written in 1607 at the court of Altan Khan's grandson, Namudai Sechen Khan, who then controlled the diminished Twelve Tümeds, the superscription of Chinggis Khan, which is not predominant in the other 17th century chronicles, allowed the lineage of Altan Khan to employ the hegemonic image of Chinggis Khan to empower their subaltern position.

Subsequently, the lineage of Altan Khan was not to obtain the hegemony ritualized in the cult of Chinggis Khan, but their expansion of the interpretative

---

[37] The importance of this reunification cannot be underestimated, for as the narrative continues after the death of Altan Khan, he is represented as the new legitimate founder of the Great State, and not Chinggis Khan. This is evident in one episode where Namudai Sechen Khan suppresses a revolt against the Ming and thereby recreates the Great State formed by Altan Khan. Cf. Jürungγ-a, op. cit., pp. 167–168.

arena of Chinggis Khan was to have further resonances. This is witnessed in the construction of Ligdan Khan of the Chakhar, who increased the symbolic implications by taking the title Chinggis Khan for himself[38] and stressing the semantic relationship even more by inviting Sa-skya lamas, as Chinggis Khan and Khubilai Khan had done, instead of lamas from the Dalai Lama's dGe-lugs-pa school.

Concluding remarks

This study of the superscription of Chinggis Khan in the *Jewel Translucent Sūtra* is only one link in establishing the semantic chain of Chinggis Khan's interpretative arena. It was not the first nor the last superscription of Chinggis Khan, but each successive case was invariably in dialogue with these developments. As noted by Duara, it 'is precisely because of the superscription over, not erasure of, previous inscriptions that historical groups are able to expand old frontiers of meaning to accommodate their changing needs'.[39] Therefore, the superscription of Chinggis Khan during the late 16th century is not unique. It continued in the rhetoric of the Manchus and the competing discourses of Mongolian nationalists and Soviet propagandists in the early 20th century, in the Chinese Communist resolution to rebuild the Chinggis Khan Mausoleum at Ejen Khoroo, and it continues into the present, as evidenced by the Mongolian Great Khural's decision to have the portrait of Chinggis Khan on the new 100 Tögrök bill, and in a contemporary political campaign, where a television advertisement proclaims: If Chinggis Khan were alive today he would vote Democratic. All of these are recent constructions of Chinggis Khan, which nevertheless reflect the symbolic representation of the superscription of Chinggis Khan as found in the *Jewel Translucent Sūtra*, yet simultaneously these modern manifestations are invariably rooted in the changing contemporary socio-political environment. As a result, through these superscriptions one can see the continuous and discontinuous nature of myth and its appropriation in the formation of ideology.

---

[38] This is evident in many of the colophons of the Kanjur, and in a letter he wrote to the Manchu ruler in 1619, wherein he titles himself 'Lord-Hero Chinggis Khan of the Forty Tümen Mongols' (*Man-zhou Shi-lu* 6.34a–36a); cf. Henry Serruys, *The Mongols in China During the Hung-wu Period (1368–1398)*, Bruxelles 1959, p. 50.

[39] Prasenjit Duara, op. cit., p. 791.

'They only weep …'
Stories about Tibetan Travellers to the Other Worlds

PER-ARNE BERGLIE

Buddhism is not unique among world religions in posing quite a number of problems concerning the core and continuity of its historical development and geographical diversity. Its lack of a central instance of authority as well as of a one-language canon, together with an astonishing ability to absorb or enter into a relationship with local religious traditions, make every attempt at analysing almost any ritual or belief complex found within a Buddhist culture quite difficult, if one also wants to add an historical dimension.

Buddhism originated within a given cultural and religious context and the dialogue between its opponents and defenders, or between adherents with different opinions, may be heard, although often with some difficulty, throughout the early textual layers in Pali, Sanskrit and Chinese. With the spread of Buddhism through the centuries, this dialogue naturally varies in strength and content depending on the participating partners and their background. Here we have one of the factors shaping the local Buddhism 'in practice'. Certain forms of Buddhism are more rewarding than others for the student of Comparative Religion who is looking for complexity, eclecticism, syncretism and heterogeneity. The tantric or esoteric forms of Buddhism have often been pointed out as good hiding-places for dissent or even heterodoxy and heteropraxy. For studies of this kind, the history of Tibetan religion seems to offer much of interest as a meeting place for South Asian Buddhism and the Central and North Asian world of ideas.

In 1970–1971, when doing fieldwork among exile Tibetans in Nepal and collecting material on ritual possession, I often became engaged in discussions with my spirit-medium informants on questions concerned with 'identity', 'consciousness' and 'soul'. Sometimes, during the seances, the possessing god was obliged to visit far-off places in order to obtain the necessary information. In the disussions after the seances, the question of 'soul travels' to distant places, or even to the worlds of gods and demons, could then naturally be raised. On such an occasion, one of the spirit-mediums told me a few stories about the Tibetan visitors to the realms beyond death, the *'das log*s. Just as the phenomenon of Tibetan spirit-mediumship in itself has been the focus of much discussion on the relationship between Buddhism and Shamanism, so the *'das log*s have been seen as good examples of Shamanic survivals within a Buddhist frame. The present paper is meant to be a contribution to this discussion.

The Tibetan travellers to the other worlds

There exist a number of publications of source material as well as a few studies of the *'das log* phenomenon.[1] The differences that may be noticed between the printed biographical texts, the oral biographies or short *'das log* stories and the observations in the field of active *'das log*s are certainly of interest. Some observations will be presented in this article.

Although there seems to be no absolute consensus with regard to the definition and delimitation of the *'das log* phenomenon, a somewhat rough picture based on the studies by Epstein and Pommaret may be outlined here as an introduction. The literary biographies seem to be rather rigidly structured.[2] In most cases, a conflict of a religious nature constitutes the starting point in the career of the *'das log*. Wishing to be a nun but forced to remain in a secular state, the future *'das log* experiences the tension between the monastic Buddhist ideal and the worldly life. The approaching

---

[1] Awaiting a complete bibliographical survey of published material covering both Western studies and Tibetan *'das log* biographies, a few titles will be given here in which further references may be found. To my knowledge the most exhaustive study is Françoise Pommaret, *Les revenants de l'au-delà dans le monde tibétain: Sources littéraires et tradition vivante*, Paris 1989. Her contribution to Donald S. Lopez (ed.), *Religions of Tibet in Practice*, Princeton 1996, 'Returning from Hell', pp. 499–510, may also be consulted. Of great interest is further Lawrence Epstein, 'On the History and Psychology of the *'Das-Log*', *The Tibet Journal* 7 (1982), pp. 20–85. A recent translation of the biography of a contemporary *'das log* is Delog Dawa Drolma, *Delog: Journey to Realms Beyond Death*, translated from Tibetan by Richard Barron under the direction of His Eminence Chagdud Tulku Rinpoche, Junction City 1995.

[2] See e.g. Epstein, op. cit., pp. 39–58, and Pommaret, op. cit., p. 502.

death causes confusion and hallucinations, and the dying *'das log* has visions of her next life while her present life is morally summarized and evaluated.³ Hearing strange sounds and roars and becoming soaked in rain, blood and phlegm, she dies. But she dies without understanding what is happening. When seeing her moaning relatives gathered around her bed, she at last understands that she has died. Then she is transported to some kind of limbo where she meets a 'guide' who takes her through the dark, frightening landscape to a city. There she is approached by other dead people, friends and relatives eager to tell their sad stories. In the different hells that she then visits she sees pains and torments of the sinners, but she may also get a glimpse of the saving and helping activities performed by the bodhisattva Avalokiteśvara. When it is time for the *'das log* to be put in front of the tribunal, her case is investigated thoroughly. As it is found out that a mistake has been made, she is sent back to the living. Having returned to this world, she has become a *'das log* and spends the rest of her life telling about her great experience and giving advice how to avoid having to spend time in the hells.

If the information gathered from the textual sources is compared to the information contained in contemporary field studies, mainly by F. Pommaret, similarities as well as differences may be noticed.⁴ In both cases, women seem to be in the majority and social and geographical marginality is evident. The overall structure of the career of the *'das log* is similar, the most obvious difference being the ability of contemporary ones to die again and again. They may even travel to the nether regions several times a month, on fixed days in the Buddhist calendar. Such a journey may last for a few hours, and after having returned the *'das log* is able to deliver very precise messages as to what has to be done in this world to improve conditions for the unfortunate relatives and friends in the other world.

During a stay among Tibetans in Nepal many years ago, I was able to collect a few stories about *'das log*s, which may add a few nuances to the phenomenon. These stories were told by a spirit-medium, *dpa' bo*, with whom I worked for six months. He told them to me when we were discussing the activities of mediums and related religious specialists. I have not been able to identify them in the literary or ethnographic material available to me. Probably there existed in Tibet, as everywhere else, a rich oral tradition

---

³ I have chosen to refer to the *'das log* with feminine pronouns and designations.
⁴ See Pommaret, op. cit., p. 149ff.

on the often connected themes of death, ghosts and visits to other worlds and strange regions.[5] I will relate here two of these stories somewhat shortened and in free translation from the longer Tibetan versions written down in the field. The first one is as follows:

> Once there was a *'das log* who said: 'I am going to die in a week from now! Do not touch my body in the week that follows. I will return to my body and stand up. Then you shall understand that I am not a *ro langs* (a walking corpse, a ghost) and that it is not a demon that has taken possession of my body.' After one week he died. After another week, his body started to move very slowly and tentatively. Then he recited the mantra of Avalokiteśvara. Then he wept for many days. He could not speak, only weep. He had been to hell, but standing in front of its king he had been told to return as he was not really dead. Several of the inhabitants in hell had come up to him telling him about their terrible situations and wanting to leave messages for him to take back to the living. When this *'das log* had finished weeping, he delivered those messages, which all contained exhortations to do good deeds for the benefit of the deceased. To become a *'das log* is very difficult, it is almost to become a *lha*, a god.

The second story is somewhat longer. It is about a female *'das log* whose name is *mKha' 'gro dkar *dros*. I have not been able to identify her.

> She was a very good *'das log*, one of the finest quality. The great man in the region where she was living decided to test her and therefore sent one of his servants to her with an invented story of a deceased relative, whose present rebirth location he wanted to find out. If she succeeded in this, she was promised a large reward. The *'das log* agreed to this and said that she would prepare a journey to try to find out whether the deceased had been reborn in heaven, in hell or among humans. She went to a solitary place with a few assistants, who were to protect her body during her absence. She put up a white tent, entered it, drank a lot of milk but did not eat anything. Then she died. First she went to hell and experienced many remarkable things. She saw the suffering creatures there in the various places of torture and helped many of them to get out of there to a better place of rebirth. However, she did not find the relative of the great man. Then she went up to the *lha yul*, the land of the gods, heaven. But the person she was looking for was not there either. Then she travelled around the world of men, but here her inquiry was in vain. So, on the fifteenth day after her death she returned to her own body. When she was able to speak, she told everything she had witnessed and delivered all the messages she had brought, and stressed the importance of helping the unfortunate ones in the hells to a rebirth as humans.

---

[5] This is still a little known part of Tibetan religion and folklore. For a contribution to the study of one aspect of this rich field, see Per-Arne Berglie, 'When the Corpses Rise: Some Tibetan ro langs Stories', *Indologica Taurinensia* 10 (1982), pp. 37–44, and the literature cited there.

But to the great man and his servants she confessed that she had not been able to locate the wanted person and therefore he could not possibly be dead. Thus they were convinced that she was a genuine *'das log* and she was handsomely rewarded.

As may be noticed, these stories add a few details to what we know about the *'das log*. As in the ethnographic material, the journey is not an isolated event. Instead, the *'das log* appears as a religious specialist whom one can consult and from whom one can request an investigation of where deceased friends and relatives have been reborn. The *'das log* is herself able to say when she is going to die and when she will be back. The duration of her journeys, furthermore, is thought to be rather long in that the *'das log* can be absent from her body for weeks. Finally, and remarkably enough, the *'das log* is herself thought to be capable of saving the sinners in hell and lifting them up to better worlds.

Buddhism or Shamanism?

Writers, both popular and scholarly, who have studied phenomena like that of the Tibetan *'das log* have often seen them as evidential remnants of a primitive and Shamanic past, loosely integrated in a Buddhist superstructure and given a Buddhist twist to teach good morals. Thus, Central Asia is made understandable against the background of North Asia, the home of the classic 'Shamanism'. But before entering a discussion of this view, let us a make a detour through South Asian Buddhism to see what this sphere has to offer.

The concept of hell, or hells, and the possibility of visiting them is present, of course, in all Indian religious traditions, although it is perhaps not regarded as a major theme. Still, it is there, more or less visible in different parts of these traditions. Buddhism first of all supplies its adherents with an elaborate cosmology in which a large number of hells and other unpleasant places are to be found.[6] Traditionally, there are five or six different worlds, all possible rebirth destinations for living beings within the Wheel

---

[6] This is not the place to give a full bibliography of Buddhist cosmology and its conception of the hells. It is sufficient to mention Daigan and Alicia Matsunaga, *The Buddhist Concept of Hell*, New York 1972, Paul Mus, *La lumière sur les six voies*, Paris 1939, and Géza Bethlenfalvy and Alice Sárközi, 'Representation of Buddhist Hells in a Tibeto-Mongol Illustrated Blockprint', in Walther Heissig (ed.), *Altaica Collecta*, Wiesbaden 1976, pp. 93–130, and the literature mentioned there.

of Life. First, we have the different heavens, where peaceful gods of all kinds enjoy the benefits of merits earned earlier. Secondly, we have the world of the aggressive *asura* gods. The third world in the hierarchy is ours, the world of men. The fourth is occupied by animals and the fifth by the *preta*s, stinking and grotesque creatures, who as men have been too gluttonous and thirsty. The sixth, and in our connection most interesting world, consists of the hells, places of torture and punishment for sinners. Someone has said that Buddhism has at its disposal the most sadistic hells known to the history of religions. This can certainly be contested and it may be noticed that the time one has to spend in any of the hells is always limited. Thus, the Buddhist cosmology is part of the moral and karmatic net which keeps everything together and governs human life.

The hells are mentioned in the earliest canonical texts, but it is in the later commentaries and scholastic *abhidharma* literature that the ideas become well-arranged and systematized. In these texts the theme is more elaborate and in some of them we find hundreds of hells mentioned, grouped in a complicated vertical and horizontal system.[7] The punishments inflicted on the sinners are described in vivid detail, and one realizes the necessity of a functional infernal bureaucracy for placing the victims in exactly the right corner of the right hell. If Buddhism sometimes gives the impression of being an intellectual and purely meditative piety, we find here a sharp contrast in the emphasis on the nauseating procedures in the hellish torture-chambers.

The scholastic masters have of course also speculated on the fundamental problem of how we know what is going on in heaven and hell. Buddhaghosa and Vasubandhu, two of the greatest commentators and exponents of Buddhist erudition, have both dwelt upon our means of knowledge of the other worlds, though not at very great length. Although their discussions, with all their implications, are surely worth a full investigation, only a summary is given here.[8] Thus, individuals obtaining a very advanced degree of spiritual development may possess the visionary gift enabling them to see over vast

---

[7] See e.g. *Saddharmasmṛtyupasthānasūtra*, preserved in Tibetan and Chinese and studied by the Matsunagas in the book mentioned in the previous footnote, and by Li-kouang Lin, *L'aide-mémoire de la vraie loi (Saddharmasmṛtyupasthāna-sūtra): Recherches sur un Sūtra Developpé du Petit Véhicule* (Publications du Musée Guimet, Bibl. d'études 54), Paris 1954.

[8] Vasubandhu analyses the modes of travelling in *Abhidharmakośa* 7.48 (with commentary). For a translation, see Louis de La Vallée Poussin, *L'Abhidharmakośa de Vasubandhu*, vol. V, p. 113f.

distances. Furthermore, it is possible to move between the worlds flying as a bird or sitting cross-legged. Or you can create a mind-made body and send it away on a mission to heaven. Or, to give a final example, you could imagine yourself going to a certain place and immediately be there. This method is reserved for the Buddha. There, thus, seem to be many possibilities and techniques available. The scholastics explain the travelling techniques while the epic literature contains many narratives of the lives and adventures of famous travellers to the other worlds. Within the Thai Buddhist tradition, the adventures of the well-known visitors to hell, Phra Malai, are dramatically performed in certain ritual contexts, and in East Asia the most famous of them all, Mulian (Moggallāna in Pāli, or Maudgalyāyana in Sanskrit), is extremely popular in Chinese vernacular fiction and drama.[9] He is visiting hell looking for his parents, especially his mother, a theme which is much stressed in order to increase the intensity and emotionality of the story. As a matter of fact, Mulian can be regarded as the very *nucleus* in one of the most important cultural processes which helped make Indian Buddhism an acceptable religion in East Asia by allowing the worship of ancestors and providing the cultic means of helping deceased relatives.

Even if what has been said above could be taken as a sufficient ideological background to the Tibetan travellers to hell, there is more in the Indian Buddhist heritage. The whole complex of ideas of death as the starting point of a journey through gloomy places is also found in Indian Buddhist texts. What in the 14th century eventually became 'The Tibetan Book of the Dead', actually parts of a large and extremely intricately woven liturgy, had its beginning in India much more than is usually recognized.[10] Thus we have Indian texts depicting in detail the setting of the highly dramatic chain of events which form the dying and death of a human being. The often frightening, though somehow illusory, experiences are not Tibetan or 'Shamanic' contributions, but are already found in the Indian texts. One of

---

[9] See e.g. Bonnie Pacala Brereton, *Thai Tellings of Phra Malai: Texts and Rituals Concerning a Popular Buddhist Saint*, Tempe 1995, for Phra Malai, and Victor H. Mair, *Tun-huang Popular Narratives*, Cambridge (Mass.) 1983, Victor H. Mair, *T'ang Transformation Texts*, Cambridge (Mass.) 1989, and Stephen F. Teiser, *The Ghost Festival in Medieval China*, Princeton 1988, esp. pp. 113–195, for Mulian.

[10] For some aspects of the background of the so-called *Tibetan Book of the Dead*, see Dieter Back, *Eine buddhistische Jenseitsreise*, Wiesbaden 1979, André Bareau, 'Chūu', *Hōbōgirin*, fasc. 5, Paris–Tokyo 1979, pp. 558–563, and Carl Suneson and Per-Arne Berglie, *The Problem of* chung yu *(Skt.* antarābhava*), the Intermediate State in the Buddhist Tradition and the Importance of the Chinese Sources* (Center for Pacific Asia Studies Occasional Paper 10), Stockholm 1990.

these texts is the *Nandagarbhāvakrāntinirdeśa*, preserved in Tibetan and Chinese and belonging to the somewhat loosely connected collection of texts called *Ratnakūṭa* dating from somewhere between AD 300 and 600.[11] In this text it is stated that the recently dead person has assumed a form and colour which indicates his future mode of existence. It is also stated that the deceased meets several obstructions and experiences auditory and visual phenomena of a hallucinatory nature. Thus he finds himself surrounded by cold and darkness. He feels a rising wind, heavy rains pour down, and he hears voices crying. He enters a house and walks through its rooms etc. It all ends up in a rebirth according to his merit. In this literary genre, death and the dying process are in an epical, mythical and ethical way inserted into the cosmology and made into a journey through a landscape which, I think, has strongly influenced the *'das log* stories as well as the experiences of the contemporary *'das log*s.

In order to argue that the *'das log* phenomenon is purely Buddhist, one may draw attention to the models given by the religious heroes and travellers like Maudgalyāyana (or, in the Tibetan context, Gesar or Padmasambhava) and the dramatic and vivid 'Book of the Dead' literature. From these sources the Tibetan *'das log* seems to be amply provided with sense, maps and experience. One may also note that the *'das log* stories strongly stress the cult of the bodhisattva Avalokiteśvara.

On the other hand, those who wish to argue that, strong Buddhist influences notwithstanding, the *'das log* is akin to Shamans, usually point to the fact that the Buddhist travellers are not 'ordinary persons' but a kind of religious 'heroes' with many supernatural powers and abilities at their disposal.[12] This is true, of course, but heroes are excellent models, and North Asian Shamans are certainly no 'ordinary persons'. Further investigation may reveal more Shamanic traits, such as the *'das log* in one of the stories that I collected: there the *'das log* saved people instead of just passively witnessing their suffering. The main problem with this line of argument is, however, that we know very little about Tibetan religion prior to the introduction of Buddhism, less than what is known about Turco-Mongol religious beliefs and practices before the arrival of Buddhism and Islam.

---

[11] For the Chinese version, see *Taishō* 310.17 (vol. XI), p. 328.
[12] See Pommaret, op. cit., p. 499f.

Concluding remarks

To understand a religious phenomenon such as the Tibetan *'das log* it would help to widen the perspectives somewhat. Buddhism is, after all, a pan-Asian religion.

A thorough study of the many Chinese stories of visitors to hell would be of great interest. Here we seem to have 'ordinary persons' dying and returning to life, and their stories bear witness of Buddhist, Taoist and many other influences.[13] The advantage of using this material for comparison is the abundance of written source material reaching far back in history. There is also a living tradition of Chinese religious specialists and spirit-mediums visiting deceased persons during their seances.[14] Such a study would provide us with examples of different ways of integrating Buddhism, spirit-mediumship/Shamanism and soul travelling.

Another line of research might possibly take as its point of departure the connection between the *'das log* and Avalokiteśvara and continue by looking at early Japanese devotional Buddhism, where the famous monk Genshin (942–1017), in order to help people towards the Pure Land, depicted his visions of the torments of hell in his writings.[15] With its emphasis on visualizations and morality, devotional Buddhism may thus incorporate and exploit the opposite of its picture of paradise and the Pure Land, that is, hell.

Finally, there is at present an ongoing discussion initiated by the anthropologists S. R. Mumford and G. Samuel as to what degree Himalayan religion is characterized by a dialogue between Buddhism and Shamanism and Tibetan religion by a so-called Shamanic Tantric Buddhism.[16] It is not

---

[13] See the articles by Robert Ford Campany, 'To Hell and Back: Death, Near-Death, and Other Worldly Journeys in Early Medieval China', in John J. Collins and Michael Fishbane (eds), *Death, Ecstasy, and Other Worldly Journeys*, Albany 1995, pp. 343–360, and Stephen F. Teiser, ' "Having Once Died and Returned to Life": Representations of Hell in Medieval China', *Harvard Journal of Asiatic Studies* 48 (1988), pp. 433–464.

[14] See, among many other studies, the modern classic Emily M. Ahearn, *The Cult of the Dead in a Chinese Village*, Stanford 1973, pp. 220–244.

[15] For a few notes on Genshin's life and works, see Robert K. Heinemann, 'This World and the Other Power: Contrasting Paths to Deliverance in Japan', in Heinz Bechert and Richard Gombrich (eds), *The World of Buddhism*, London 1984, p. 223, Daigan and Alicia Matsunaga, *Foundation of Japanese Buddhism,* vol. I, Los Angeles–Tokyo 1987, p. 216f., and Robert E. Morrell, *Kamakura Buddhism: A Minority Report*, Berkeley 1987, p. 16f.

[16] Stan Royal Mumford, *Himalayan Dialogue: Tibetan Lamas and Gurung Shamans in Nepal*, Madison 1989, and Geoffrey Samuel, *Civilized Shamans: Buddhism in Tibetan*

my intention to enter into this very interesting discussion here, but simply to make the observation that there may always have been a dialogue going on in Buddhism between upholders of different streams in the tradition. It did not start with Tantrism or with the spread of Indian Buddhism to other cultures. Instead, I think it can be traced from the very beginning of Buddhism, although the traces are fainter in some parts of the tradition and more visible in others. Especially what we call Tantrism may have offered a good hiding-place for ideas and practices not recognized by the clerical orthodoxy.[17] To understand the processes which have shaped the Tibetan *'das log* phenomenon, we need to look not only at the meeting of Buddhism and Central Asian popular religion, but also at the 'Shamanic' complex within Buddhism itself.

Societies, Washington 1993. For a different view, consult Todd Gibson, 'Notes on the History of the Shamanic in Tibet and Inner Asia', *Numen* 44 (1997), pp. 39–59.

[17] This observation was made in James H. Sanford, 'The Abominable Tachikawa Skull Ritual', *Monumenta Nipponica* 46 (1991), p. 1. Cf. Per-Arne Berglie, 'The *āveśa* Ritual in Tantric Buddhism and Ritual Possession in Tibet' (paper read at the Fourth International Conference of the International Society for Shamanic Research, Chantilly, Paris 1997).

LANGUAGE

Regional Aspects of the Turkic Influence on Mongolian

Maria Magdolna Tatár

Turkic-Mongolian contacts have been studied ever since scholars obtained some knowledge about these languages and the obvious similarities in their grammars and vocabularies. Mongolian was regarded as an especially important link between Turkic and Manchu-Tungusic languages and its Turkic loan-words were investigated both by the adherents and the opponents of the Altaic hypothesis. Such loan-words are to be found in any layer of Mongolian. There are also many Mongolian words borrowed into various Turkic languages, especially of the Kipchak group. These contacts explain why Mongolia, although a part of Inner Asia and culturally influenced by Buddhism and only sporadically by Islam, should and must be included in studies concerning Central Asia.

While hardly any scholars at present are for the Altaic hypothesis in Europe, it has many defenders in Mongolia. For example, D. Tömörtogoo in his interesting historical survey of the Mongolian language takes the Altaic affinity as the undisputed origin, the cardinal point for the development of the Mongolian language.[1] A common problem is that both earlier studies and recent publications often compare general 'Turkic' and 'Mongolian' without taking the exact dialects into consideration and often even without trying to establish a chronology. One of the reasons for the popularity of this hypothesis in Mongolia is probably that in lack of enough dialectological material there are no extensive etymological works carried out about the exact sources and receptive dialects until lately. Actually, there are more scholarly works treating Mongolian elements in Turkic languages[2] than

---

[1] D. Tömörtogoo, *Mongol xėlnij tovč tüüxen xėlzüi* I, Ulaanbaatar 1992, p. 2.

[2] See O. F. Sertkaya, 'Mongolian Words and Forms in Chagatay Turkish', in *Olon ulsyn mongolč ėrdėmtnij V ix xural*, Ulaanbaatar 1992, and G. Kara, 'Kirghiz

vice versa. Still, two works could be mentioned here: Rassadin's work about Turkic elements in Buryat[3] and an article by Róna-Tas[4] referring to the fact that both *k*- and *g*-initials are to be found in the Chuvash-Turkic loan-words in Mongolian and stating that some phonetic problems can be explained by the fact that Chuvash-Turkic had at least two dialects. These works are from a methodological point of view important contributions indicating a beginning to distinguish the different regional units one from the other in the larger area and to define the actual Turkic languages which influenced the various Mongolian dialects. Optimally, the results of such research could help to establish a chronology as well. Because these problems are not elaborated and lack summarizing references, the characteristics of different borrowings are often less visible, and the general impression of a 'common origin' can easily continue. The recently published dictionary of foreign words in Mongolian by Sùxbaatar,[5] a very interesting and useful book, contains very few words of Turkic origin while it registers not only foreign words but also common loan-words like *čixer* 'sugar', if they are not of Turkic origin. The reason for this difference in treatment must be that most Turkic words are understood as of common Altaic origin.

In this paper I intend to demonstrate the regional differences connected to the different layers of the Turkic loan-words in the Mongolian dialects. The following divisions have been made:

I. Borrowings which occur due to long-lasting contacts between Turks and Mongols living in the same area, presumably after establishing the Chinggiside empire

One example is *dede* 'uncle' in the West Mongolian Dòrvòd dialect,[6] which until recently had everyday contacts with Central Asian Turks and even absorbed Turkic substrates during and after the Jungarian period. Another interesting word is Buryat *xarma* 'sausage of meat; food made of clotted

---

Onomatopoetic Words of Mongolian Origin', in *Olon ulsyn mongolč èrdèmtnij V ix xural*, Ulaanbaatar 1992.

[3] V. I. Rassadin, 'O tjurkizmax v burjatskom jazyke', in *K izučeniju burjatskogo jazyka*, Ulan–Ude 1969.

[4] A. Róna-Tas, 'A magyar-bolgár-török érintkezés jellege', in *Magyar őstörténeti tanulmányok*, Budapest 1977.

[5] O. Sùxbaatar, *Mongol xèlnij xar' ùgiin tol'*, Ulaanbaatar 1997.

[6] E. Vanduj, *Dòrvòd aman ajalguu*, Ulaanbaatar 1965, p. 152.

blood, mixed with fat, but not a sausage',[7] especially in the Ekhirit dialect and its Kachuga subdialect spoken along the left-side tributaries of the river Lena.[8] It is *not* connected with Yakut *xarba* 'internals, stomach',[9] as perhaps could be expected in this vicinity. It is a participle of *qar-* 'to mix',[10] represented in the Oghuz and Kipchak languages. So the exact meaning is 'mixture' – a meaning that already exists in Turkic; cf. Kazak *xarma et* 'minced meat, braised or cooked in its own steam'.[11] It is noteworthy that the word is not documented in the geographically close Yakut language but in a Kipchak language spoken far away. Such words are first of all important in the study of the particular dialect and its contacts, but less important concerning the Altaic hypothesis.

II. Words known in most dialects, sometimes with regional developments of their semantics

For example, Khalkha *dzaram* (Classic Mongolian *ǰarm-a*) 'bran, peelings, separated from the flour, meal',[12] is to be found in most dialects, even in the archaic Dagur language.[13] In the isolated Boo-an language it exists in the expression *dzarma òr* 'an empty peel'.[14] The two words in this expression actually mean the same in Turkic and Mongolian. The word *ǰarma* is a participle of Turkic *yar-* 'to split', borrowed from a language where *ǰ-* corresponds to Common Turkic initial *y-*, as it does, for example, in Kirghiz, whereas e.g. the Mansi language borrowed *jōrem, jōrme, jarma* (and other dialectal variants) 'bran'[15] from a Turkic form in *y-*. This is one of the few

---

[7] K. M. Čeremisov, *Burjatsko-russkij slovar'*, Moskva 1973, p. 556a.
[8] A. G. Mitroškina, 'Govor kačugskix (verxolenskix) burjat', *Issledovanija burjatskix govorov II*, Ulan–Ude 1968, p. 67.
[9] P. S. Afanas'ev, M. S. Voronkin and M. P. Alekseev, *Dialektologičeskij slovar' jakutskogo jazyka*, Moskva 1976, p. 282.
[10] Sir Gerard Clauson, *An Etymological Dictionary of Pre-Thirteenth Century Turkish*, Oxford 1972, p. 642.
[11] B. Bazylxan, *Mongol-kazax tol'*, Ulaanbaatar 1966, p. 267b.
[12] Ja. Cėvėl, *Mongol xėlnij tovč tajlbar tol'*, Ulaanbaatar 1966, p. 267b.
[13] Namsaraj Xasartani, *Dagur kele mongγol kelen-ü qaričaγulul*, Köke qota 1983, p. 524.
[14] Cin, Nay and Siyuing, *Boo-an kelen-ü üges* (Mongγol töröl-ün kele ayalγun-u sudulul-un čuburil 011), Köke qota 1986, p. 198.
[15] B. Munkácsi and B. Kálmán, *Wogulisches Wörterbuch*, Budapest 1986, p. 176a.

Turkic words to be found in Sùxbaatar's dictionary.[16] Widely used in different dialects as this word is, it must rather be considered to be a loan-word and not a foreign one. It is to be found in the list of Róna-Tas about Turkic agricultural terms in Mongolian.[17] Nevertheless, it is interesting that such an agricultural term became so widely spread in the receptive Mongolian dialects. However, it is *not* documented in Buryat and it is not known among the Darkhats, i.e. in the northern territories. In this case, the semantic differences are historically interesting. In Kalmuck the word also means 'millet',[18] while in Kirghiz *jarma* means 'shavings, peel, soup made of roast cereals'.[19]

III. Words borrowed into different Mongolian dialects independently, possibly at different times from different languages

The Dagur word *isur* 'lining of a garment',[20] for example, is a borrowing from Yakut *is* 'interior, internal organs of the body, fur used as undergarment' with the Dagur suffix *-r*. The word is well known in Turkic languages,[21] but the *-č* > *-s* development is undoubtedly Yakut. The same specific meaning, namely *ičkilik* 'lining', is to be found in Kirghiz,[22] and obviously in Yakut, too (cf. *ista* 'to line a garment',[23] which was borrowed into the South Samoyed languages as well: Koibal *isti, iste*[24]). On the other hand, the archaic Khalkha word *ičreg* 'genital organs'[25] is a euphemism, semantically close to related word forms in all Turkic languages. Especially interesting are Kazak *išti* 'pregnant'[26] and Yakut *istex* > Evenki *iskek* 'roe of fish'.[27]

---

[16] O. Sùxbaatar, op. cit., p. 111.
[17] A. Róna-Tas, op. cit., p. 271.
[18] G. J. Ramstedt, *Kalmückisches Wörterbuch*, Helsinki 1935, p. 467b.
[19] K. K. Judaxin, *Kirgizsko-russkij slovar'*, Moskva 1965, p. 235b.
[20] Namsaraj Xasartani, op. cit., p. 460b.
[21] Cf. Clauson, op. cit., p. 17a–b, and E. V. Sevortjan, *Étimologičeskij slovar' tjurkskix jazykov I–III*, Moskva 1974–1980, vol. I, pp. 388–389.
[22] K. K. Judaxin, op. cit., p. 307a.
[23] E. K. Pekarskij, *Slovar' jakutskogo jazyka I–III*, Moskva 1958, pp. 973–974.
[24] A. Castrén, *Versuch einer koibalischen und karagassischen Sprachlehre*, St. Petersburg 1857, p. 146b.
[25] Ja. Cèvèl, op. cit., p. 311b.
[26] B. Bazylxan, op. cit., p. 81b.
[27] A. V. Romanova, A. N. Myreeva and P. P. Baraskov, *Vzaimovlijanie èvenkijskogo i*

Still, they are not the source of the loan-word in Khalkha, because their suffixes differ from that in Khalkha. Its source must be a dialect similar to the one used in the Turkic runic inscriptions, where *ičräki* 'internal' is to be found.[28] The Khalkha word is a much earlier borrowing than the Dagur one. In both cases, their semantics became narrower and they came to mean very specific objects, which is not an unusual development for loan-words.

IV. Appearance of local semantic development

One example is West Mongolian *xartsaxa* 'waist' (anat.)[29] < Turkic *kurša:g* 'belt',[30] which is a derivation from *kur* 'belt, girth of a tent'.[31] This word is widespread in Oghuz and Kipchak languages and is to be found as a loan-word in the languages of neighbouring regions (e.g. Persian, Russian and the languages on the Balkan).[32] Phonetically, the West Mongolian word must descend from Turkic languages spoken in Central Asia and Kazakstan, while semantically it is closer to the Turkic languages of the northern group (cf. the Ust'-Yan dialect of Yakut *kurtan'n'yk* 'heart',[33] Yakut > Evenki *kurtax* 'stomach',[34] as well as Koibal *kurtana* 'hip'[35]). The semantic development 'clothing on the body' > 'a part of the body dressed by the actual clothing' possibly occurred in these languages independently (cf. Russian *pojas* 'belt' > *pojasnica* 'waist').

---

jakutskogo jaxykov, Leningrad 1975, p. 187.
[28] Kül Tegin B and Tonyuquq; cf. G. Ajdarov, *Jazyk orxonskix pamjatnikov drevnetjurskoj pis'mennosti VIII. veka,* Alma–Ata 1971, p. 358.
[29] Z. Coloo, *BNMAU dàx' mongol xèlnij nutgijn ajalguuny tol' bičig II. Ojrd ajalguu,* Ulaanbaatar 1988, p. 393.
[30] Sir Gerard Clauson, op. cit., p. 664b, and G. Doerfer, *Türkische und mongolische Elemente im Neupersischen I–IV,* Wiesbaden 1963–1964, no. 1565.
[31] Sir Gerard Clauson, op. cit., p. 660b, and G. Doerfer, op. cit., no. 1553.
[32] Cf. G. Doerfer, op. cit., no. 1565.
[33] P. S. Afanas'ev et al., op. cit., p. 127b.
[34] A. V. Romanova et al., op. cit., p. 191, and P. S. Afanas'ev et al., op. cit., p. 127.
[35] A. Castrén, op. cit., p. 91a.

V. The testimony of the earlier archaic Dagur language

In spite of interesting details, which reveal a position in between Central Asia and the Yakuts with some possible influence of earlier Turkic populations in Mongolia, many of these loan-words cannot be dated. However, in the case of archaic Dagur (perhaps a descendant of Khitay) it is possible to estimate a chronology, which makes its loan-words extremely important. Compare the following examples:

V a–b

Dagur *balag* 'dust, soil'[36] originates from the Turkic *balyk* 'mud'.[37] The Dagur expression *balag karo:* 'big wall of soil/mud' reveals further connections. From the word meaning 'mud' developed Middle Turkic and Eastern Turkic *balyq* 'wall built of unbaked bricks'[38] and 'town'.[39] The word is borrowed into Pre-Classic Mongolian as well: *balɣasun* 'wall'[40] > Classic Mongolian 'town', probably under Turkic influence. However, also the form *balaɣ* 'sand dunes'[41] existed in Classic Mongolian, with a specific meaning. The second word in the Dagur expression, *karo:* 'big wall, fortress', is interesting as well. Its Middle Turkic parallel *korig* 'enclosure' is explained by Clauson as a loan from Mongolian[42] (cf. Mongolian *qori'an* 'enclosed place'), while Hungarian linguists explain this word and its Hungarian counterpart *karám*[43] as a word of Turkic origin. Both Dagur words are shorter than the Classic Mongolian forms: *balag* does not have the typical Mongolian suffix *-sun* and the long vowel at the end of *karo:* must go back to a final -Vɣ. The vowel in the last ending was probably not a velar *-ï-*, as it is in Middle Turkic and Classic Mongolian, but *-u-*. This variant was

---

[36] Namsaraj Xasartani, op. cit., p. 475b.
[37] Sir Gerard Clauson, op. cit., p. 336a.
[38] E. V. Sevortjan, op. cit., vol. II, p. 59.
[39] Sir Gerard Clauson, op. cit., p. 335b.
[40] N. N. Poppe, *Mongol'skij slovar' Mukaddimat al-Adab I*, Moskva–Leningrad 1938, p. 100a–b.
[41] F. D. Lessing, *Mongolian-English Dictionary*, Bloomington 1982, p. 78b.
[42] Sir Gerard Clauson, op. cit., p. 659b.
[43] *A magyar nyelv történeti-etimilógiai szótára I–IV*, Budapest 1984, vol. II, p. 375a, and *Etymologisches Wörterbuch des Ungarischen I–VI*, Budapest 1992–1997, p. 695a–b.

attested by Erdal in the inscriptions of Kül Tegin, Bilgä Kagan and Tes,[44] i.e. *karo:* is borrowed from a Turkic language, which was closer to the language of the inscriptions than the source of the Classic Mongolian was. (The Hungarian form originates from variants with an *-a-*, as e.g. is to be found in the Ongin inscription and in the Kipchak languages.) This means that both words are closer to Turkic forms than the Classic Mongolian forms are.

V c

The word *gat* 'stake, pole, nail'[45] occurs in Dagur in the expression *altan gat* 'golden nail; the Polar Star, the North Star', while the usual word for 'nail', namely *xadasn*,[46] has the same suffix *-sun* as the Mongolian dialects. This is a well-known word in Mongolian languages and dialects: Classic Mongolian *γadasun*, *γadaγusun*, Khalkha *gadas*,[47] Buryat *gadaha(n)*,[48] Kalmuck *γasn*, *γassn*.[49] The form used in the traditional name for the star must be the older one in Dagur, while the common technical term is more probably a new borrowing from some Mongolian dialect. The Turkic etymology of the word has been described several times.[50] Furthermore, a shorter form like the Dagur one is to be found in Kirghiz (*kada* 'pole'),[51] and in Solon (*gata*, most probably a Dagur loan). Evenki *gatahun* is borrowed from Mongolian.[52] However, the shorter Turkic form cannot originate in *any* Mongolian dialect or language, only in Dagur, which is hardly the case. Both *-sun/-san* and *-Vn* are typical Mongolian additions. On the other hand, Soyot *kadax*[53] manifests a regular Turkic development, which must

---

[44] M. Erdal, *Old Turkic Word Formation I–II*, Wiesbaden 1991, cf. vol. I, pp. 193–194.
[45] Namsaraj Xasartani, op. cit., p. 450b.
[46] Namsaraj Xasartani, op. cit., p. 138a.
[47] Ja. Cével, op. cit., p. 131a.
[48] K. M. Čeresimov, op. cit., p. 138b.
[49] G. J. Ramstedt, op. cit., p. 146b, and Z. Coloo, op. cit., p. 344.
[50] Cf. M. Räsänen, *Versuch eines etymologischen Wörterbuchs der Türksprachen*, Helsinki 1969, p. 243, Sir Gerard Clauson, op. cit., p. 597, and lately, L. Ligeti, *A magyar nyelv török kapcsolatai a honfoglalás előtt és az Árpád-korban*, Budapest 1986, p. 15, who erroneously wrote that Mongolian has only forms with *-d-*.
[51] K. K. Judaxin, op. cit., p. 313a.
[52] *Sravnitel'nyj slovar' tunguso-man'čžurskix jazykov I–II*, Leningrad 1975, vol. I, p. 144a.
[53] A. Castrén, op. cit. p. 92a.

have been the source of the longer Mongolian form *yadayusun*. The word is doubtless a development of Turkic *qad-/qaz-* 'to stick into, to drive in, to nail', whose Mongolian counterpart is *qada-* 'to drive in, to nail'. The alternation *-d-* in Classic Mongolian, *-t* in Dagur and *-s-* in the West Mongolian *yassn* (>*yasn*) shows the $d > t$, $d > \delta > z$ development which is well known in Turkic languages.[54] This alternation not only proves the Turkic origin of the word but also the fact that the word must have been borrowed three times:

1. Into Dagur from a Turkic language which had *-t-* in the middle position (e.g. Yakut);

2. Into Classic Mongolian from a Turkic language which had *-d-* in the middle position (e.g. Tatar);

3. Into West Mongolian from a Turkic language which had *-z-* in the middle position (e.g. the Mrass dialect of Shor).

V d

Dagur *bo:s* 'pregnant (of animals)'[55] is a widespread word: Classic Mongolian *boyus* 'embryo; pregnant (of animals)', Khalkha *boos*,[56] Kalmuck *bos* 'pregnant (of animals)'[57] < Middle Turkic *boyaz* 'pregnant (of animals)'.[58] It is known in Yakut, Tuva and Bashkir as well as in the Turkic languages of the Altay region and Central Asia, and it has also been borrowed into Kamas: *bos* 'id.'.[59] The most interesting fact is that this generally known loan-word has an unusual counterpart in Dagur, namely *bo:r* 'id.'.[60] This is a regular form according to rotacism: the final *-z* is substituted by *-r*, as is common in the Chuvash-type languages. However, I have not been able to find this word in Chuvash. The following explanations are possible:

1. Dagur once preferred an *-r* on the syllabic limit; cf. *elpur < elbeg* 'abundant, plentiful', *erdegu < ebdeku* 'to break', *borka:gu < bosyaqu* 'to raise, to erect'. Therefore, an internal development cannot be excluded.

---

[54] Cf. L. Ligeti, op. cit., pp. 105–107.
[55] Namsaraj Xasartani, op. cit., p. 480b.
[56] Ja. Cėvėl, op. cit., p. 92b.
[57] G. J. Ramstedt, op. cit., p. 54a.
[58] M. Räsänen, op. cit., p. 78b, and E. V. Sevortjan, op. cit., vol. II, p. 169.
[59] A. Castrén, op. cit., p. 161.
[60] Namsaraj Xasartani, op. cit., p. 480b.

However, it is possible, that in Turkic loans like *bo:r* and *bur* < *bös* 'belt',[61] the characteristic *-z/-r* change is connected to a Chuvash-type Turkic language.

2. Dagur borrowed this form from a Chuvash-type Turkic language. This means that such a language must have existed somewhere close to Manchuria, or that the Dagurs must have lived somewhere close to Chuvash-type Turkic speakers. This question cannot be answered yet. Still, it is noteworthy to mention here the research conducted by Róna-Tas about the earliest Samoyed-Turkic contacts.[62] In this case, the borrowing must have happened at a very early stage, which Clauson called the first period,[63] probably in the 5th and 6th centuries. However, the exact date is most uncertain, and so is the source.

V e

While *bo:r* perhaps indicates contacts with some Chuvash-type language, Dagur *šatag/xatag* 'broken'[64] probably refers to other Turkic languages. It is a regular form of Turkic *čat-* 'to fasten, unify'.[65] However, in some languages, not the unifying but the splitting dominates the semantics, as in Kirghiz *čatkal* 'a deep couloir between two mountains'[66] and Turkish *čatal* 'gespalten'.[67] This semantical development is explained by Turkish dialectal *čatak* 'space between two hills'.[68] The word is unknown in Khalkha, Buryat and Western Mongolian dialects, as well as in Manchu-Tungusic languages. It means that Dagur speakers probably had early contacts with a Kipchak or Oghuz speaking population as well.

---

[61] All examples: Namsaraj Xasartani, op. cit. pp. 456a, 458b, 481b, 480b.
[62] A. Róna-Tas, 'On the Earliest Samoyed-Turkic Contacts', in *Congressus Quintus Internationalis Fenno-Ugristarum*, Turku 1980.
[63] Sir Gerard Clauson, 'The Turkish Elements in 14th Century Mongolian', *Central Asiatic Journal* 5 (1959–1960), p. 301.
[64] Namsaraj Xasartani, op. cit., p. 518b.
[65] M. Räsänen, op. cit., p. 101a; for the suffix, cf. M. Erdal, op. cit., p. 224.
[66] K. K. Judaxin, op. cit., p. 851a–b.
[67] M. Räsänen, op. cit., p. 101a.
[68] *Türkiye'de Halk Ağzından Derleme Sözlüğü*, vol III, Ankara 1993, p. 1087a–b.

Concluding remarks

These examples show how complicated the background of the Turkic loans is even in Dagur, an archaic and isolated language in Manchuria far from most Turkic languages except Yakut and Fu-yü. At the same time they indicate that much clarifying historical information could be obtained through further analysis of them. The final conclusion in the Altaic debate with explanations that would be satisfactory to both parties will be possible only after the dialectological and chronological classification of the Turkic loanwords in Mongolian, which this paper is meant to be a contribution to.

Remarks on the Mongolian Vowel System

Vivan Franzén and Jan-Olof Svantesson

Although Mongolian, the most important language in the Mongolic language group, has a long tradition as a literary language dating back to the 13th century, a thorough modern investigation of its phonetics and phonology has not yet been carried out. With this in mind, a number of linguists at Lund University have set up a research project for a large-scale investigation of Mongolian phonemes.[1]

The aim of this article is to shed some light on vowel length in initial syllables and non-initial syllables in Mongolian – an issue about which there are different opinions. The quality of first-syllable /i/ and /e/ as well as the quality of epenthetic vowels in non-initial syllables is also discussed.

The object of our investigation is the Khalkha dialect as spoken in Ulan Bator, i.e. what is usually called Standard Khalkha Mongolian. The technical phonetic analyses of the Mongolian vowel system, monophthongs as well as diphthongs, have been processed in Lund at the Department of Linguistics.

The material

The phonetic data presented here are based on recordings made in Ulan Bator in May 1990. The main recordings were performed with three male speakers of Khalkha origin: Basbajar (BB), Davaadorž (DD) and Xürelbaatar (XB). All three were born and grew up in Ulan Bator. At the time of the recording they were all living there. They were 21, 26 and 36 years of age,

---

[1] The project 'Modern Mongolian Phonology' is supported by the Swedish Council for Research in the Humanities and Social Sciences.

respectively. The informants read a list of words illustrating various phonetic phenomena repeating each word 3–5 times. The recordings were analysed in the ESPS Waves program on a Sun workstation at the Department of Linguistics at Lund University. In the following pages, diagrams of the preliminary results of the recordings are presented. More detailed diagrams and discussion will be presented in a forthcoming monograph on Mongolian phonetics and phonology from our project.

Vowel phonemes

There are seven basic vowels in Mongolian:

(1) i   u
     e   ʊ
         o
     a   ɔ

These vowels occur both long and short. Four of the vowels mentioned in (1) form diphthongs with /i/. In initial syllables there are three kinds of contrasting vowels (as to the absence of short /e/, see below, p. 112), viz.:

(2) Short vowels   Long vowels   Diphthongs
      i   u   i: u: ui
           ʊ   ʊ: ʊi
           o   e: o:
      a   ɔ   a: ɔ: ai   ɔi

Duration

The duration of each vowel in short and long initial syllables and in non-initial ones was measured from spectrograms and waveform displays using a material consisting of disyllabic words illustrating each combination of monophthongic vowels in the first and second syllable. Whenever possible, words with an initial dental consonant and a vowel followed by /l/ or /r/ were chosen. The words were read in the sentence frame *bi: _ gisĕŋ*, 'I said _.'

REMARKS ON THE MONGOLIAN VOWEL SYSTEM

Figure 1 below shows an example of short and long vowels in initial syllables of disyllabic words (speaker BB).

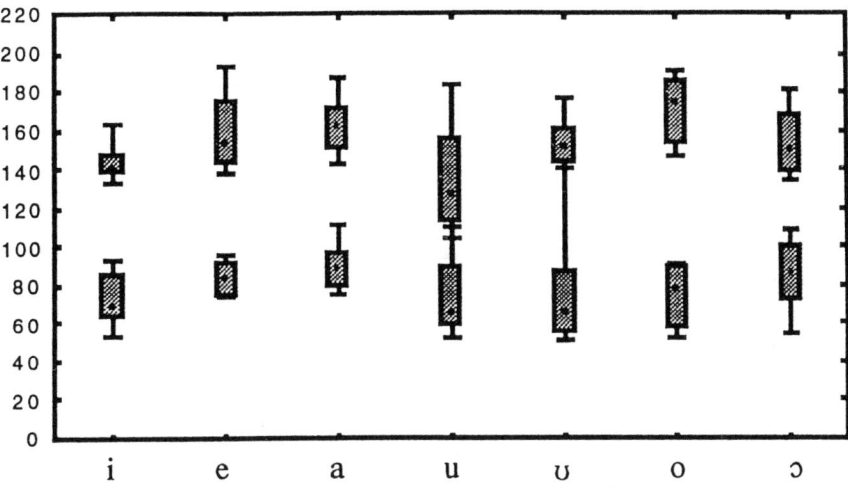

Figure 1. Duration in ms of short and long initial-syllable vowels (BB)

In the upper row are the long vowels and in the lower, the short ones. Each individual box plot presents all the values for the particular vowel. The point in the box is the median. The box itself contains 50% of all the values. Above the box are 25% of all the values and underneath, the remaining 25%. The horizontal lines represent maximum and minimum values.

Measurements of the duration for each vowel and all speakers are summarized in Table 1 and Figure 2:

	First syllable			Second syllable		
	Double	Single		Double	Single	
BB	154	78	(51%)	97	53	(55%)
DD	128	64	(50%)	78	46	(59%)
XB	127	56	(44%)	76	40	(53%)

Table 1. Mean vowel duration (ms) for all vowels

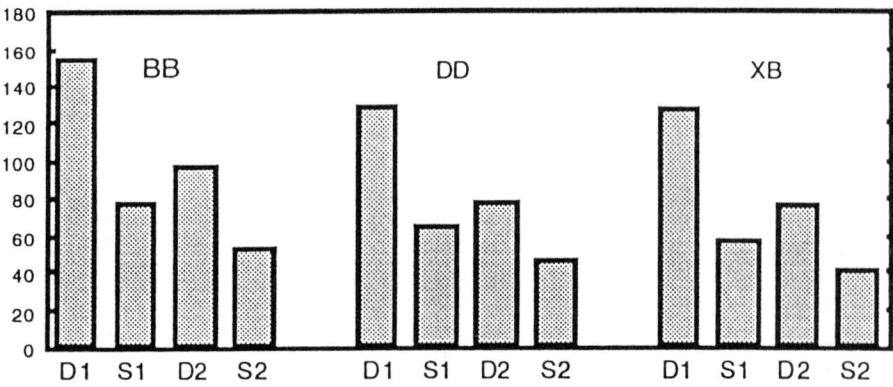

Figure 2. Mean vowel duration (ms) for all vowels and all speakers

A 'single' vowel (S) is here defined as one phoneme, orthographically written with a single letter, and a 'double' vowel (D) is a phoneme written with two letters. An initial-syllable vowel is referred to as (1) and the vowel of a non-initial syllable as (2). D1 thus means a vowel written with two letters in the first syllable.

From these measurements we can see that the average duration of a single vowel is 49% of the duration of a double vowel in the initial syllable. In the second syllable this ratio is 55%. The duration ratio is then approximately the same in initial and final syllables. It can also be noted that the duration of a double vowel in a non-initial syllable is only slightly longer than the duration of a single vowel in the initial syllable, and much shorter than the duration of a double vowel in the initial syllable.

Another observation is that short first-syllable /e/ and /i/ have merged so that the short vowel /e/ does not occur in initial syllables. From Figures 3 and 4 it can be seen how close they are.

Formant frequencies of monophthongs

The first three formant frequencies of each vowel were measured for the three informants on the basis of the same material and the same method as were employed for measuring vowel length. The following figure is an example of how F1, F2 and F3 could be visualized:

REMARKS ON THE MONGOLIAN VOWEL SYSTEM

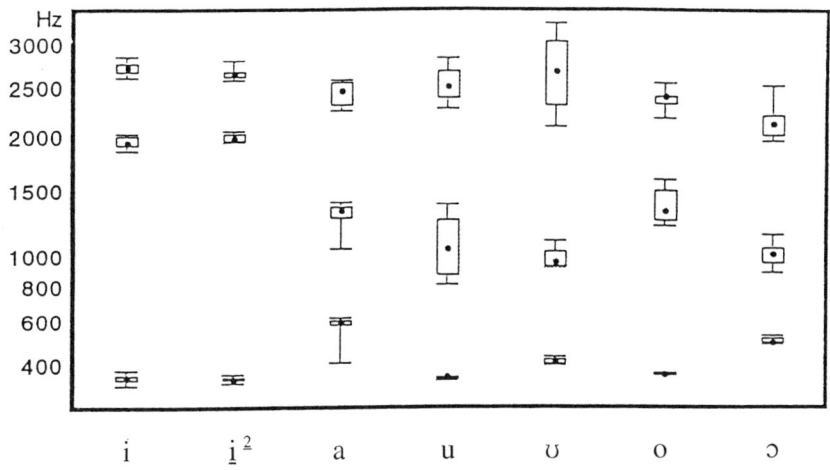

Figure 3. Formant frequencies for short first-syllable vowels (BB)

In order to make the picture still clearer F1 and F2 have been plotted on a diagram formed by a mel scale:

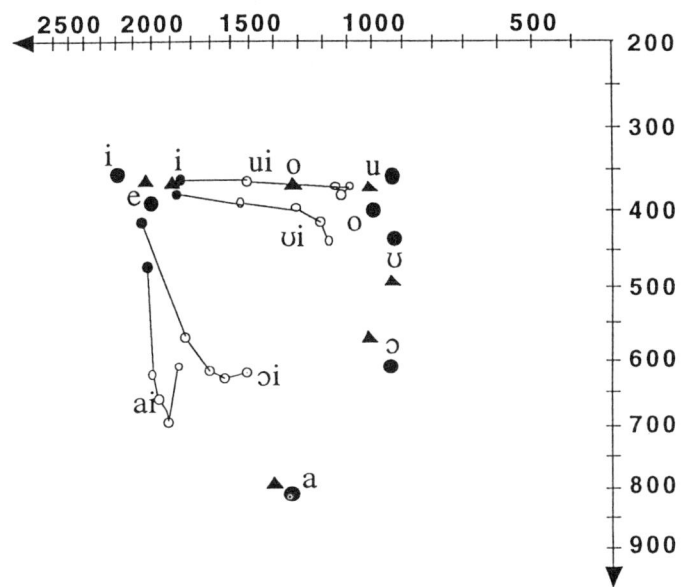

Figure 4. First-syllable short and long monophthongs and diphthongs (DD)

---

[2] i̱ represents the sound that orthographically is written as short *e*.

Explanations of the different symbols in Figure 4:

- ● represents long monophthongs
- ▲ represents short monophthongs
- ○ represents the starting point and ● the end point of diphthongs

The quality of initial-syllable short and long vowels is approximately the same, the short ones being slightly centralized. The only exception is /o/, where the short vowel has a much higher F2 than the long one and is more like [ə] or even [ʉ] than [o].

Our investigation of some other Mongolian dialects (Khalkha and South Mongolian, i.e. Khalkha spoken in Inner Mongolia)[3] shows similar tendencies, while Khalkha formant frequencies published by Rialland and Djamouri in 1984[4] (Northern Khalkha) and Jōo in 1973[5] and 1976,[6] show a higher F2 for /u/ in addition to the F1 difference.

The vowels given here as /u/ and /o/ have traditionally been described as 'central', and sometimes even 'front'. The vowel /u/ is usually written as *u* or *ü* and /o/ is written as *ó* or *ö*. The vowel /ʊ/ is usually given as *u*, and /ɔ/ as *o*. This description goes back to Ramstedt[7] (who used the then current term 'mixed' instead of 'central'), and furthermore, to Castrén's[8] description of Buryat. Although many researchers seem to have doubted the phonetic correctness of this description (for instance, many, including Ramstedt, have observed that '[u]' is not identical with the cardinal vowel [u]), it has remained standard. One reason for this seems to be the great authority of Ramstedt's work. Another reason is the influence of Old Written Mongolian, where the vowels etymologically corresponding to Khalkha /u, ʊ, o/ and /ɔ/

---

[3] Jan-Olof Svantesson, 'Vowel Harmony Shift in Mongolian', *Lingua* 67 (1985), pp. 283–327.

[4] Annie Rialland and Rédouane Djamouri, 'Harmonie vocalique, consonantique et structures de dépendance dans le mot en mongol khalkha', *Bulletin de la Société de Linguistique de Paris* 79 (1984), pp. 333–383.

[5] Hakutarō Jōo, 'Jikken onseigaku ni yoru Mongorugo no kansatsu' [The Mongolian Language from the Point of View of Experimental Phonetics], *Onsei no kenkyū* [The Study of Sounds] 16 (1973), pp. 207–229.

[6] Hakutarō Jōo, 'Mongoruo no boin chōwa' [Vowel Harmony in Mongolian], *Gengo* 5:6 (1976), pp. 53–61.

[7] Gustaf John Ramstedt, 'Das Schriftmongolische und die Urgamundart phonetisch verglichen', *Suomalais-ugrilaisen seuran aikakauskirja* 21:2 (1903), pp. 1–56.

[8] Matthias Alexander Castrén, *Versuch einer burjätischen Sprachlehre nebst kurzem Wörterverzeichnis*, St. Petersburg 1857. Reprinted in 1969 by Zentralantiquariat der DDR, Leipzig.

were most probably pronounced as /y, u, ø / and /o/, respectively. A third reason may be that full recognition of the phonetic facts was felt to lead to difficulties in the description of Mongolian vowel harmony, both within structuralist and generative phonology. Linguists from Inner Mongolia, e.g. Cenggeltei[9] and Dobu,[10] have described these vowels in the same way as was done here.

The vowels of non-initial syllables

The number of contrasting vowels in initial and non-initial syllables differ greatly, due to vowel harmony and vowel reduction. In non-initial syllables, there are two kinds of full vowels, monophthongs and diphthongs. There are also reduced vowels, which occur only in non-initial syllables. They have short duration and are somewhat centralized (see Figure 5). In our view,[11] the place and quality of the reduced vowels can be predicted. Therefore, they can be regarded as epenthetic vowels, which are not present in underlying forms but are inserted by rules. The contrasting possibilities of non-initial vowels are, however, reduced further by vowel harmony.

The present investigation is supported by the fact that the duration of a full non-initial vowel is close to, though somewhat longer than that of a short vowel in initial syllables (see Table 1 and Figure 2). The following full vowels occur in non-initial syllables:

(3)   i   u   ui
      e   ʊ   ʊi
          o
      a   ɔ   ai   ɔi

The same material was used for the analysis of short (reduced) vowels in non-initial syllables. The first two formants in the middle of the vowels were measured and compared to the formants in the first syllables. The

---

[9] Cenggeltei, *Odo üy-e-yin Mongyol kelen-ü jüi* [Grammar of Modern Mongolian], Köke qota 1979.
[10] [Dobu] Daobu, *Mengguyu jianzhi* [Short Description of Mongolian], Beijing 1983.
[11] See Jan-Olof Svantesson, *Mongolian Syllable Structure* (Working Papers 42, Dept. of Linguistics), Lund 1994, pp. 225–239, and id., 'Cyclic Syllabification in Mongolian', *Natural Language and Linguistic Theory* 13 (1995), pp. 755–766.

results for all three informants were plotted on a diagram formed by a mel scale:

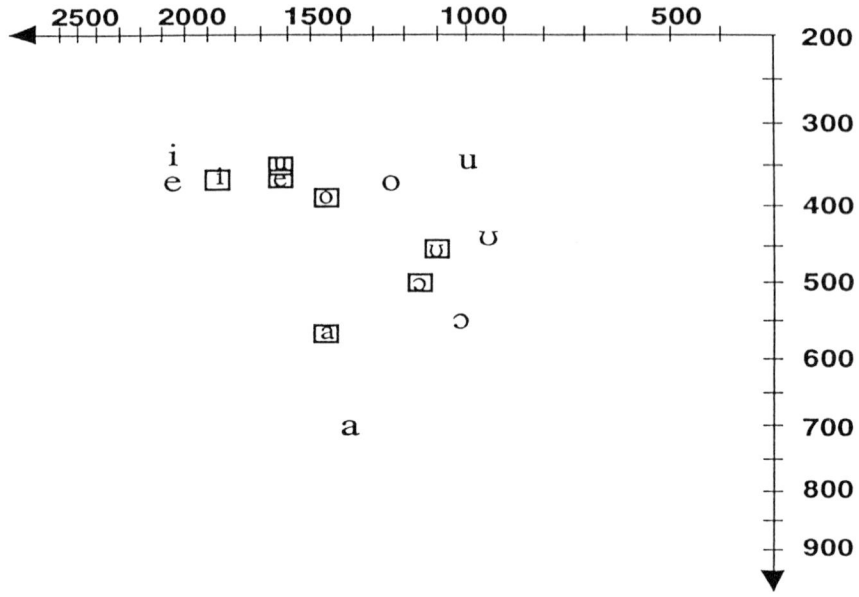

Figure 5. Diagram showing the average F1 and F2 values for the vowel in the first syllable and F1 and F2 for a reduced vowel in the second syllable in disyllabic words (average over the three speakers)

As is indicated by the Cyrillic Mongolian orthography, the quality of a single vowel in the second syllable is heavily influenced by the quality of the vowel in the first syllable and may be regarded as a reduced variant of this. Thus we will write [ă] for a reduced vowel if the vowel in the first syllable is [a(ː)], etc. (e.g. <baatar> 'hero' [baːtăr], <xural> 'meeting' [xʊrŏl]).

The results show that a reduced vowel acoustically is a centralized variant of the vowel in the first syllable. The only exception is [ŭ], which is more or less identical to [ĕ]. This is consistent with the Cyrillic Mongolian script, which writes [ŭ] as <э>, i.e. in the same way as [ĕ] and [ĭ]. On the other hand, the Cyrillic script implies that [ŏ] is identical to [ă], since both are written <a>, and this is not supported by the acoustic data, which show that the quality of [ŏ] is rather close to [ʊ], but quite different from [ă] and [a]. Thus, a spelling like <*xʊrʊl> 'meeting' would be more accurate than the official spelling <xʊral>.

In other words, the quality of a short vowel in a non-initial syllable depends on the nearest preceding full vowel in the following way:

(4) | Preceding full vowel | Epenthetic vowel |
|---|---|
| i | ĕ |
| u | ĕ |
| e | ĕ |
| o | ŏ |
| ʊ | ŭ |
| a | ă |
| ɔ | ɔ̆ |

The quality of a short vowel in a non-initial syllable can be predicted from the quality of the vowel in the preceding syllable as has been shown above. The vowel in question is a reduced centralized variant of the vowel in the preceding syllable.

Conclusion

Our investigation of Mongolian vowels shows that orthographic signs do not always stand for what is expected. Double letters in the first syllable represent much longer vowels than double letters in second syllables. Vowels written with a single letter show differences in first and second syllables, too, but in this case we also found definite quality differences. In the first syllable, short e is actually [i]. In the second syllable the short vowel is a centralized variant of the vowel in the first syllable.

With these data we have pointed to some of the discrepancies that can be found in literature on Mongolian phonology and phonetics. Needless to say, much work remains to be done in this field.

Towards a Sociolinguistic History of Sinkiang

JOAKIM ENWALL

The purpose of this paper is to take a look at the background material for a sociolinguistic history of Sinkiang, to outline basic tasks for this research and to make some references to points of particular interest.[1] The possible conclusions hinted at are often tentative and quite speculative.

One preliminary question is why choose Sinkiang, an obviously anachronistic concept from a historical perspective, and how to define this area. From the point of view of multifarious cultural and linguistic contacts, Sinkiang presents an unusually complex and interesting picture reflecting changes in language usage conditioned by migration, the spread of religions, military expansion and trade relations.[2]

The question of defining the geographical area of research is more complicated. Is Sinkiang to be understood as synonymous with the quite recently established Chinese province/autonomous region of Sinkiang; or is it perhaps to be interpreted as the Uighur 'Šäriq Turkistan', i.e. Eastern Turkestan, which is rather defined as being the area inhabited by a Turkic group whose present self-designation is Uighur? The definition adopted here is variable, with the area between the Tianshan and the Kunlun Mountains, i.e. the Tarim basin, as the main focus, but including the areas bordering on this region where linguistic interaction has been significant.

There are several ways of investigating sociolinguistic processes, but in this case the focal point is the use of languages, and more particularly

---

[1] The author is currently engaged in writing a sociolinguistic history of Sinkiang as a project sponsored by the Swedish Council for Research in the Humanities and Social Sciences.
[2] Michael Dillon, *Xinjiang: Ethnicity, Separatism and Control in Chinese Central Asia* (Durham East Asian Papers 1), Durham 1995.

writing systems, as a reflection of ethnic, religious, commercial and military relations in the area. In several instances these functions have been divided within one society and we find in the long course of history cases of both diglossia and triglossia – as e.g. in Kroraina, where Loulan is the best known example, with a triglossia for civil (Tokharian), military (Chinese) and religious (Loulan Prakrit) affairs – at least at a certain point in its historical development.

I will give a brief outline below of the sociolinguistic setting of each of the major ethnic groups in the area and thereafter try to define some general tendencies, which are also of importance for understanding the sociolinguistic situation in Sinkiang today.

Ancient ethnic setting

The archaeological finds in the region date back to several thousand years BC and include the famous mummies discovered mainly along the south-eastern border of the Takla-makan desert. It has hitherto been impossible to identify these archaeological finds with any particular ethnic or linguistic group, although there has been significant speculation about the apparent Indo-European character of the mummies found and the possible connection with a supposed south Tokharian population, e.g. in Cherchen.

Ancient peoples mentioned in the Chinese historical annals include the Xiongnu, sometimes referred to as the Huns of the East, the Yuezhi and the Wusun. Their languages were probably Altaic, but no compelling evidence has been forwarded to support this assumption, although it seems most plausible. Later, several Mongolian and Turkic peoples dominated or passed through the area, but little is known about the linguistic conditions of these groups.[3]

At the beginning of the Common Era, or even somewhat earlier, Buddhism was introduced to the Tarim basin by Indian missionaries. Indian languages, Sanskrit and the north-western Prakrits, subsequently played an important role in the area, especially within the field of Buddhism, but also significantly within the spheres of administration and commerce. The Indian influence on Saka, Tokharian, Tibetan and Uighur terminology is very strong, which

---

[3] Cf. L. N. Gumiljov, *Drevnie turki*, Moskva 1993, and Wolfgang-Ekkehard Scharlipp, *Die frühen Türken in Zentralasien: eine Einführung in ihre Geschichte und Kultur*, Darmstadt 1992.

even indicates the high prestige of Indian learning and the importance of Indian society in general to the formation of the Buddhist kingdoms of the Tarim basin, such as Khotan and Kroraina.[4]

The Tokharians

The Tokharian language constitutes a separate branch of the Indo-European languages. It, somewhat paradoxically, belongs to the *kentum* or generally western group of Indo-European languages and thus not to the *satem*, or basically eastern group, like the Indo-Iranian languages. It can be supposed that the Tokharians, during their migration eastwards, adopted many of the Iranian loan-words present in the extant written materials.

The texts in Tokharian, all written in the Brahmi script, were found from the beginning of this century onwards along the northern Silk Road, mainly in Maralbashi, Kucha, Karashahr and Turfan. The texts represent two strongly divergent dialects, which according to glottochronological estimates were divided approximately 1000 BC. The dialects are usually referred to as Tokharian A and Tokharian B.[5] The Tokharian A texts were found only in the monastery ruins in the eastern part of the area, while texts in Tokharian B were found at virtually all sites, which excludes the possibility of a strict geographical division between the dialects. The fact that only Tokharian B was used for profane purposes like private letters and caravan passes could indicate that Tokharian A had already by the time of the earliest extant texts been reduced to serving solely as a written and no longer as a spoken language, while Tokharian B continued to be the spoken language in most parts of the area.[6] The texts all date from the 6th to 8th centuries AD, and in the 7th and 8th centuries unofficial translations into Tokharian were added to Kuchean documents issued in Prakrit, which indicates a considerable importance of the language at that time.

Tokharian influence on neighbouring languages and peoples can, however, be traced further back, both linguistically and through comparative

---

[4] T. Burrow, *The Language of the Kharosthi Documents from Chinese Turkestan*, Cambridge 1937, pp. v–ix.

[5] Georges-Jean Pinault, 'Introduction au Tokharien' (Lalies: Actes des sessions de linguistique et de littérature 7), Paris 1989, pp. 5–224.

[6] This type of difference between Tokharian A and B is noted in Annemarie von Gabain, *Einführung in die Zentralasienkunde*, Darmstadt 1979, p. 14, while it is not explicitly stated in other works on Tokharian.

mythology. For the latter we have the Tokharian concepts of the celestial horses and the unicorn, appearing at least 1,000 years earlier than the extant Tokharian texts in historical Chinese mythological literature. As to loan-words, one clear example is the word for 'honey', in modern Chinese 'mì', found in Chinese texts from the 3rd century BC onwards. The proto-Chinese pronunciation of the character used was *miet*, to be compared with proto-Tokharian *myät*.

Another way of investigating the whereabouts of the Tokharians prior to the period of the unearthed texts is to look at loan-words in the Prakrit language used for administrative purposes in both the northern settlements, like Kucha, and in the Kroraina kingdom, including Niya. Many important terms were borrowed from Tokharian, which again shows that this must have been a prestigious language. A problem of interpretation is, nonetheless, posed by the fact that the Tokharian variety supplying loan-words to Niya and Loulan Prakrit was not identical with either of the Tokharian dialects used in the texts found in the North. There was, most probably, a southern dialect which was the substratum language in the kingdom of Kroraina and in Niya, but which was not committed to writing.

In Kumārajīva's translation of the Buddhist scriptures into Chinese in the late 4th century we can also find – in the choice of terminology etc. – evidence of the fact that his mother tongue was Tokharian.

After the fall of the Han dynasty, the Buddhist cities along the northern Silk Road experienced independence for some 400 years. Then, with the establishment of the Tang dynasty in AD 618, the Chinese began recapturing the area, starting in 630 and completing the task around 658, when Kucha was made the regional centre. This Chinese influence led to a decline in the monastic culture of the area, although Tokharian continued to be in use for at least two more centuries.

The Chinese

The Chinese presence in the region dates back to ancient times, but it was with the establishment of the system of military colonies, or *tuntian*, that the Chinese influx became more important and permanent, this process being initiated in the Han dynasty, around 200 BC, and strengthened during the early stage of the Tang dynasty. The Chinese influence over the area was much reduced after the Chinese defeat in the battle against the Arab

Muslim army at Talas in 751, which in fact stopped their westward expansion for good. This led to an increasing Islamic influence in the region, though no large-scale dominance came about until almost three centuries later. It also favoured the power of the Turkic peoples and the Tibetans; the latter manifested in the Tibetan occupation of Khotan and the area along the southern Silk Road in the 8th century.

After the Chinese defeat at Talas, the region remained quite isolated from China proper until the late 19th century, although the region had formally been integrated into China by the Qing empire in 1757–1759.

The Sogdians

The Sogdians, speaking a Middle Iranian language, originally lived near the lower reaches of the Oxus river (Amu-darya). Commercial contacts with Sogdian merchants had been frequent from the early centuries of the Common Era, but it was not until the restoration of Zoroastrianism in Sogdiana in the 6th century that there was a migration of Sogdians into the Tarim basin. In that area the Kök-Türks adopted the Sogdian language as their written medium.

In China proper Sogdian missionaries introduced Manichaeism in the late 7th century. Shortly afterwards places of worship were built, especially for usage by Sogdians and Iranians living in the Chinese capital. In 758, after the rebellion of An Lushan, the Chinese asked the Uighurs for military support. The Uighurs liberated Luoyang in 762. During their five month occupation of the city they came into contact with Manichaeism and subsequently brought with them four Manichaean monks of Sogdian descent to their capital Karabalghasun, where Manichaeism was proclaimed as the state religion. After the fall of the Uighur empire in 840, Manichaeism was brought to Qocho near Turfan, where it continued to be practised, albeit alongside Buddhism and Nestorian Christianity. Subsequently, Manichaeism also spread to Khotan; it was mentioned in a notice about a Khotanese embassy to China in 961.[7] In the 11th century the Sogdian language died out in the Tarim area and was replaced by Uighur. There is, on the other hand, a continuation of the language at present with the Yagnobian language in the Pamirs.

---

[7] Peter Bryder, *The Chinese Transformation of Manichaeism: A Study of Chinese Manichaean Terminology*, Lund 1985, p. 11.

The Sakas

The Sakas living in the Khotan region are relatively well documented in both Chinese and Tibetan chronicles. Furthermore, after the early 20th century discovery of texts in the Khotan Saka language, an Iranian language until then unknown, the knowledge about Khotan has been greatly increased.[8]

The Sakas originated from the area north of the Tarim basin but subsequently spread over a vast territory, including the area north of the Black Sea. In the early centuries AD, their administrative language was a north-west Indian Prakrit, Gandhari. From AD 330 onwards, Saka was used as state language, as well as the language of religion and commerce. After temporary hegemony by the Ruanruan and the Hephthalites in the 5th and 6th centuries, Khotan came under Chinese power in 644.

In the mid-8th century the Tibetans occupied Khotan and the area along the southern Silk Road as far as Miran for approximately one hundred years.[9] From this period we find extensive writings about the region in Tibetan, e.g. important works on the history of Khotan; for example the 'Prophecy of the Li Country' (*Li yul luṅ-bstan-pa*).[10] In 1006 Khotan was conquered by the Muslim ruler of Kashghar, Yusuf Qadir Khan.

The aforementioned name Khotan appears in Prakrit texts from Kroraina, while the indigenous name for the country was Hvatan, a name of disputed etymology. The above-mentioned texts in Khotanese Saka – or rather, texts discovered in the sand since the beginning of this century – date from the 4th to 11th centuries. There are no signs that Saka continued to be used for any greater length of time after the Turkic conquest.

The Mongols

In the early 13th century, Chinggis Khan's troops entered the Tarim basin and the Uighur ruler offered himself as Chinggis Khan's vassal. Uighur culture and learning enjoyed a position of high prestige among the Mongolians and the Uighur script system was subsequently borrowed for writing the

---

[8] Cf. Harold W. Bailey, *The Culture of the Sakas in Ancient Iranian Khotan*, New York 1982.

[9] For an extensive and well-informed account, see B. A. Litvinskij (ed.), *Vostočnyj Turkestan v drevnosti i rannem srednevekov'e: Ėtnos, jazyki, religii*, Moskva 1992.

[10] Cf. R. E. Emmerick, *Tibetan Texts Concerning Khotan*, London 1967.

Mongolian language. After the death of the khan and the splitting up of the empire among his sons, Mongolian power was less felt in the region, but there was a certain influx of Mongolians, especially in the North-West.

The Uighurs

In AD 744 the Uighurs established an empire in the Orkhon valley, in western Mongolia, taking over the power within a Turkic confederation from another Turkic tribe, the Eastern Türks.[11] The writing system used was runic Turkic, a script adapted from Aramaic. From approximately AD 760 onwards, their state religion was Manichaeism. With the Kirghiz destruction of the Uighur empire in northern Mongolia in 840, a group of Uighurs migrated eastwards to the Chinese province of Gansu, where this group is nowadays officially defined as *yugu,* in Chinese, or Yellow Uighur in English. The main part of the Uighurs emigrated further westwards, first to Qocho near Turfan, and later also to Kucha. There they borrowed a writing system, earlier adopted by the Kök-Türks from the Sogdians. This writing system subsequently became known as the Uighur script. Due to Chinese influence the direction of writing was changed from a horizontal left-to-right order to vertical writing. In this form it was later borrowed both by the Mongols and the Manchus.[12]

In this script the Uighurs recorded Manichaean, Nestorian Christian and Buddhist literature.[13] With the conversion of the Uighurs to Islam in the 11th (Kashghar) to 14th centuries (Qocho), the Uighur script came into disuse and was replaced by the Arabic script. The literary languages *par préférence* were Arabic and Persian, but at the same time there were various attempts at representing Uighur in Arabic script, with some of the peculiarities pertaining to the Persian orthography.

---

[11] Colin Mackerras, 'The Uighurs', in Denis Sinor (ed.), *The Cambridge History of Early Inner Asia,* Cambridge 1990, p. 317.
[12] Cf. Feng Jiasheng, Cheng Suoluo and Mu Guangwen (eds), *Weiwu'erzu shiliao jianbian, shang, xia, (neibu kanwu)* (Zhongguo minzu wenti yanjiu congkan 2), Beijing 1955. New edition 1981.
[13] Jens Peter Laut, *Der frühe türkische Buddhismus und seine literarischen Denkmäler,* Wiesbaden 1986.

JOAKIM ENWALL

From the Mongolian empire to the Chinese empire

After the fall of the Mongolian Yuan dynasty in China, the Uighur principalities were very much left to themselves until the Chinese annexation of Sinkiang, one hundred years after the establishment of the Manchu Qing dynasty, in the 1750s.

A group of the West-Mongolian Oirats, the Jungars, became the rulers of the area north of the Tianshan Mountains in the 17th century, and from this area – Jungaria – they tried to expand their power into the Tarim basin. Their efforts were, however, put to an end by the Chinese annexation and incorporation of the area into the Chinese empire under the name 'Xinjiang', i.e. 'The New Border Region', in 1757–1759.

Most everyday matters in the Uighur-dominated oasis cities were still run by the Uighur authorities and few Han Chinese migrated into the area. From 1815 onwards there were several uprisings against the Chinese authorities. In 1865 one of the rebellion leaders, though himself not an Uighur, Yakub Beg, started out with a small armed force to gain power over the region and two years later he became the ruler of Kashghar. The area under his command included not only the nearby cities of Khotan and Yarkend, but also Urumchi, Turfan and Qomul (Hami). His reign did not, however, enjoy popular support as his tax-collectors and secret police were as ruthless or even more so than their Chinese predecessors. In 1877 the Qing troups defeated Yakub Beg and re-established Chinese control.[14]

In the 19th century, foreign interest in the region increased, particularly from the Russians and British, and the competition for power over the region has later been termed 'The Great Game'. During the previous one hundred years, the Russians had been advancing in Central Asia, and it appeared to the British that their next goal was Eastern Turkestan, and from there perhaps British India.

After Yakub Beg

Both the British and the Russians established consulates in Kashghar. Their activities and aspirations have been thoroughly described in Peter Hopkirk's

---

[14] Linda Benson and Ingvar Svanberg (eds), *The Kazaks of China: Essays on an Ethnic Minority* (Studia Multiethnica Upsaliensia 5), Uppsala 1988, p. 35.

TOWARDS A SOCIOLINGUISTIC HISTORY OF SINKIANG

The Great Game.[15] During this time, Chinese power was severely weakened through the fall of the Qing dynasty in 1911 and the subsequent political turmoil of the 1910s and 1920s.

In 1893 the Swedish Mission Board decided to set up a printing-office in Kashghar, and by 1901 publishing activities were initiated on the basis of cyclostyled publications. During the early years there was a certain variation in the Uighur orthography, but the appearance of a spelling guide in 1929[16] the orthography became standardized for all publications issued by the Swedish press in Sinkiang. The printing-office remained active until 1938, when the missionaries were forced to leave because of Islamic rebel forces.[17]

Already in 1933, an Eastern Turkestan republic had been proclaimed with Kashghar as its centre, but with the rise of Soviet-backed Sheng Shicai the republic was crushed and Sheng became the military and political leader of Sinkiang, only formally under the Nanking government and based in Urumchi.

In 1921 the Uighurs in Tashkent had arranged a conference at which they decided to revive the term Uighur as a self-designation for the Turkic people in Sinkiang speaking a fairly unified Turkic language and claiming ancestry from the ancient Uighur empire. Earlier self-designations had been simply 'turk' or names of geographical origin, like 'xotänlik', i.e. person from Khotan. The ethnonym was first established in the Soviet Union and soon afterwards in Sinkiang. In 1944 a second Eastern Turkestan republic was established, but it was abolished when the Chinese regained power in the late 1940s.

Consolidation of Chinese rule

Since the establishment of the People's Republic of China in 1949 and the subsequent full incorporation of Sinkiang in the following year, the state policies towards national minority languages have varied considerably. In

---

[15] Peter Hopkirk, *The Great Game*, Oxford 1990.
[16] Gustaf Ahlbert, *Spelling Book for the Language of the Six Cities*, Kashghar 1929. In Uighur.
[17] Gunnar Jarring, *Prints from Kashghar – The Printing-office of the Swedish Mission in Eastern Turkestan – History and Production with an Attempt at a Bibliography* (Transactions 3), Swedish Research Institute in Istanbul, Stockholm 1991, p. 10.

the early 1950s, nationalities institutes and research institutions were set up all over the country and survey projects were arranged regarding languages, history, customs, religious practices and traditional economic structures. In the mid-1950s, several large-scale conferences on these questions were held and this was followed by reform work for the many existing writing systems and the creation of scripts and orthographies for the hitherto unwritten languages.

After the Qing incorporation of Sinkiang, a large number of Uighurs had been removed to Jungaria, the area north of the Tianshan Mountains. Their dialect, identical with that of the Uighurs in the Soviet Union, was termed the Taranchi or soil-tillers' dialect. Following the Soviet example the Chinese minority language authorities adopted this dialect as the standard written language to be used in the region, in spite of significant differences from the dialect spoken in the Uighur heartland, in Kashghar and Khotan.

In the 1950s, the Chinese immigration to the area increased, partly on the basis of the *tuntian*-system (see p. 122 above), now renamed as *bingtuan*, with Han Chinese paramilitary agricultural colonies around the Takla-makan desert.

As a result of the main political movements in China, several large groups were sent to Sinkiang, both voluntarily and involuntarily, from the early 1950s onwards. These groups included traditional class enemies, well-educated urban youth, cadres, prisoners of war and intellectuals.

In the 1960s, the traditional Arabic script used for Uighur was replaced by a Latin writing system based on the spelling conventions in the Hanyu Pinyin scheme adopted for writing Chinese by the People's Congress in 1958. To the basic scheme borrowed from the Pinyin scheme there were additions of letters for sounds not found in Chinese. These graphemes were basically modelled on Soviet Central Asian examples.

The present situation

The proportions of ethnic groups in Sinkiang have changed significantly since the establishment of the People's Republic of China. Today, for the first time, the official Chinese population in Sinkiang approaches half of the population of the region. This tendency is clearly visible in the population statistics:[18]

	Census 1953	Census 1982	Census 1990
Uighur	3,640,125	5,949,655	7,194,675
Kazak	594,500	903,335	1,106,989
Kirghiz	70,000	112,973	139,781
Mongol	59,000	117,460	137,740
Hui	200,000	681,527	570,789
Han	300,000	5,286,533	5,695,626

In some areas, as e.g. the Bayangol Mongolian Autonomous Prefecture, the Mongolians constitute a minority, but they still have quite considerable language rights, like Mongolian television broadcasts and radio. This has led to a conflict between Uighurs on the one hand and the authorities and Mongolians on the other, as the Uighurs feel that the extensive use of Mongolian is a manipulation of the actual ethnic composition of the area, a kind of Chinese *divide et impera* among the various nationalities.

The control over religious activities became markedly diminished after the 11th Party Congress in 1979, but the authorities still continue to keep a vigilant eye on the educational activities among the Muslims, especially in the *madrasa*s, the religious schools. These are usually considered illegal by the state; many of them have been closed and subsequently secretly reopened. Religious contacts with neighbouring countries have also increased significantly, particularly with Afghanistan and Iran. In this connection groups of young Uighurs have been trained by the Talibans in Afghanistan for guerilla warfare within the framework of *jihad* against the Chinese. Over the last few years, many instances have occurred of bombing and killing Chinese military personnel and Uighurs being accused of collaboration with the Chinese authorities. The first major instance was the fighting in the Uighur village of Baren near Kashghar in 1990, which resulted in 30 persons being killed and many injured, on both the Uighur and the Chinese sides.

The number of people living in present-day Sinkiang is disputable since, according to an anonymous employee of the statistics bureau in Urumchi, there is serious manipulation of the census results regarding the number of

---

[18] Cf. Linda Benson and Ingvar Svanberg (eds), *China's Last Nomads: The History and Culture of China's Kazaks,* New York 1998, p. 16.

Uighurs. Even according to Uighur sources in exile, the number of Uighurs could be several times higher than officially reported in state statistics. Furthermore, the number of Chinese is impossible to estimate due to the *hukou*-system, which includes in the official statistics only people who have a *hukou*, i.e. residence permit in Sinkiang. As a result of the relatively slow economic development of the Chinese inland many poor, but ambitious, Han Chinese peasants have left places where they are officially registered and migrated to more prosperous areas offering better opportunities for work. Of this so-called floating population, *liudong renkou*, estimated to between 60 and 120 million people altogether, a significant part has made its way to Sinkiang, particularly after the large resettlement programme in the Three Gorges area. This group in Sinkiang, consisting mainly of young men, has been largely employed in the swiftly growing petroleum industry, where virtually no Uighurs are employed. The figures for economic growth in the Sinkiang area thus reflect almost exclusively the state of affairs for the Han Chinese population in the area, while the Uighurs tend to be more and more economically marginalized. According to official statistics (1992), 41% of Uighurs live under the poverty line. The unemployment rate among young people is set at approximately 25% by Uighur organizations in exile. Recently, this increasing unemployment has led to political unrest among the young Uighurs, with severe outbreaks of violent protests and an even more violent crushing of the protests, for example, in Ghulja (Yining), Jungaria, north of the Tianshan Mountains, in March 1997.

The present situation is thus characterized by an intensified conflict and a societal division between Han Chinese and Uighurs, which in many ways reminds of a traditional colonial setting, and which contains many political complications, e.g. the economical and hence political dependence of the former Soviet Central Asian republics on trade with China, republics where there are many Uighurs living in exile. Unless a significant change is brought about regarding the economic conditions of the Uighurs and other Turkic peoples living in Sinkiang, this tense situation is not likely to change and hard-core groups, like the Afghanistan-trained Uighur Talibans, will probably gain further support among the Uighur population.

In the contemporary development we do, however, see counter-tendencies, such as increased interest in poverty relief and basic education for the poorest groups in the border regions, sometimes in cooperation with international and foreign development-aid organizations, but the results of these efforts still remain to be seen and they may as well be counter-balanced by other events. Even such economic development projects as the highway across the Taklamakan desert between Korla and Niya and the railway between Urumchi and Kashghar, scheduled to be opened on 1 October, 1998, are likely to lead to an even greater influx of Han Chinese and a further marginalization of the Uighurs.

Political Aspects

Russia and Post-Soviet Central Asia
Reintegration Ahead?

BO PETERSSON

After the dissolution of the Soviet Union in 1991 there was some disorientation among the Russian leadership concerning which foreign policy course to take. During the initial period after the break-up, Russia was rather accommodating towards the Western powers. This was above all evident in its relation with the United States which was awarded top priority in the country's foreign policy. Universal human values were made the centrepiece of policy, military force was renounced as a means of solving contemporary political problems, and cooperative, multilateral strategies were emphasized instead.

Already during 1992 there were tendencies indicating a pending shift of paradigms.[1] By 1993, the so-called Near-Abroad Doctrine was definitely hatched.[2] Now, relations with the former Soviet republics were given top priority on the foreign policy agenda.[3] Henceforth, a clear distinction could be discerned between the still relatively soft-spoken Russian foreign policy *vis-à-vis* the Western powers, constituting significant parts of the Far Abroad, and the tougher stance towards the former Soviet republics of the Near

---

[1] Hannes Adomeit, 'Russia as a "Great Power" in World Affairs: Images and Reality', *International Affairs* 71:1 (1995), pp. 35–68. See also John Löwenhardt, *The Reincarnation of Russia: Struggling with the Legacy of Communism, 1990–1994*, Harlow 1995, and Mark Webber, *The International Politics of Russia and the Successor States*, Manchester 1996.

[2] Mark Webber, op. cit., pp. 97–100.

[3] See, among a plethora of sources, Andrej V. Kozyrev, 'Vnešnjaja politika preobražajuščejsja Rossii', *Voprosy istorii* 1 (1994), pp. 3–11, Alexei G. Arbatov, 'Russian Foreign Policy Priorities for the 1990s', in Teresa Pelton Johnson and Steven E. Miller (eds), *Russian Security After the Cold War: Seven Views from Moscow*, Washington and London 1994, pp. 1–41, and Shireen T. Hunter, *The Transcaucasus in Transition: Nation-Building and Conflict*, Washington DC 1994, pp. 147–157.

Abroad. Some commentators have aptly differentiated between a 'dinner-jacket policy' in the first case and a 'flak-jacket policy' in the latter case.[4] When the new Russian military doctrine was introduced in the autumn of 1993,[5] care was taken to spell out the need to safeguard the rights of the approximately 25 million Russians living within the borders of the Commonwealth of Independent States (CIS) but outside those of the Russian Federation.[6] Harassment and discrimination of such Russians were explicitly singled out among the security threats that might prompt Russian military actions. In international fora, like the UN and the OSCE, Russia tried consistently to acquire recognition of its prime right to function as peace-keeper within the territory of the former Soviet Union. Seemingly, this quest proved to be quite successful.[7] During 1992–1993 Russian military units became actively involved in conflicts in several post-Soviet republics, most notably in Tajikistan, but also Moldova and Georgia.

Reintegrationist winds

As of today there is widespread consensus within the Russian political élite on Russian foreign-policy orientations towards Central Asia.[8] All major political actors seem to agree on the desirability of achieving some reintegration within the borders of the former Soviet Union. The infamous resolution adopted by the Duma in March 1996 declaring as null and void the Belovezhskaya agreement of December 1991 that established the CIS and toppled the Soviet Union, is so far the most evident indication of the prevailing winds.

---

[4] Cynthia Barner-Barry and Judith A. Hody, *The Politics of Change: The Transformation of the Former Soviet Union*, New York 1995, p. 323.

[5] Brigitte Sauerwein, 'Russia's Military Doctrine: Addressing New Security Requirements', *International Defense Review* 1 (1994), pp. 5–6, and Gerhard Wettig, 'Die neue russische Militärdoktrin', *Osteuropa* 44:4 (1994), pp. 330–337.

[6] Neil Melvin, *Russians Beyond Russia: The Politics of National Identity* (Chatham House Papers), London 1995, and Paul Kolstoe, *Russians in the Former Soviet Republics*, London 1995.

[7] Vladimir Baranovsky, 'Conflicts In and Around Russia', *SIPRI* [Stockholm International Peace Research Institute] *Yearbook 1996: Armaments, Disarmament and International Security*, p. 278.

[8] Cf. Mohiaddin Mesbahi, 'Russian Foreign Policy towards Central Asia: The Emerging Doctrine?', in Ingmar Oldberg (ed.), *Priorities in Russian Foreign Policy: West, South or East?*, Proceedings of a Conference in Stockholm, 3 June, 1996, FOA [Försvarets forskningsanstalt] Defence Research Establishment, Stockholm 1996.

In order to get the upper hand *vis-à-vis* his main rival in the presidential race of 1996, the Communist Gennadii Zyuganov,[9] President Yeltsin skilfully exploited this climate. On 1 April, 1996, he triumphantly announced the quadripartite agreement between Russia, Belarus, Kazakstan and Kirghizstan on the establishment of an inner CIS circle of cooperation on economy and humanitarian matters.[10] Almost at the same time, another inner circle consisting of Russia and Belarus was established, indicating a thrust towards even closer integration, and indeed hinting at the eventual and complete merger of the two states.[11] We will in the following discuss these two treaties somewhat more in detail. Suffice it to say here that there is no doubt that the policies of the Yeltsin administration promote and enhance reintegration within the borders of the former Soviet Union. Both leaders of Russia and Belarus expressed their desire to make the complete merger of these two states the first foreign-policy priority of 1997.[12]

One of the most important motivating forces behind the shift of emphasis in Russian foreign policy was the above-mentioned fact that some 25 million Russian ex-Soviet citizens found themselves in diaspora after the downfall of the Soviet Union. As regards Central Asia, estimates of the number of Russian residents are hampered by the fact that the Soviet-time census of 1989 is still the last one to have been carried out in these countries. According to those dated figures, 6.5 million lived in Kazakstan (amounting to some 40% of the total population), 1.6 million in Uzbekistan (8%), 0.9 million in Kirghizstan (21.5%), 0.4 million in Tajikistan (7.5%) and 0.3 million in Turkmenistan.[13] Of course, much has happened since then, including brain drain of well-educated and/or privileged Russians after the dissolution and a bloody civil war in Tajikistan, producing an exodus of its own.

In keeping with the Near-Abroad Doctrine, Russian policy makers have over the last years steadfastly endeavoured to make the non-Russian former Soviet republics comply with the principle of dual citizenship for diaspora Russians. If implemented, this would give the Russian Federation a potent and legitimate instrument of influence, since Russia in such a case would

---

[9] For Zyuganov's election platform, where the reintegration theme figured prominently, see *Sovetskaja Rossija*, 19 March, 1996.

[10] *Rossijskaja gazeta*, 2 April, 1996.

[11] *Rossijskaja gazeta*, 3 April, 1996.

[12] See e.g. *OMRI Daily Digest* 46:1, 6 March, 1997.

[13] See e.g. Alf Grannes and Daniel Heradstveit, *Etnisk nasjonalisme: Folkegrupper og konflikter i Kaukasia og Sentral-Asia*, Oslo 1994, pp. 273–280.

have a clear-cut obligation to see to the interests of its citizens living abroad. In December 1993, a treaty on recognizing the principle of dual citizenship was signed between the Russian Federation and Turkmenistan.[14] In September 1995, Tajikistan was the second country to sign such a protocol. Subsequently, Russia has also negotiated texts of such agreements with Kirghizstan and Belarus.[15]

The institutional framework

It is small wonder if reintegration-prone Russian politicians have felt a certain frustration when looking at the achievements within the existing framework of the CIS. These are actually somewhat meagre. This is partially accounted for by the CIS organizational structure itself, where decision by consensus constitutes the general rule.[16] Whereas political leaders have often used lofty rhetoric at CIS summits, there has been a glaring discrepancy between words and deeds, which is probably best explained by conflicting state interests and a lack of common political will.

The most concrete achievements of CIS cooperation have been made in the military sector. Cooperation in this field is structured by the Treaty on collective security of May 1992, which is a separate treaty and not part of the CIS Charter. All Central Asian states are parties to it save Turkmenistan, which has regulated its military cooperation with Russia by means of a bilateral agreement. According to the treaty, the contracting parties are not to enter any alliances or groups directed against any other party, they are to initiate consultations in the event of threats to their security or sovereignty, they are to extend military assistance to each other in case of military aggression from outside powers and they are to develop some degree of

---

[14] For the text, see Šoxrat Kadyrov, *Turkmenistan: 4 goda bez SSSR*, Bergen 1996, pp. 222–223.

[15] Bo Petersson, 'Tadjikistan: ständiga konflikter i en artificiell stat?', in Bo Petersson and Ingvar Svanberg (eds), *Det nya Centralasien: Fem forna sovjetrepubliker i omvandling*, Lund 1996, p. 89.

[16] According to its charter, the CIS has a council of heads of state that is convened at least twice a year and a council of heads of government that are to get together at least four times a year. Within this structure, no provisions are made for supranational powers. The rule of consensus prevails. There are, however, certain supranational traits in the international economic committee established separately in 1994; Mark Webber, op. cit., pp. 91–93.

integration with regard to their military forces.[17] However, the treaty does not provide for a joint command, instead there is a rather loose coordination staff. The treaty does not provide for joint operational planning nor coordination of military education. There are no common systems of command and control.[18]

Some multilateral agreements have subsequently been added to the treaty, most notably one on aerial defence of February 1995, aiming at coordination of radar usage and anti-missile early-warning facilities.[19] So far, Turkmenistan has, together with Azerbaijan and Moldova, chosen to remain outside this framework.[20] In view of the practical problems involved,[21] however, the implementation of the agreement may provide yet another example that there is often a wide distance between what is said on the CIS summit meetings, on the one hand, and what eventually materializes, on the other.

Concrete steps have been taken to establish practical cooperation as regards border control. All Central Asian states are party to an agreement to that effect, concluded in May 1995.[22] The most conspicuous part of CIS military activities is, however, without doubt the one pertaining to peace-keeping operations on the territory of the former Soviet Union. Here, the CIS frame has in practice come to provide the means of a forwarded Russian territorial defence.[23] CIS peace-keeping has in essence followed the dictum of a Russia-first policy.[24]

The Tajik case

The case of Tajikistan stands out as the most clear-cut example of peace-keeping activities according to the Russian conception. When this was written – in March 1997 – armed clashes still occurred in the country, but

---

[17] See Mark Webber, op. cit., p. 193.
[18] Mark Webber, op. cit., pp. 167–168.
[19] Vladimir Baranovsky, op. cit., p. 271.
[20] Zdzislaw Lachowski, 'Appendix 16B: Foreign Military Presence in the OSCE Area', *SIPRI Yearbook 1996. Armaments, Disarmament and International Security*, pp. 745–746.
[21] Zdzislaw Lachowski, op. cit., pp. 745–746.
[22] Vladimir Baranovsky, op. cit., p. 271.
[23] Witness e.g. the statement by Yeltsin that the outer borders of Tajikistan for all practical purposes are to be regarded as the outer borders of Russia. See Bo Petersson, op. cit., p. 87.
[24] Cf. Vladimir Baranovsky, op. cit., p. 272.

the most acute and bloody phase of the civil war took place in the latter part of 1992. In December 1992, Russian, Uzbek, Kazak and Kirghiz forces moved in under the auspices of the CIS. The military reinforcements were dispatched into the area to supplement the Russian 201 Motor Rifle Division which since the Soviet period was already in position in Tajikistan. All in all, Russia held a huge dominance in the manpower of the CIS contingent, whereas the participation of Kirghizstan and Kazakstan was only of token character. Soon after the dispatch there was a formal agreement that peace-keeping CIS forces were to be stationed in Tajikistan, and since then several supplementing agreements have been reached on the extension of the mandate of the peace-keeping forces. Pledges to neutrality notwithstanding, the CIS forces clearly sided with the Tajik nomenklatura Communist camp against the oppositional alliance consisting of Islamists, Democrats and Pamiri nationalists. The CIS action most decisively turned the winds of war, and the armed forces of the opposition had to seek refuge in neighbouring Afghanistan or in the mountain lands of Pamir.

The Russian motives for action seem, among other things, to have been fear of irredentist tendencies thriving in Tajikistan and causing further unrest in the region, but also fear of Islamic fundamentalism gaining a foothold in Tajikistan. According to a prevalent Russian line of thinking, this would have posed a threat to other neighbouring countries, and ultimately, perhaps to the Russian Federation itself.[25] Undeniably, the then Islamic Renaissance Party was a hub in the wheel of the Tajik oppositional struggle. Still, the factor of religion was probably not as crucial for the development of the conflict as was the influence of regionally based and clan-related friction. One could also discern other factors behind the Russian action. For Russia, it was vital to improve its geostrategic positions, and here was a chance to demonstrate the country's great power prowess in the Near Abroad. Also, the Russian minority in Tajikistan, today supposedly amounting to some 3.5% of the total population,[26] supplied part of the rationale.

---

[25] For an example of this mode of thinking, see the statement by the Commander-in-Chief of the Russian Ground Forces, Col.-Gen. Vladimir Semenov, according to which the greatest potential threat to Russia comes from the possible spread of Islamic fundamentalism from the south and south-east, *OMRI Daily Digest* 2:1, 3 January, 1996.
[26] According to *CIA World Factbook*.

Military cooperation between Russia and Central Asia

Military cooperation with Russia is hailed by the ruling élites of the Central Asian countries. It helps the states protect themselves against external threats, including Islamic fundamentalism, and maybe even more significantly, safeguards domestic stability and, at the same time, the position of those very élites.[27] There are no challenges to Moscow's hegemony in the military field. Maybe precisely because of this, there were surely Russian reactions to the fact that the Secretary-General of Nato, Javier Solana, in March 1997 went to Central Asia to discuss the subject of Nato enlargement with the political leaders of the region.[28]

Apart from the general state of affairs, there are some common traits as regards the military relations of the post-Soviet Central Asian states to the Russian Federation.[29] First of all, they have all concluded bilateral agreements with Moscow on cooperation on military matters. Second, Russia is entitled to keep on using military installations on the territories of all the five states. Third, there is substantial technical cooperation as regards arms technology and arms development. Fourth, Russian military units are to some extent present on the soil of all these states. Finally, Russian military men, i.e. citizens of the Russian Federation, are allowed to serve in the national armed forces of all states in the region.

The latter point may actually have almost as thorough-going consequences as the actual basing of Russian troops on their national territory. In all five states the military rank-and-file is primarily made up of representatives of the ethnic home nation, whereas the majority of the officers corps consists of Russians. On an average, some 90% of the officers are Slavs, primarily Russians, in the national armed forces of the five countries.[30] In Kazakstan, 70% of the officers decided to leave military service between 1992 and 1995, which should be seen in conjunction with the large exodus of Russians from the country.[31] As a result, the Kazak army today fills only about two

---

[27] Zdzislaw Lachowski, op. cit., p. 750.
[28] *OMRI Daily Digest* 53:1, 17 March, 1997.
[29] Cf. Paul George, Bengt-Göran Bergstrand, Susan Clark and Evamaria Loose-Weintraub, 'Military Expenditure', *SIPRI Yearbook 1996: Armaments, Disarmament and International Security*, p. 340.
[30] Zdzislaw Lachowski, op. cit., p. 750, and Šoxrat Kadyrov, op. cit., p. 190.
[31] Between 1992 and 1995 some 900,000 people emigrated, about half of whom were Russians. Whereas ethnic Russians represented as large a percentage of the population as did the Kazaks in Soviet times, the Russians today constitute only about 30% as

thirds of its need for officers.[32] This situation will no doubt change in some years as education and training bear their fruit, and by that time one of the potential Russian influence-wielding instruments will lose much of its effectiveness.

The number of Russian military stationed in Central Asia varies considerably from state to state.[33] One is not surprised to find that Tajikistan, due to the civil unrest in the country, is heading the league. In 1996, about 24,000 foreign troops were stationed there. Of these some 16,000 were preoccupied with border control along the border to Afghanistan, whereas the remainder took part in the CIS peace-keeping effort. The vast majority of the military making up the CIS force is still Russian, and the backbone of it is still the 201 Motor Rifle Division. However, a battalion from Uzbekistan and a company from Kirghizstan also form part of the force. While having participated from the outset, Kazakstan withdrew its contingent in September 1995.[34]

In 1994, 15,000 Russian military men were still stationed in Turkmenistan.[35] However, most of them were withdrawn in the following year, leaving behind only about 2,000 Russians in border force units.[36] Like Kirghizstan but more consistently so, Turkmenistan adheres to a policy of neutrality, hence the wish of the autocrat ruler, Sapurmurad Niyazov, or *Turkmenbashi*, that the Russian troops be withdrawn. In Uzbekistan and Kirghizstan the numbers of Russian military men amounted in 1994 to 5,000 and 3,500, respectively.[37] In Kazakstan there were about 1,000 Russian military men. In addition, Russia has leased the space-launching site of Baikonur, as well as the supporting city of Leninsk for a period of 20 years. Also, there is a joint Russian-Kazakstani force on the border to China consisting of about 15,000 men.[38]

In January 1995, quite a stir was caused by the announcement that Russia and Kazakstan had agreed, in principle, on merging the armed forces

---

compared to the 50% made up of the Kazaks. See Paul George et al., op. cit., pp. 339–340.

[32] Paul George et al., op. cit., pp. 339–340.

[33] Zdzislaw Lachowski, 'Conventional Arms Control and Security Dialogue in Europe', *SIPRI Yearbook 1995: Armaments, Disarmament and International Security*, p. 781.

[34] Vladimir Baranovsky, op. cit., p. 268, footnote 120.

[35] Zdzislaw Lachowski, op. cit., p. 781.

[36] Šoxrat Kadyrov, op. cit., pp. 189–191.

[37] Zdzislaw Lachowski, op. cit., p. 781.

[38] Zdzislaw Lachowski, ibid., and Paul George et al., op. cit., p. 342.

of the two countries. They were to set up a joint command for planning and training, and another joint command for border control, the latter of which is already in existence. Apart from this, however, the agreement does not seem to have been implemented to any significant degree.[39] Even so, it is there on paper, and it might be developed at a later date.

The new inner circles

The CIS constitutes a rather blunt instrument for achieving substantial reintegration, and the two separate agreements on establishing inner circles of cooperation should be seen in that light. In the text of the 29 March, 1996 agreement on establishing closer cooperation between Russia, Kazakstan, Kirghizstan and Belarus,[40] it is underlined that other states of the former Soviet Union are welcome to join as well. The four states have evidently had the European Union as a source of inspiration, which becomes clear from a view of the organizational set-up. Thus, there is a council consisting, according to the practical need, of heads of state, heads of government or heads of specialized ministries. Even though nothing is said about the specific decision rules, the council has the right to take decisions that are compulsory for members of the new commonwealth. Furthermore, there is also a counterpart to the EU commission, a so-called Integration Committee, and a parliamentary body, the so-called Inter-Parliamentary Committee.

As for substance, the main focus is on economic, social and humanitarian issues, and the cooperative efforts are to cover everything from the establishment of a common market of goods to the integration of information systems. By the end of 1996, the states were to have established an area of common customs tariffs, as well as hammered out a system for the common administration of relevant rules thereon. Moreover, they have the ambition to decisively accelerate cooperation within the monetary field as well as within the credit, currency and financial areas. Even though some caveats are added, there is also an ambition to establish a common currency. Finally, there are some provisions for trying to coordinate planning and implementation of foreign policy, and also for creating a system of promoting

---

[39] Vladimir Baranovsky, op. cit., p. 272.
[40] *Rossijskaja gazeta*, 2 April, 1996.

security in the area.

As was mentioned above, another circle of cooperation, closer still to the Russian Federation, was established during the first days of April, 1996, with Belarus as the junior partner. One would imagine that the news about this broke rather unexpectedly to the Kazak and Kirghiz leaders. According to the treaty[41] establishing the so-called Community of Sovereign Republics (SSR, from *Soobščestvo Suverennyx Respublik*), the parties are to coordinate their foreign policies and general positions on international questions, cooperate in matters of security and work out common principles of military development. Furthermore, they are to synchronize the stages, timetables and extent of their economic reforms, standardize their monetary, credit and budgetary systems and create conditions for a common currency. However, it is spelled out that the participant states will retain their state sovereignty and territorial integrity as well as the main attributes thereof. Yet, one is tempted to ponder over which areas indeed remain to be independent in, as the treaty seems to foresee a close symbiosis between the contracting parties. Also, the timetables are pretty tight, and as far as the economic, monetary, budgetary and credit spheres are concerned, the harmonization and coordination was to be achieved already by the end of 1997.

The organizational set-up of the SSR is such that the main body will be the Supreme Council, consisting of heads of state, heads of government and parliamentary speakers. The Council will make decisions by consensus. Also, there will be an Executive Committee, organizing the practical work of implementing the treaty, and a Parliamentary Assembly, above all having the right of legislative initiative *vis-à-vis* the national parliaments. This treaty, too, clearly spells out that the framework is open for accession by other states that share its goals and principles. It remains to be seen, however, to what extent this kind of tightly-knit cooperation could attract other states. As has already been touched upon, Russia and Belarus have through their presidents expressed their desire to pursue the integration between the two states even further and ultimately achieve a full federation. Might this development, then, be a likely option for any of the five states under consideration here?

---

[41] *Rossijskaja gazeta*, 3 April, 1996.

Proceeding reintegration, but problems ahead?

At the time of the break-up of the Soviet Union, the Central Asian states were by far the most reluctant when it came to acquiring independence. Neither economically nor politically were they ready for this. It is therefore small wonder that schemes involving reintegration attract them, especially since the economic situation is still bad, or outright dismal in the case of Tajikistan. The latter would probably join either of the two leagues of states at once, were it only to be admitted, but the truth is that the other members at this stage probably would try to keep it out as long as possible. The civil unrest is costing the state dearly, and admitting Tajikistan would for the other states be like throwing money into the ocean.

Still, one can conclude that whereas speculations were frequent around the year 1991 concerning whether Turkey or Iran would fill the vacuum left by the Soviet Union in Central Asia, one can now safely say that the answer is, and will be, Russia. The remaining question is how far reintegration will go. The Soviet Union will hardly be re-established, but other organizational frameworks of close cooperation may arise in its place. We have already seen two examples of this. The near future will show to what extent the Belarus formula can lure the Central Asian states into even closer cooperation with the Russian Federation.

One should underline, however, that cooperation within new frameworks is by no means devoid of problems. A truly dynamic integration scheme would probably presuppose an undisputed Russian economic dominance, or at least a Russian economy that could serve as a motor in the area. This is not necessarily so today, even if Russia is certainly far stronger than its junior partners. In the past few years it has actually lost much ground to international competitors. The case of Turkmenistan offers a drastic and illuminating example. In 1994, the Russian share of Turkmenistani foreign trade turnover fell steeply, from 50% to 7.5%, leaving Russia only in fourth position after Ukraine, Kazakstan and Turkey.[42] Even if the drop has not been equally drastic in the other republics, the tendency is there.[43] Recent

---

[42] Šoxrat Kadyrov, op. cit., pp. 152–154.
[43] Lena Jonson, 'Comments on Nato Enlargement and the CIS', in Ingmar Oldberg (ed.), *Priorities in Russian Foreign Policy: West, South or East?*, Proceedings of a Conference in Stockholm, 3 June 1996, FOA Defence Research Establishment, Stockholm 1996, p. 71. Not even in disaster-ridden Tajikistan is Russia the main trading partner but has fallen behind Switzerland, Holland and Turkey. See *OMRI Daily Digest* 57:1, 21

rumours have it that Kazakstan is not all that happy with the quadripartite customs union of 1995, which provided a major foundation for the treaty between Russia, Kazakstan, Belarus and Kirghizstan, and may actually be considering a withdrawal from it.[44]

As indicated above, Kazakstan has otherwise been the most eager among the Central Asian states to draw closer to Russia. This fits rather well with President Nazarbayev's repeated proposals for establishing a Euro-Asian commonwealth,[45] in which Kazakstan, and its president personally, supposedly would play a prominent part. Whereas President Lukashenko of Belarus seems inclined to extinguish Belarusian independence by forming a fully-fledged union with the Russian Federation as a senior partner, Nazarbayev is, however, rather involved in the balancing act of strengthening Kazakstani statehood through the process of *rapprochement* with Moscow. His quest for a Euro-Asian union may be instrumental in this. By reaching accords with Moscow he might also succeed in reducing the destabilizing potential of the still substantial Russian diaspora, situated above all in the northern part of the country.[46]

On the part of Uzbekistan, statements have been rather ambiguous. Its president, Islam Karimov, has been heard to caution against giving the CIS framework supranational powers of decision. He has also stressed the necessity of observing total equality among the states and of having similar scope and pace of economic reform. That is, no state would be allowed to go faster than the slowest one of the pack, and Tashkent not being the most eager among reformers, this would fit the Karimov regime well. Furthermore, Karimov has suggested that the CIS be given an economic role rather than a military one, and Tashkent has repeatedly promoted the thought of strengthening links between the Central Asian states to counterbalance Russian influence.[47] From the Russian point of view, Uzbek regional great-

---

March, 1997. Cf. also *UNDP Human Development Report 1995*, Dushanbe, p. 13, according to which foreign trade with Belgium, the Netherlands, the United States and Switzerland accounted for more than 70% of the national foreign trade turnover.

[44] *OMRI Daily Digest* 55:1, 19 March, 1997.

[45] Ingvar Svanberg, 'Kazakstan – ett land mellan Europa och Asien', in Bo Petersson and Ingvar Svanberg (eds), *Det nya Centralasien: Fem forna sovjetrepubliker i omvandling*, Lund 1996, p. 31.

[46] Vladimir Baranovsky, op. cit., p. 273. For a scenario where the destabilizing potential of the large group of Russians is borne out, see Daniel Yergin and Thane Gustafson, *Russia 2010 and What It Means for the World* (The Cera Report), New York 1993, pp. 155–156.

[47] Paul George et al., op. cit., p. 378.

power ambitions will most certainly be a problem in the long run. Indicatively, Uzbekistan was one of the very first ex-Soviet states to establish its own military. Apart from Uzbek economic and strategic interests in the region, there is a substantial Uzbek diaspora in the neighbouring countries, above all in the highly unstable neighbouring countries of Tajikistan and Afghanistan. This, together with a still unsettled border controversy with Tajikistan, helps to account for the rather high Uzbek profile in the area.

Turkmenistan, as led by its headstrong *Turkmenbashi*, seems determined to cling to its policy of neutrality. It has thus refrained from participation in the 1992 Treaty on collective security as well as in the CIS peace-keeping operation in Tajikistan. The dismantling of the lion's share of the Russian military presence is another case in point. Kirghizstan, on the other hand, seems to be the state giving Russia least to worry about so far, but then again this country is probably the least significant of the five Central Asian states from a strategic and economic point of view.

It goes without saying that Tajikistan has produced the worst problems for Russia, even though the dialogue between the government and the opposition as of March 1997 finally seemed to make significant progress. As the protracted hostage-taking affairs of February–March 1997 indicated, the Tajik development might hold a few unpleasant surprises still. Suffice it to say here that the unpredictability and volatility of the region has been amply demonstrated by the example of Tajikistan. Regional and clan-related loyalties have often produced dynamics and logic of their own, often opaque and incomprehensible to outside observers. So even though Russia has re-established itself as the most influential actor in the region, Moscow still has a host of problems to face.

Democracy versus Stability in Kazakstan

MARIANNE ØHLERS

The official goal of nation-building in Kazakstan is based on the principles of democracy and market economy. Both of these principles are, however, likely to generate threats to the present power structure in the country. President Nursultan Nazarbayev seems to be well aware of this and it looks as if he fears that the introduction of a genuine democratization and privatization process will split his power base. That is why stability is a very important keyword in Nazarbayev's speeches.

It is not surprising that stability is an important factor for the new Kazakstani state.[1] Even though there are no immediate open conflicts, the country is in many ways divided. One of the most important boundaries is between Kazaks and Russians.[2] Estimates for 1996 indicate that Kazaks now make up 48% of the population, a rise from 39.7% since the last census in 1989, while Russians account for 34% of the population, a fall from 37.8% in 1989.[3] The Russian minority is worried about the rapid growth of the ethnic Kazak population, which is expected to comprise a majority in the year 2000. The Russians still dominate the northern and eastern parts of Kazakstan and prosperous cities like Karaganda, Kustanai, Akmola and Almaty, while the majority of the Kazaks live in less developed regions like Kzyl Orda, Atyrau, Mangistau and Aktöbe in the countryside

---

[1] In this article a distinction is made between Kazakstani referring to all the citizens of Kazakstan and Kazak referring to the ethnic group.

[2] There are approximately 100 different nationalities in Kazakstan. The largest groups are Kazaks, Russians, Ukrainians, Germans, Uzbeks, Tatars and Belarusians.

[3] The rapid changes in the ethnic composition are the result of a growing Kazak birth rate, large Kazak immigration from other former Soviet republics, China and Mongolia, and emigration by Russians and other Slavs. See *EIU Country Report*, 1st Quarter 1997, p. 13.

of western and southern Kazakstan.[4] This demographic structure may be a threat to the national unity of Kazakstan.

The Soviet legacy – a deeply centralistic way of handling the society – is another complicating matter. The form of government and public administration in Kazakstan has not changed much since 1991. An important explanation of this rigidity is the absence of a strong national liberation movement in Kazakstan. Since the republic gained its independence as a result of the disintegration of the Soviet Union, there was no external enemy and therefore no joint national struggle.[5] Consequently, to put it bluntly, a Kazakstani national identity, which is meant to legitimize the new government, has not been founded yet, although the outer frame – the Kazakstani sovereign state – became a reality already in 1991.

President Nazarbayev intends to construct a Kazakstani nationalism as a force to keep the society together and secure stability. The aim of the present article is to specify the meaning of nationalism in Kazakstan and to point out the conflicts of interests met within the Kazakstani society.

The Kazakstani sense of nationhood

According to the constitution, Kazakstan is a multiethnic society and according to President Nazarbayev the multiethnicity is a possible reason why there have not yet been any serious conflicts in Kazakstan:

> It is because of this unique polyethnicity [...] that Kazakstan has avoided the sad destiny of our nearest neighbours who have been driven to brother-killing wars.[6]

President Nazarbayev cannot blame the Kazaks for their minority status in their own country nor the other ethnic groups which were forced to live in Kazakstan by the Soviet imperial system. In his end-of-year message for 1996 President Nazarbayev declared 1997 to be the year of both remembrance

---

[4] Anvar Daurenbekov, 'Life and Death in Kazakhstan', *Focus Central Asia* 16 (1995), p. 16.

[5] The breakdown of the Soviet Union came as a shock for the government and for most people in Kazakstan. President Nursultan Nazarbayev was until the last minute eager to keep the Union as one body and Kazakstan gained sovereignty as the last Soviet Republic in December 1991.

[6] Nursultan Nazarbaev, 'Za mir i soglasie v našem obščem dome. Doklad Presidenta N. A. Nazarbaeva na pervoj sessii Assamblei narodov Kazaxstana', *Kazaxstanskaja Pravda*, 24 March, 1995.

with special attention to the victims of Stalinism and harmony as an appeal of keeping the ethnic and social peace.[7] Officially the President praised multiethnicity as a reasonable basis for a new non-Soviet identity. Now, multiethnicity is in itself a much used and tainted concept in the former Soviet ideology and in reality Kazak history, culture and language is after all meant to form a strong part of the national identity for all citizens in the future, which, on the other hand, is a challenge because of the *de facto* lack of national cohesion. Kazakstan has not existed as a consolidated independent state before, and the Kazak national identity never had a chance to develop – first because of its fragmented clan-based nomadism and later as a consequence of two centuries of foreign domination. According to the Turkish scholar Kemal Karpat, Kazak ethnicity, on which a Kazakstani national identity is to be founded, is a blend of tribal identity and Folk Islam (culture and traditions) and later shaped by the meeting with the Russian colonizers who made the Kazaks aware of the meaning of language and territory.[8]

The Kazak khanates contra kinship and tribalism

Tribal structure – local kinship and clan membership – has traditionally been stronger than the connection to the superior leader, the khan. The first and only premodern unification of the Kazak nomads into one Kazak state was established in the early 16th century by Qasim Khan, who intensified and centralized the earlier unification of the Kazak tribes.[9] During Qazim Khan's leadership, the Kazaks consisted of about 1 million nomads, who spoke the same Turkic language, used the same form of nomadic pastoralism and were joined in a common cultural and social organization.[10] The khanate

---

[7] *EIU Country Report*, 1st Quarter 1997, pp. 12–13.

[8] Kemal Karpat, 'Roots of Kazakh Nationalism', in Marco Buttino (ed.), *In a Collapsing Empire: Underdevelopment, Ethnic Conflicts and Nationalisms in the Soviet Union*, 1993, pp. 331–332.

[9] Already in the late 15th century – Janibek and Kirai, sons of Barak Khan from The White Horde of the Mongolian empire, broke away from the Uzbek federation under Khan Abu'l Khayr. They established a khanate (Qazaq Orda) – a political confederation in the south-western parts of Kazakhstan. For further reading, see e.g. Martha B. Olcott, *The Kazakhs*, Stanford 1987, Zeki Velidi Togan, 'The Origin of the Kazaks and the Özbeks', in H. Paksoy (ed.), *Central Asia Reader: The Rediscovery of History*, Arnmonk (N.Y.) 1994, and Elisabeth Bacon, *Central Asians under Russian Rule*, Ithaca 1980.

[10] The Kazaks are descendants of Turkic and Mongolian tribes, that came from the Mongolian plateau in the mid-sixth century and settled on the Eurasian Steppe; see Ahmed Rashid, *The Resurgence of Central Asia: Islam or Nationalism*, Karachi 1994,

of Qazim Khan lasted till the middle of the 16th century, when it was split into three khanates – Ulu Zhuz, Orta Zhuz and Kichi Zhuz.[11] In Soviet and Western literature, these khanates are known as the Great Horde, the Middle Horde and the Little Horde, respectively.[12] Ulu Zhuz had control over the southern regions of present-day Kazakstan, while Orta Zhuz dominated the central and north-eastern parts and Kichi Zhuz the western parts of Kazakstan bordering on the Ural river. The authority of the khan was only relevant as long as it protected the grass steppe from other nomadic pastoralists. Pasture for the animals – a necessity for surviving – meant more than the affiliation to the state-nation. By this system the *aul*[13] and local tribal authority formed the primary social and economic base.

The tribal structure constitutes a weak and fragmented basis for a multiethnic identity. This is a fact with both negative and positive aspects for Nazarbayev's solution of the national question. The positive aspect is that the Kazak nation does not constitute a united threat for the other nationalities in Kazakstan. The negative aspect is that the division between Ulu, Orta and Kichi Zhuz may even lead to intraethnic conflicts. A worsening of the economic crisis can increase the distance between rural Kazaks in the economically backward regions and the government. When the central government is no longer able to meet the needs of the countryside, the traditional power structure will still be there to define the political, economic and social loyalty of the individual. Folk Islam, the common language and the commitment to territory are on the other hand elements which tie together all Kazaks.

---

p. 110.

[11] There are still many speculations on when and why the original khanate was divided in three khanates. One reasonable explanation is that the tripartition was due to the fast growing population and that each area contained both summer and winter pastures. Another explanation is that the tripartition was practical for the military protection of the steppe; see Martha B. Olcott, op. cit., p. 11, Lawrence Krader, *Peoples of Central Asia*, Indiana University, 1963, p. 192, and H. Paksoy (ed.), *Central Asian Reader*, p. 33.

[12] The Kazak word *žuz* 'one hundred' refers to the earlier Mongolian organization of the military in units of hundreds. Kemal Karpat suggests a translation of *žuz* into the English 'part', 'particle' or 'ingredient' and argues that it refers to three units as parts of a greater unit, probably the khanate of Qasim Khan; see Kemal Karpat, op. cit., footnote 16, p. 322.

[13] The *aul* was the migratory unit of the Kazaks, which generally consisted of several extended families belonging to the same clan.

Folk Islam

The religion among the Kazak steppe nomads around the 10th century was a blending of local beliefs and the influence of Islamic Sufi teachers. The contact between this version of Folk Islam[14] and established Islamic centres in the southern oases of Central Asia was superficial until the 18th century. At that time classical Muslim institutions were introduced throughout the steppe by orders from the Russian empress, Catherine the Great. She believed that Islam would tame the 'wild' nomadic Kazaks and facilitate the task of the Russian administration. However, the institutionalization of Islam never penetrated Folk Islam, which is today reappearing as a very popular, moderate and individual belief. Sufism – the spiritual and mystic tradition of Islam – as practised by Kazaks is in contrast to what is generally referred to by the term 'fundamentalism' in the West. It is a deeply personal, silent expression of faith which does not need mosques, formal prayers and mullahs to retain its essential spirit. This belief in tolerance and moderation is winning converts, at a time when many people have had enough of ideologies. But Sufism is a non-political movement without the ability to function as an organized counterpart to the threat of fundamentalism.[15] It is a fact that the political version of Islam had its renaissance in Kazakhstan, with economic and spiritual backing from, for instance, Turkey, the Arab countries and Pakistan.

As a whole, Islamic faith is functioning as a mechanism that separates the Kazaks from the Soviet past and claims that they are a part of the Islamic world. However, whereas Sufism does not advocate a distance to non-Muslims, it is not unlikely that the influence from politicized Islam can be a destabilizing factor for the building of a nation. It is primarily religious Uzbeks, Tajiks, Chechens, Tatars, Uighurs or Mongols who dominate the established Muslim community in Kazakhstan. These non-Kazak Muslim minorities see Islam as an effective means to diverge themselves from Russians, secularized Kazaks and other non-believers. Islam presents a link to their ethnic identity and their national homeland.[16] One could imagine that the non-Kazak Muslims will be more disposed to use Islam than a Kazakstani national identity as the common ethnic basis in a possible conflict.

---

[14] For a general background on Folk Islam among the Kazaks, see e.g. Kemal Karpat, op. cit., pp. 314–319.
[15] Ahmed Rashid, op. cit., p. 247.
[16] Ibid., p. 133.

Language

Language is often seen as one of the most important national symbols in the struggle for group acknowledgement.[17] In Kazakstan language did not have a major impact on Kazak nationalism until the second half of the 19th century, when the literary language was created. Until the 1930s, when the Soviet administration introduced the Latin script in Central Asia, they wrote their language with Arabic letters. In 1938–1939 the Soviet authorities replaced Latin with an adapted form of the Cyrillic alphabet. By this policy it became possible for the Soviet system to influence and control the Kazak language and simultaneously it became impossible for the coming generations to read old Arabic and Persian texts. At the same time Russian language education was made compulsory. During the Soviet years Russian became the professional and interethnic language and there were practically no good Kazak primary schools, no Kazak books and no university where it was possible to learn and practise the Kazak language.

Today Kazakstan has one of the most liberal language laws in the post-Soviet Republics. In the 1993 constitution Russian was given a prominent position as the language of interethnic communication, while Kazak had official language status. But due to a sustained opposition of ethnic Russians to the secondary status of their language, Russian was granted official language status in 1995.[18] The consequence of this move is that Russian is supposed to be used equally with Kazak, now the national state language, in all official, central and local bodies.[19] On 22 November, 1996, a new language law was approved by the lower house of parliament. According to this new law, non-Kazaks in government service are required to be proficient in Kazak by the year 2006, while it is stipulated that ethnic Kazaks must know the Kazak language by January 2001.[20] It is not only because of a deliberate governmental policy that Russian is beginning to lose its dominating position. It is also due to the new wave of urbanization. An increasing number of young rural Kazaks are moving to the cities and they push kazakification forward in the multiethnic and cosmopolitic cities of

---

[17] Donald Horowitz, *Ethnic Groups in Conflict*, University of California Press 1985, p. 222.
[18] See e.g. *Kazaxstanskaja Pravda*, 30 December, 1993, 22 June, 1994, 22 September, 1994, and 24 March, 1995, for comments on the language law.
[19] 'New Constitution to be Approved by a Referendum', *Focus Central Asia* 12 (1995).
[20] *EIU Country Report*, 4th quarter 1996, p. 10.

Kazakstan.

However, in the near future Russian will remain the *de facto* official language, as Kazak is not used very actively in Kazakstani public life, simply because the non-Kazaks and even many Kazaks do not know the language well enough. This quite important and large group of Kazaks prefers to speak Russian, which is the language they grew up with as a result of the strong russification during Soviet rule. It places the Kazak language in a difficult position as a national symbol, both for Kazaks and non-Kazaks. Even though attempts like the Tenge (the new national currency), where the value is spelt in Kazak, street names in Kazak, the new flag, Kazak television programmes etc., are mainly of symbolic importance, they might be more important for Kazak identity than for Kazakstani nationhood.

Territory

The loss of free admission to the grazing lands is also a part of the Kazak collective consciousness that does not include Russians or other non-Kazaks. Tsar imperialism, Soviet collectivization, cultivation of the virgin lands and confiscation of land for military and nuclear purposes destroyed the nomadic economy. The Kazaks came under Russian control already during the 18th century as a result of the pressure from the east where a new Manchurian dynasty was established. The Kazak khanates recognized the Russian empire as the superior military force in the region and the khan of Kichi Zhuz, Abu'l Khayr, was the first to swear loyalty to the Russian empress in 1731. The khans from Orta Zhuz followed in 1732 and 1740, while the khans from Ulu Zhuz stayed under Jungar control till 1756 and then under the protection of the Kokand khanate till the first half of the 19th century, when the Russians consolidated their hold by establishing a series of military outposts throughout the steppe and seriously began to colonize the Kazak lands. This did not happen without resistance from the Kazaks. Under Khan Kenisari Qasimov, the Kazaks rebelled against the Russians. He died as a hero in 1847 and his resistance gained a permanent place in Kazak history.

The Kazak oath of allegiance to the Russian empire is for many Russians still a symbol of voluntary annexation of the Kazak territory, while Kazaks often refer to the old alliance with the Russians as a strategical and temporary one. The violent civil war in the Kazak steppe after the Russian revolution showed clearly that most Kazaks wanted independence not only from the

Russian empire but from any Russian superiority. Instead of supporting the new Bolshevik regime they created the Alash Orda Autonomous Government, which attempted to rule small parts of the steppe from 1917 to mid-1919 and fought with the White forces to defeat Bolshevik rule.

The present borders of Kazakstan are much more fixed in the minds of Kazaks than in the minds of Russians. Serious attempts to secession among Russians in the north will most likely be met with a military solution from the Kazakstani government.

Soviet influence on Kazak nationhood

The major contribution of the Soviet system to Kazak national identity was the recognition of Kazakstan as a Union Republic in 1936. The Soviet nationality policy created the territorial and political basis for the realization of the present-day sovereign nation, with its recognition of the Kazaks as a titular nationality inhabiting a well-defined territory. But in the name of development, modernization and internationalization it also created the multiethnic and ethnically divided state with a latent potential for conflicts. Especially two factors have had impact on this development:

1) The Soviet Union used the Kazak steppe as a 'virgin land' for Russians and other Slavic peoples and as a human 'dumping-ground' for unwanted nationalities in Russia, such as Koreans, the Volga Germans and Chechens.
2) Development and internationalization meant in reality an economic, political and cultural favouring of some ethnic groups instead of others and resulted in the creation of advanced and backward nationalities both locally in the former republics and at the union level.

The Soviet structure legitimized Russians as the leading nationality both locally as well as at the union level. Simultaneously the government in power implemented the so-called *korenizacija* ('anchorage') policy in the late 1920s, with the aim of rooting the communist ideology via indigenous cadres. By institutionalizing ethnicity in the administration, *korenizacija* contributed to the consolidation of nationalities in two essential ways. First, the policy supported the native languages and created local national intelligentsias and political élites. The national cadres did not lose their positions despite Stalin's increasing sovietization via russification.

Dinmukhamed Kunayev, First Secretary of the Kazak Communist Party until 1986, who was removed on account of Gorbachev's anti-corruption campaign, is a good example of a leader who learnt to play Moscow's game, without losing respect among the Kazaks. Second, the cultural and political policy of resemblance implemented by the Soviet nationality policy created modern national and cultural city élites who rather identified themselves as Kazaks than as Soviet citizens. However, non-Kazak engineers, technicians and other white-collar workers were meanwhile imported to build up the economy of Kazakstan. This meant that the majority of Kazaks continued to live in less developed steppe regions, while Russians and other Slavic groups worked in the privileged Soviet industry.

The separation between different ethnic groups and the internal division among the Kazaks show the weakness not only of a Kazakstani identity but also of the Kazak national identity, which alone is hard to imagine as a basis for a multiethnic Kazakstani identity. In reality, President Nazarbayev's solution of the national question looks more like kazakification combined with openness towards Russian demands. The revitalization of the Kazak language, the restoration of traditional names, the revision of the history and the celebration of Kazak and Islamic holidays help to prevent Kazak dissatisfaction, while obedience to Russian demands serves to appease Russian dissatisfaction in order to maintain national stability. Fear of instability seems stronger than the need for democratization and privatization, and that is a possible explanation why a serious change of the political and economic system is yet to come. In continuation of this, a relevant question would be: What will implementation of democracy and privatization mean to Kazakstan? Will sweeping reforms worsen or reduce the potential for ethnic conflicts?

Stability or transition?

As Donald Horowitz emphasizes in his article 'Democracy in Divided Societies', there is a strong tendency to confuse inclusion in government with inclusion in the community and exclusion from government with exclusion from the community in ethnically divided societies.[21] When ethnic boundaries appear unchangeable as in Kazakstan, inclusion and exclusion

---

[21] Donald Horowitz, 'Democracy in Divided Societies', in Larry Diamond and Marc F. Plattner (eds), *Nationalism, Ethnic Conflict, and Democracy*, Baltimore 1994, p. 35.

will also appear permanent. This may affect the distribution of important material and non-material matters, including the prestige of the various ethnic groups and the identity of the state as belonging mostly to one group. The favouritism of one ethnic group often becomes visible among policies that have non-ethnic purposes, as for example, administrative decentralization, economic restructuring and a measure of electoral democracy.[22]

The breakdown of the Soviet Union in 1991 changed the traditional balance of power within the now sovereign republics. Even though the remaining Russians, due to their traditional choice of education and employment, might still be the economically and technically advanced part of the population, they lost their political and economic superiority when Kazakstan became an independent state. A clear example of exclusion from government is the composition of Parliament in 1994, where the Kazaks constituted the majority. They occupied 60% of the seats, while the Slavs occupied only 33%. As much as 85% of the Kazaks in Parliament came from Ulu Zhuz and thus had the same geographical and tribal background as the President.[23] Likewise, out of a total of 19 ministers in the present government, only 5 are Russians.[24] The new language law can also be seen as an example of a future exclusion of citizens who do not know Kazak from governmental and state positions. Citizenship is another example of favouring Kazaks as the ethnic group on which the identity of the state is based. According to the Kazak constitution, it is not possible to receive dual citizenship, unless you belong to the Kazak diaspora:

> The right to receive citizenship in the Republic of Kazakstan together with keeping another citizenship is recognized for all who have been forced to leave their territory, and also for Kazaks who are citizens in other states if this is not against the law in the actual state.[25]

In reality this means that the Kazak diaspora can have dual citizenship

---

[22] Donald Horowitz, 'How to Begin Thinking Theoretically about Soviet Ethnic Problems?', in Alexander Motyl (ed.), *Thinking Theoretically about Soviet Nationalities: History and Comparison in the Study of the USSR*, New York, 1992, p. 2.
[23] Yuri Kulchik, 'Central Asia after the Empire: Ethnic Groups, Communities, and Problems', in Roald Z. Sagdeev (ed.), *Central Asia: Conflict, Resolution and Change*, The Center for Post Soviet Studies, 1995, p. 110.
[24] *EIU Country Report*, 1st quarter 1997, p. 4.
[25] *Konstitucija Respubliki Kazaxstan, Glava 2, Statja 4*, 1993.

while other ethno-national groups like Russians, Germans, Ukrainians and Uzbeks are not allowed to keep Kazak citizenship if they wish to receive one in a second country. From a Kazak point of view, it is logical to encourage the approximately two million Kazaks outside Kazakstan to come home, as a return of the diaspora will increase the Kazak share of the population. On the other hand, dual citizenship to Russians would mean that almost half of the population in Kazakstan could be Russian citizens and that would make it easier for the northern regions bordering on Russia to claim the right of secession and annexation to the Russian Federation. The question of dual citizenship – like the question of language status – is a matter of perpetual disagreement between the Kazak government and the Russians. From a Russian point of view it is an example of the exclusion of Russian rights in the Kazakstani society.

Recommendations from the Western world have generally been focusing on the will and ability of the post-Soviet and East European states to start democratic and market economic reforms. It has been very difficult to achieve the necessary Western political and economic support without accepting the recommended direction. But while democracy and privatization on paper are two very important indicators for a successful transition towards a sovereign, liberal and Western-style nation-state, they also include very sensitive aspects for a country like Kazakstan. A symptomatic example is the massive migration of particularly Russians and Germans. A sociological survey of the Slavic population in the Taldy–Kurgan province shows that the main reasons for migration are the loss of access to power and material goods and a desire to gain control over their own economical situation. According to the survey, two thirds of the Russians from this region wish to emigrate. As to the motivation for their wish to leave, 22% state a fear of losing their ethnic culture and language, while 7.8% refer to ethnic discrimination. The rest mention the enlargement of personal material possibilities and provisions of better living standards.[26] President Nazarbayev dislikes migration but he prefers to emphasize ethnic reasons rather than economic reasons:

---

[26] 'Migration: Economic Crisis and Danger of Discrimination', *Focus Central Asia* 17 (1995), p. 6.

> [...] the reasons for the present migration are not only to be found in the economic problems, but also in the fact that the descendants from the massive emigration of Russians, Ukrainians, Belarusians, Germans and other peoples, wish to return to their historical fatherland to participate in the building of the national states.[27]

When President Nazarbayev points to the physical need for peoples' historical fatherland, this could be interpreted as an excuse for not doing anything essential to keep the non-Kazak ethnic groups in Kazakhstan. Nurbulat Masanov, a Kazak historian, sees the massive emigration as an invisible ethnic cleansing. He accuses Nazarbayev of accepting the migration as a way to avoid the Russian problem and as a means to release economic and material resources. When a lot of people leave the country, they leave dwellings, jobs and financial means for the Kazak diaspora to take over. From a Russian viewpoint, it is a way to undermine Russian domination in some regions. Contrary to Nazarbayev, Masanov regards the massive migration as a disadvantage for the Kazakstani state. He sees it as a brain-drain of technically advanced and qualified ethnic groups.[28]

Nazarbayev's superior strategy for the solution of the national question and avoidance of ethnic conflicts seems well-considered and democratic. He has created a constitution with reasonable rights and possibilities for all citizens in Kazakhstan. However, his orientation in real policy is not liberal and is based not on individual rights, but on group and ethnic interests. He uses the ethnic aspect and the fear for ethnic conflicts to legitimize his autocratic rule. The civil war in Tajikistan and in the Chechen part of Russia is for Nazarbayev a good reason for keeping control of the power at the expense of development of democracy and market economy. For the President, transition can easily mean a redefinition of the political and economic power in Kazakhstan. In the case of free and democratic elections, for example, for the Parliament, and a less restrictive presidential policy towards political opposition, one could imagine a more honest opposition to the regime. A genuine privatization of land and means of production would probably in the same way create contesting power bases outside Kazak and presidential influence. With this in mind, Nazarbayev has been changing from a would-be democrat to an authoritarian leader whose image

---

[27] Nursultan Nazarbaev, 'Za mir i soglasie v našem obščem dome. Doklad Presidenta N. A. Nazarbaeva na pervoj sessii Assamblei narodov Kazaxstana', *Kazaxstanskaja Pravda*, 24 March, 1995.
[28] 'Komu vygodna ėmigracija?' (an interview with Nurbulat Masanov), *Doživem do ponedel'nika*, 19 May, 1995.

is very much like the images of the presidents of Uzbekistan and Turkmenistan.

A good explanation for a slow transition in Kazakstan is the growing markets in South East Asia and China. They are proving that it is easier for authoritarian regimes than for weak democracies, to fulfil the fundamental economic indicators emphasized by the World Bank. It seems easier for an authoritarian regime to resist the pressure from different groups of interests. Both South Korea and Taiwan are striking examples of countries where economic success has been followed by spectacular political liberalization since the late 1980s. A comparison of Russia and China, two countries in great transition, showed in 1994 that the Russian liberal way with both democratic and market economic reforms experienced a 12% decrease in the economy, while the Chinese economy increased 13%.[29]

Democracy and multiethnicity

A good argument for not implementing democratic reforms in Kazakstan is that the population is not experienced in an individualistic tradition. This mentality was developed in the Soviet Union and it fits well to socially or ethnically defined group behaviour. In his article 'How to Begin Thinking Comparatively about Soviet Ethnic Problems', Donald Horowitz emphasizes that the Western understanding of democracy is closely connected to the Western modern tradition of placing the individual in focus.[30] Election is the keyword in Western democracies and can be seen as a mechanism which counts individual votes to obtain a valid result. The mentality of Western individualism does not fit very well with ethnically defined political group behaviour. The elections held in Kazakstan have all been marked by collective voting with the head of the family, the village, the kolkhoz or the factory collecting the personal votes to assure that the ballots were cast 'correctly'.

Anatoly Kotov, an official spokesman, identifies the government as liberal–democratic with certain enlightened authoritarian elements in his article 'Conversation about Democracy in Kazakstan',[31] where he emphasizes

---

[29] Ferry Versteeg, 'Democracy and Growth or the U.S. vs. the Asians?', *Focus Central Asia* 18 (1995), p. 8.
[30] Donald Horowitz, op. cit., p. 12.
[31] In *All over the Globe*, 17 June, 1996, pp. 1–2. Anatoly Kotov is senator of the

the necessity of the authoritarian element in a post-totalitarian country like Kazakstan:

> [...] only a powerful unitary state is capable of deciding the question of how to incorporate political freedom with the economic necessity of speeding up the process of social modernization.[32]

The suppression of any kind of political opposition is a clear example of the authoritarian element in the regime. Undoubtedly parties and movements like the Russian-dominated LAD ('Harmony') and the three main Kazak movements Alash, Zheltoksan and Azat together with different Kossack movements are ethno-national and nationalistic, but it is difficult to regard them as a threat against unity due to the fact that they are not supported by very many people. The tendency towards political apathy is widespread and can be seen as a consequence of the long tradition of authoritarian political systems in the region. Furthermore, the new political parties are suffering from a lack of organizing ability and insignificant economic means, which makes it even more difficult to mobilize the necessary public support. The fact that their different political actions have been banned several times by the authorities also abstains the public from involvement. In April 1996 a new mass movement with the Kazak name Azamat and the Russian name Graždanin ('Citizen') was established. It was formed by Petr Svoik, the former head of the State Committee for Anti-Monopoly and Price Policy, and it is supported by a wide range of intellectual supporters – primarily people with an academic background, artists and politicians. Even though the movement is multiethnic and an example of Kazakstani opposition, Nazarbayev does not seem very eager to listen to them. Azamat organized a silent protest in Almaty on 17 November, 1996, as a reaction against the country's increasing social problems. The authorities tried to ban the demonstration which was seen as illegal and the organizers were given warnings and fines.[33]

The problems of democracy in ethnically divided societies and in societies in great transition are huge and it is hard to blame the government as long as there are crucial economic problems to be solved as well. But in order to avoid conflicts in ethnically divided societies it is very important to build

---

Parliament in Kazakhstan and secretary of the Standing Committee on Legislation and Judicial–Legal Reform.

[32] Ibid., p. 2.
[33] *EIU Country Report*, 1st quarter 1997, p. 11.

up a multiethnic democratic system as soon as possible. And there is a basis for this kind of system in Kazakstan, where a lot of people are educated in an international frame, even though it was a Soviet international frame. What is happening today is that ethnicity more and more defines and controls the political possibilities of the individual. Contrary to President Nazarbayev, Donald Horowitz emphasizes that the more difficult way – democracy as a stabilizing factor instead of stability for its own sake – is a solution which can last:

> To have failed once makes things more difficult the next time. To have failed twice makes the next time problematic altogether. Many states will soon be in this position. In planning for a state that is to be democratic and multiethnic, earlier is assuredly better.[34]

Enlightened authoritarianism and privatization

Just as the keyword in Western democracy – individual voting – collides with ethnically bound group understanding and collective loyalty, the assumption of market economy – privatization – collides with the Soviet and traditional Kazak understanding of collective ownership. In the Kazak traditional society, the steppe region was understood as common property, even after it was split into three *zhuz* regions, since the *aul*s migrated across the steppe from winter to summer pastures. In the command economy of the Soviet Union it was formally the workers, and with it the people, who collectively owned the means of production, land and property.

Kazakstan was the first post-Soviet Republic which actually introduced a privatization law in 1991 (it was improved in 1993). At that time it was the aim of the government to privatize all small- and medium-sized enterprises in the nearest future. In the middle of 1994, 10,000 small enterprises in the service sector were privatized, which was only 1/5 of the planned number. The aim of the second privatization programme for 1993–1995 was to mass-privatize middle-sized and large enterprises through the sale of shares to private investment funds. For this purpose Kazakstani citizens received vouchers. Time has shown that the privatization plans more or less vanished in the fight for control over economic resources. The second round of privatization has primarily been used as a means to collect and unite property

---

[34] Donald Horowitz, op. cit., p. 54.

in the hands of the existing Kazak nomenclatura, seeing that the government actually is in a position to control the investment funds and redistribute the new private companies for its own profit. The Kazak-dominated government has openly supported those investment funds which dominate southern Kazakstan, where Ulu Zhuz – the 'presidential *zhuz*' – has its traditional support. When major industrial projects are put on the block, most of the property will be lawfully transferred to clans in southern Kazakstan.[35] This 'ethno-privatization' is, of course, a disadvantage for the Russian population, a major part of which is engaged in the industrial sectors. For this reason any mention of collective property has been removed from local legislation, along with the right for employees to decide on the redemption of the property of state enterprises.

The traditional division of territory between the three Zhuzes might be another good reason why privatization, especially that of land, is a major subject. So far the government has authorized itself to keep land as state-owned by declaring the state as protector of the national interests of the Kazak rural population.[36] But the new market system with its general economic crisis and the widening gap between rich and poor and between different regions may strengthen the tribal structure. The government is no longer able to guarantee free social services like subsidized food products, housing, medical coverage and education. Communication and transport services are also becoming increasingly expensive and this isolates the rural population from the city. Because of the lack of support from the government the rural population turns to the traditional social structure and that might affect the local authorities to demand influence over resources placed in their region. This could lead to intertribe rivalry; while Ulu Zhuz has the central political power, most of Kazakstan's mineral and oil resources are located in the central, northern and western parts of Kazakstan in the regions of Orta and Kichi Zhuz.[37]

---

[35] Yuri Kulchik, op. cit., p. 102.
[36] Nurbulat Masanov and Nurlan Amrekulov, *Kazaxstan meždu prošlym i buduščim*, Almaty 1994, p. 13.
[37] Tulegen Askarov, 'Kazakh Groups Might Pose Opposition to Unitary Kazakhstan', *Focus Central Asia* 19 (1994), p. 10.

A way to lasting peaceful coexistence

One of the most essential governmental tasks in a transition period from planned economy to market economy is to guarantee that the resources are used and distributed for the sake of all individuals. At the same time the state itself should be a good example.[38] The problem in Kazakstan is that President Nazarbayev's authoritarian power base has a breaking effect on the development. This might worsen the interethnic and intraethnic rivalry, due to the unwillingness to share the political and economic power with either Kazaks from Orta or Kichi Zhuz or Russians. Contrary to all the declarations about Kazakstan's advancement towards a market economy, government control of the economy is becoming more evident than in the last years of the communist regime. The collapse of the communist regime did not bring about any essential changes in the composition of the power élite but only an alteration in its ideological visage.

President Nazarbayev has chosen stability as the keyword for a peaceful coexistence in his multiethnic society. So far peace prevails in Kazakstan and initially the concentration of political and economic power seems sensible since division of power could have crucial consequences in a country which is already ethnically split. Still, it remains to be seen if the chosen policy will to an even greater extent deepen and freeze the existing polarization of society. When one's ethnic background determines whether an individual is included in or excluded from political decisions, there is a great risk that the difference between rich and poor, advanced and rural will also be determined by ethnicity.

The regime's solution can be criticized for lack of dynamism. During the communist era, people were alienated from political life and the decision-making process. This alienation did not disappear after the country's independence. Fear of imagined ethnic conflicts made the regime restrain a serious involvement of people in the transition process. An important consequence of this is that the opposition to the presidential power is practically non-existent except for a very mild resistance among Kazaks and Russians. The presence of foreign investors, new foreign political alliances, diplomats, foreign scholars and students functions as a mirror of

---

[38] 'Transition Report' (European Bank for Reconstruction and Development), 1994.

a different reality. The complex ethnic structure combined with the increasing economic crisis, cannot guarantee that Kazaks, Russians and other ethnic minorities will continue to be pacified by the traditional Soviet-style government.

War and Change in Afghanistan
Reflections on Research Priorities[*]

KRISTIAN BERG HARPVIKEN

Insufficient knowledge of the social and political transformation in Afghanistan during the war is an obstacle to finding solutions to the conflict. This is the basic assumption of this paper, in which I will elaborate on some of the war-initiated processes that I consider to be insufficiently studied. New research on these processes could provide essential input to the building of peace.

Recent publications on the peace process in Afghanistan have revealed the extent to which negotiators have had minimal insight into Afghanistan's social and political make-up.[1] To some extent the explanation is that negotiations have taken place under a cold-war logic, according to which only the international dimension of conflict was a legitimate concern. However, no mediation processes have fully neglected the need for a domestic political solution.

Academic interest in Afghanistan grew throughout the 1960s, resulting in a number of high-quality publications within history and social science. Research suffered a dramatic setback from the onset of war, as the indigenous academic environment became severely affected by the political conflict and the opportunities for foreigners to do fieldwork became increasingly constrained. Although the war led to a dramatic increase in publications on Afghanistan, many of the wartime analyses are severely biased, and they

---

[*] I am grateful for comments on earlier versions of this paper from J. 'Bayo Adekanye, Mohamad Ehsan and Arne Strand. The responsibility for the final version remains entirely mine.

[1] Diego Cordovez and Selig S. Harrison, *Out of Afghanistan: The Inside Story of the Soviet Withdrawal*, New York 1995, and Barnett R. Rubin, *The Search for Peace in Afghanistan: From Buffer State to Failed State*, New Haven 1995.

are rarely based on primary material.² Travelling and working in the country have become easier since the communist abdication in April 1992, but this has not stimulated a new wave of research. The requirement now is for empirically solid, fieldwork-based studies.

Research themes emphasized in this paper are guided by an interest in contributing to an understanding of the current conflict, and ultimately in inspiring solutions to it. This is not a denouncement of other research priorities, but it reflects the conviction that whatever the short-term developments will be, Afghanistan is in dire need of a debate about its future, informed by knowledge about its recent past. Furthermore, the lack of references to any particular theoretical or methodological framework is not incidental. There is both room and need for a variety of approaches; what is important is that the dialogue between researchers, as well as between researchers, policy-makers and people, is strengthened. Hence, the selection of themes is policy-oriented, and their presentation here is general. The six themes of the paper secure a wide catch: the politicization of society, the militarization of society, war economy, the technological revolution, migration and the international dimension.

1. Politicization

Afghanistan before the war was a country whose population cared little about politics at the national level. The so-called palace politics of Kabul barely affected living conditions beyond the capital. If people had to throw their support behind any political candidate, the choice would reflect little but local loyalties based on kinship and economic relations. Yet, rulers in Kabul have historically lacked the resources to control the country, and

---

[2] For a useful bibliography, see Schuyler Jones, *Afghanistan* (World Bibliographical Series, vol. 135), Oxford 1992. Another useful source is the historical dictionary by Ludwig W. Adamec, *Historical Dictionary of Afghanistan*, Metuchen (New Jersey) 1991. A useful collection of essays that can inspire new research is Ewan W. Anderson and Nancy Hatch Dupree (eds), *The Cultural Basis of Afghan Nationalism*, London 1991. Although the quality of contributions is more uneven, the following seminar reports are also useful: Rasul Amin (ed.), *Social and Cultural Prospects for Afghanistan*, WUFA [Writers' Union of Free Afghanistan] Journal of Afghan Affairs, Special Issue, 5:4 (1990), Rasul Amin (ed.), *Rebuilding Afghan Political and Legal Institutions*, WUFA Journal of Afghan Affairs, Special Issue, 7:1 (1990), E. Eide and T. Skaufjord (eds), *From Aid During Times of War to Aid for Reconstruction and Development*, Norwegian Afghanistan Committee, Peshawar 1992, and Suroosh Irfani and Fazal-ur Rahman (eds), *Afghanistan: Looking to the Future*, Institute of Strategic Studies, Islamabad 1991.

being in power has depended on alliances with various forces, most often the tribes. The 1973 coup, in which former prime minister Daud dethroned the king, Zahir Shah, was the first instance of an Afghan ruler taking power solely with the force of the army.[3]

With the onset of war, intense ideological struggles were introduced into the most remote valleys. Although traditional loyalties continued to play a role, they did so within a different context, one in which people also saw their participation in a movement with national ambitions as one aspect of their personal identity. The most recent empirically solid work on the politicization initiated by the war is Olivier Roy's *Islam and Resistance in Afghanistan*.[4] The fundamentalist Taliban movement, which emerged in late 1994 and currently controls two thirds of the country, including the capital, Kabul, has yet to be analysed. Peace proposals for Afghanistan often assume that pre-war arrangements can again stabilize the country, an assumption that neglects the deep politicization brought about by the war.[5] In fact, had these arrangements functioned, there would most probably have been no war.

1.1. Large-scale identities

Numerous political parties were established in Afghanistan from the early 1960s, when new political openings were provided under the so-called New Democracy initiative. The parties, whether Islamist, Marxist-Leninist or Maoist in orientation, had much in common. The scene of their political battles was Kabul, particularly the university campus. Their recruits were young people who, in their encounters with modern science, had developed a deep dissatisfaction with Afghan traditionalism and wanted swift political and economic change.[6] While all these movements presented themselves in strong ideological terms, their membership was as much decided by belonging to a network based on kin, common place of origin or enrolment at the same institution. The popular support for these movements was extremely

---

[3] Asta Olesen, *Islam and Politics in Afghanistan*, Richmond 1995.

[4] Olivier Roy, *Islam and Resistance in Afghanistan*, Cambridge 1986. Roy's book, first published in French in 1985, has not only become a reference work on Afghanistan; it is also a frequently quoted source on political Islam.

[5] Kristian Berg Harpviken, 'Transcending Traditionalism: The Emergence of Non-State Military Formations in Afghanistan', *Journal of Peace Research* 34:3 (1997), pp. 271–287.

[6] Olivier Roy, op. cit.

small, but it was from this environment that the key figures of the conflict were to come, communists and Islamists alike.[7]

The politicization of Islam is crucial. Islam was the common denominator for the resistance. Core Islamistic political organizations with a potential for expansion were in existence and the international radicalization of Islam meant inspiration, political support and funding. Not least, in a population strongly Muslim in a popular religious sense, Islam provided a rich repertoire for collective action, exemplified in *jihad* (struggle in defence of one's religion) and *hijrat* (the escape of Muhammed from Mecca to Medina; refuge to protect one's religious belief). There is a need to understand better the distinction between fundamentalist and modernist Islamic movements when it comes to recruitment, principal objectives and popular support. This was demonstrated by the emergence of the Taliban, whose initial success largely reflected dissatisfaction with the irreconcilable line of the Islamists. Ethnic differences have become important dividing lines, with different movements seen to represent primarily the Pashtun, Tajik, Uzbek or Hazara populations. Apparently, ethnic divisions became more prevalent with the disappearance of the Soviet threat.[8] There are several possible explanations for this: the new political awareness makes the traditional Pashtun domination in national politics unacceptable; new political and military organization makes protest an opportunity; the Soviet-inspired nationality policy of the communist regime has strengthened ethnic identities.[9]

The movement towards adherence to larger-scale identities is insufficiently studied. Emerging from what is said above, one crucial concern must be the interplay between religion, ethnicity and the formation of political groups.[10] The apparent contradiction between modern and traditional organization should be addressed. In my view it is exactly the ability to rely on traditional

---

[7] The coming government party, the People's Democratic Party of Afghanistan (PDPA), had around 5,000 members, from the technocratic élite of bureaucrats, officers and students. About 200 members were within the armed forces (Henry S. Bradsher, *Afghanistan and the Soviet Union*, Durham (North Carolina), 1983). For a comprehensive pre-war political history, see Louis Dupree, *Afghanistan*, 3rd ed., Princeton 1980.

[8] Barnett R. Rubin, *The Fragmentation of Afghanistan: State Formation and Collapse in the International System*, New Haven 1995, pp. 264–265.

[9] E.g. Kristian Berg Harpviken, *The Dynamics of Identity: Shifting Scales in Recent Mobilisation among the Hazara of Afghanistan*, unpublished manuscript, 1995, 40 pages. See contributions on ethnicity in Afghanistan in Jean-Pierre Digard (ed.), *Le fait ethnique en Iran et en Afghanistan*, Colloques Internationaux (Editions du CNRS), Paris 1988.

[10] Robert L. Canfield, 'Afghanistan: The Trajectory of Internal Alignments', *Middle East Journal* 43:4 (1989), pp. 635–648.

networks that has been the major success criterion for the so-called modern organizations.[11] Changes reflecting the policies of the People's Democratic Party of Afghanistan (PDPA) or the Soviet Union are almost neglected, probably because research itself was so politically influenced during the war. New source material should now be available thanks to the opening of Soviet archives.[12] Existing studies of political change in Afghanistan tend to treat the relations between the communist government and the population as static rather than dynamic, failing to grasp the extent to which the government interacted with all parties.

1.2. New leaders

Looking at Afghanistan's present-day leadership, it consists of people who all have a share in the responsibility for the current state of affairs. In other words, the country is in dire need of unifying leaders, but has no Nelson Mandela. This is largely the result of the war itself. War rarely promotes those leaders that one needs in peacetime, but there is more to it than that. The communists, once in power, targeted leaders with a potential for rallying an opposition faction, including religious leaders, village leaders and political opponents within the Maoist or Islamist groups. The Islamists targeted intellectuals with a capacity for opposing their line of resistance politics, effectively joining hands with the Kabul regime in securing the political arena for the Islamist-communist confrontation. Independent members of the country's intelligentsia, as well as many local leaders, were killed or escaped to a country outside the region.

Simultaneously, the war has fostered a change in the forms of leadership.[13] Traditional local leadership was based on patron–client relations. The local leader had to be able to gather support from his followers, and from his sovereign, the state administration. Support from below is dependent on the ability to mediate resources; support from above is dependent on the ability

---

[11] Kristian Berg Harpviken, *The Dynamics of Identity*, and Kristian Berg Harpviken, 'Transcending Traditionalism'.

[12] Odd Arne Westad, 'The Foreign Policy Archives of Russia: New Regulations for Declassification and Access', *The Society for Historians for American Foreign Affairs Newsletter* 23:2 (1992), pp. 1–2.

[13] Asger Christensen, *Aiding Afghanistan: The Background and Prospects for Reconstruction in a Fragmented Society* (NIAS [Nordic Institute of Asian Studies] Reports no. 26), Copenhagen 1995.

to prevent conflict and prepare the ground for state interference. Maintaining a leadership position consists of balancing these conflicting interests within a multi-tiered patron–client system. This traditional form of leadership was challenged during the war, and many resistance organizations, particularly the Islamist ones, were hierarchical, with a greater potential for large-scale mobilization and quick action and with lesser checks on leadership.

1.3. Silent majority?

Soon after the Soviet invasion, Pakistan, which was fronting for the United States in supporting the Afghan resistance, granted recognition to six resistance parties thereby effectively excluding dozens of others from foreign support. The parties recognized were all Islamic, primarily Sunni Muslim, and had an established working relationship with Pakistan's Foreign Office and intelligence.[14] Membership in one of these parties was also obligatory for becoming registered as a refugee. Pakistan effectively stopped all other political initiatives, resulting in a divided resistance susceptible to outside control.[15] Military and financial support was dependent on military efficiency, not political popularity. The effects became clear after the 1992 communist abdication. Of seven Pakistan-based parties, only three survived, the common denominators being efficient military organizations, foreign support and the will to apply violence to gain power.[16] Other groups had problems making their voices heard in the ongoing violent conflict.

The indication is that the parties currently dominating the political scene in Afghanistan are anything but representative of the population.[17] The

---

[14] Riaz M. Khan, *Untying the Afghan Knot: Negotiating Soviet Withdrawal*, Durham (North Carolina) 1991.

[15] Mohammad Yousaf and Mark Adkin, *The Bear Trap: Afghanistan's Untold Story*, London 1992.

[16] These parties were Jamiat-e Islami, Hezb-e Islami and Ittehad-e Islami. The parties that have more or less withered away during the past four years are Harakat-e Inqelab, Hezb-e Islami (Khales), National Islamic Front of Afghanistan (NIFA) and Afghanistan National Liberation Front (ANLF). Furthermore, there was a number of Shiitic groups, most of whom joined Hezb-e Wahdat in 1989; see Kristian Berg Harpviken, *Political Mobilization Among the Hazara of Afghanistan 1978–1992* (Report no. 9, Department of Sociology, University of Oslo), Oslo 1996.

[17] This was also the analysis of the United Nations, when its 1994 mission concentrated on creating a 'public space', meeting numerous personalities not affiliated with the battling parties and arranging virtual mass meetings both in Afghanistan and in refugee centres elsewhere (Barnett R. Rubin, *The Search for Peace in Afghanistan,* p. 136). The

country has a 'silent majority', and it might be by enhancing the expression of this majority's view that one can foster a peaceful solution to the conflict. The challenge here is not only to lay bare the facts of political loyalties but also to promote a debate on how to provide an opportunity for the silent majority to influence the political process.

2. Militarization

The processes of politicization and militarization are closely intertwined. Indeed, one of the central arguments above is that much of what is seen to be politicization is actually militarization, making open political debate impossible. When militarization is here treated independently, it is because it entails a number of distinct issues, such as the impact of modern warfare and the potential for demobilization. Yet, it needs to be emphasized that it is exactly in analysing and disentangling phenomena within the broader politicization–militarization complex that one of the major research challenges lies.

2.1. Modern warfare

Present writings on Afghanistan often assume that the post-communist fighting in the country is merely a return to a normal state of affairs, based on a conception of the inherently warlike Afghan. In contrast, some analysts have attempted to establish the difference between modern war and a traditional, tribal mode of warfare, also called feud. The feud is a limited kind of warfare: fighting appears only during times of leisure, it does not go beyond the group's primary area, infrastructure is not destroyed, casualties are limited, and women and children are spared.[18] Hence, pre-war Afghanistan was a society with a conflict level exceeding that of many other societies, but the conflicts and their effects were restrained by a comprehensive set of norms. It is exactly these norms that were violated when the communist government and the Soviets exposed Afghanistan to total warfare. The

---

1994 U.N. initiative was brought to a halt by the emergence of the Taliban movement.
[18] Louis Dupree, 'Post-Withdrawal Afghanistan: Light at the End of the Tunnel', in A. Saikal and W. Maley (eds), *The Soviet Withdrawal from Afghanistan*, Cambridge 1989, pp. 29–51.

population adapted to the requirements of modern warfare and with external aggression gone, it has become evident that traditional warfare norms have withered.

A different mode of explanation would emphasize the organizational change brought about by the war. The military organizations of Afghanistan today are very different from those existing before the war. They are larger in scale, they are more formally hierarchical, and they consist of permanent troops. Changes in military organization are closely linked to the politicization process, including the trend towards larger-scale identities.[19] A major cause of the emerging military relations is, of course, the external threat; the brutality with which the communist regime approached the local communities is truly astonishing.[20] However, the scope and durability of the military mobilization would be unthinkable without a change of leadership, the introduction of new technology and extensive foreign support.

2.2. Conditions for demobilization

Afghanistan has a young generation that has never experienced the absence of war. Not only does this mean a generation suffering from war-traumas; it also means a generation that is more competent to make war than to undertake most other activities. Thus, for any settlement to hold in Afghanistan, demobilization becomes a major challenge. With the resistance entering Kabul after the communist abdication in April 1992, one would have expected the communist government's military to dissolve. Exactly the opposite happened; their skills were in demand, creating competition between different resistance groups in making the best offers to the élite troops of the former regime, often co-opting whole units *en bloc*.

However, there have been examples of indigenous demobilization. With the fall of the PDPA government in 1992, many resistance fighters and commanders felt *jihad* was over and withdrew from fighting.[21] Being part

---

[19] Kristian Berg Harpviken, *The Dynamics of Identity*.

[20] Fredrik Barth, 'Cultural Wellsprings of Resistance in Afghanistan', in R. Klass (ed.), *Afghanistan: The Great Game Revisited*, London 1987, pp. 187–202, and M. Nazif Shahrani, 'Introduction: Marxist "Revolution" and Islamic Resistance in Afghanistan', in M. N. Shahrani and R. L. Canfield (eds), *Revolutions and Rebellions in Afghanistan*, Institute of International Studies (UCLA), Berkeley 1984, pp. 3–57.

[21] Asger Christensen, op. cit., p. 68. When the Taliban emerged in late 1994 in protest against the incompetence and 'heresy' of the other political parties, the core of its

of the traditional Islamic network, these people had a non-military retreat, hence an opportunity to withdraw with dignity. Apparently, demobilization is facilitated when people have access to a different position which is more attractive than continuing fighting, in terms of both economic security and social status. In the past few years, demobilization has become a major theme in the study of conflict settlements, yet no study has been undertaken on demobilization in Afghanistan, in spite of the fact that indigenous instances of demobilization have taken place.

2.3. Might is right

As long as conflicts are resolved by military means, it is military might and not political support that will decide matters in Afghanistan. This is most clearly seen in the withering away after 1992 of the parties that had no strong military organization or external sources of supply.[22] In a sense, this is the 'silent majority' theme revisited: it is the few who possess the military means to enforce their claims who get heard, there is no space where the population is heard, and political change becomes hostage to the manipulation of military–political leaders who are hardly accountable to anyone. The current domination of military power in politics fosters a vicious circle of violence that needs to be broken, yet military forces continue to enjoy foreign support, while any group opposing the continued violence is unable to make itself heard.

3. War economy

The war has initiated a profound change in the economy, inspiring new demands, altering transport and distribution networks and providing new business opportunities. A distinct war economy has developed, parts of which are closely integrated with the new political and military organizations. The war economy includes drug production, smuggling and processing, the importing and smuggling to neighbouring countries of a variety of capital-intensive goods, the taxation of transport by armed groups, the taxation of

---

network was formed by traditional religious leaders (*ulama*), who had withdrawn from fighting in 1992. Some had in fact demobilized after the Soviet withdrawal in 1989.

[22] Barnett R. Rubin, *The Fragmentation of Afghanistan*, p. 265.

local residents by local leaders, arms trade and the looting of private and public buildings following the conquering of new territory.

3.1. Basis for conflict

The war economy generates its own interests and resources which then become further incentives or bases for the continuation of conflict. Economic success, hence also political survival, becomes dependent on the control of certain resources, such as access to the border or control over a territory that contains specific assets (for example, minerals or fields suitable for poppy cultivation). Hence, when the Taliban in early September 1996 took control over three more provinces in eastern Afghanistan, including Jalalabad on the main road from Kabul to Peshawar, this was a major blow for the government, which lost direct access to the country's borders.[23] When Ahmad Shah Massoud in the late 1980s allowed Soviet arms transport to go through against a certain compensation, this was also motivated by the economic needs of his organization. It is likely that most political decisions in present day Afghanistan are motivated by the wish to secure a group's resource base in the short to medium term, not by the contribution it makes to a long-term solution at the national level.

3.2. Independence of political formations

Afghanistan has a weak state, controlling only a share of the country's territory, with coercive capacities that are at best on a par with those of its adversaries. In other words, the government has no monopoly over the means of coercion. As a matter of fact, it is also an open question whether it is a legitimate government, even though the international community has so far decided not to tamper with its recognition.

In analysing the current situation, there are two contradicting positions. On the one hand, it is claimed that with the collapse of the PDPA government and the drying up of external resources, there has been a shift of power from the new commanders back to traditional leadership figures.[24] On the

---

[23] Kabul fell to the Taliban on 27 September, 1996, in a relatively bloodless overtaking, as the government forces fled their positions.
[24] Asger Christensen, op. cit., p. 67.

other hand, it is claimed that the 1992 change led to an economic revival for many commanders, with their new independence being further strengthened by the downgrading of foreign patronage.[25] This divergence of views might be explained by local differences, but it is more likely that both underestimate the extent to which there is continuity in change. I tend to believe that the most successful 'modern' leaders are those who have managed to accommodate traditional sources of loyalty and existing forms of organization.

3.3. Business prevents peace?

The war economy favours a few at the expense of many. Before the war, most economic transactions involved a benefit for both parties. Now, in what is still effectively a war situation, the one who possesses the means of coercion can enforce his will, obtaining a benefit by threatening evil. Unfortunately, the few who gain will find it in their interest to protect their business opportunities, which again presuppose some state of war. With time, the war economy penetrates much of society, making most people dependent on it, hence also making it resistant to change. If a functioning government were to be established in Afghanistan, it would have to target the war economy. That is an extremely demanding task, yet one that is necessary to restore human dignity, to secure the government's survival and to rebuild Afghanistan's international relations. The problem is not easily addressed, but problem-solving gets easier with more substantial knowledge of how the war economy operates.

4. Technology shock

Afghanistan was, and most certainly is, one of the world's least developed countries, ranked 169 of 174 countries on the United Nations Development Programme's 1996 Human Development Index.[26] The war has led to the destruction of much of the country's infrastructure, including buildings, roads, electric-power supply and industrial installations. However, the war

---

[25] Barnett R. Rubin, *The Search for Peace in Afghanistan,* p. 97.
[26] UNDP (United Nations Development Programme), *Human Development Report 1996,* New York 1996.

has also introduced an extremely traditional society to a technological revolution, particularly in those sectors that were important for the war effort.

4.1. Weaponry

Probably the most significant technological change has been in military equipment. In pre-war Afghanistan, weapons were fairly common, but Lee Enfield rifles were the most advanced and even those were relatively rare. Remote valleys, whose inhabitants had barely been visiting their neighbouring valley and where wooden ploughs were still dominant, suddenly became exposed to modern military equipment like tanks, helicopters and even Stinger heat-seeking ground-to-air missiles.[27] More advanced weaponry increases the effectiveness of military formations: more people are killed in battle since a relatively small group can inflict large-scale damage. The link to the militarization of society is clear; indeed the militarization rests on access to advanced weaponry.

The new availability of arms is not only a political problem; it is also a criminal one. In Pakistan, there is great concern over the role that 'surplus arms' from the Afghanistan conflict play in both political and criminal violence in the country.[28] This concern also applies to Afghanistan, although its current chaotic situation makes it difficult to disentangle the effects. Undoubtedly, arms collection should be an integrated part of a settlement in Afghanistan. Further knowledge of the impact of weaponry would be an asset in the current situation, but it is even more important to come up with good ideas on how to bring about disarmament.

4.2. Media

The war has led to a media revolution in the country. Every family now has a transistor radio, the BBC news (in indigenous languages) being the favourite

---

[27] David C. Isby, *War in a Distant Country. Afghanistan: Invasion and Resistance*, London 1989, and Mark Urban, *War in Afghanistan*, 2nd ed., London 1990.
[28] Chris Smith, 'The Impact of Light Weapons on Security: A Case Study of South Asia', *SIPRI* [Stockholm International Peace Research Institute] *Yearbook 1995: Armaments, Disarmament and International Security*, Oxford 1995, pp. 583–593.

programme. There has also been an upsurge in the distribution of printed material, but more so in the refugee settlements abroad than in the countryside of Afghanistan. Newspapers and magazines have often been party publications and are propagandistic rather than informative in nature.[29] There are two effects of the media revolution. First, information on national and international politics has become widely available, leading to a different sense of being situated in the larger world. Second, the population is frequently exposed to political propaganda.[30] There are reasons to question the effectiveness of this propaganda; the priority given to the relatively neutral BBC is encouraging, as is the apparent loss of popular support for the political parties resulting from post-communist fighting. The media revolution is one of the most important war-induced changes, particularly because it has an inherent potential in the event of a political resolution process.

5. Migration

The conflict in Afghanistan since 1978 has led to the largest coerced movement of people in recent times, with about 5 million refugees in Iran and Pakistan and estimates of internally displaced persons ranging from 1 to 2 million.[31] Repatriation started after the Soviet withdrawal in 1989, but it became substantial only after the fall of the communist government in April 1992. By now, about half of the refugees have returned. The escalating conflict from 1994, particularly in Kabul, led to the displacement of up to half a million people, mostly within Afghanistan.[32]

---

[29] Paul Bucherer-Dietschi, 'Change and Continuity: Documentation for Action and History', in R. Amin (ed.), *Social and Cultural Prospects for Afghanistan,* WUFA Journal of Afghan Affairs, Special Issue, 5:4 (1990), and Jan-Heeren Grevemeyer, 'Anmerkungen zur Literatur der afghanischen Widerstandsbewegung', *Orient* 34:2 (1993), pp. 195–198.
[30] David Busby Edwards, 'Summoning Muslims: Print, Politics and Religious Ideology in Afghanistan', *The Journal of Asian Studies* 52:3 (1993), pp. 609–628.
[31] Michael Knowles, *Afghanistan: Trends and Prospects for Refugee Repatriation* (Refugee Policy Group), Washington DC 1992.
[32] USCR (U.S. Committee for Refugees), *World Refugee Survey* (Immigration and Refugee Services of America), Washington DC 1995, pp. 99–100.

5.1. Escape

Some research has been done on refugees who left in the 1980s, but the methods and conclusions were largely elementary. Most of these studies focused on what motivated flight.[33] The data sources are typically interviews with non-random samples of refugees, often several years after flight. Major reasons for escape emerge as being anti-Islamic government, fighting or bombing, threat of army conscription and belonging to a targeted group. Escalation in outflow is related to shifts in warfare. One of the studies touches on the interplay of coercive factors with attracting factors in the country of destination.[34] One feature of the Afghan refugee experience is the so-called 'refugee warrior' community; resistance groups established camps in exile where the families stayed while the men participated in the struggle across the border.[35] It is a puzzle that groups which were similarly situated in relation to all acknowledged refugee-driving factors still have enormous differences in flight rates. I believe that refugee studies suffer from focusing on either individual motivations or structural forces, while variations in escape rates are more likely to be understood by looking at relations between people, both within the primary group and between the potential refugee and people settled at the destination.

5.2. Exile

In exile, refugees have been exposed to societies different from their own in terms of belonging, culture as well as economic and technological development. Children up to mature age may never have seen their home country. Having had to live in dense settlements, often with people from a different part of the country, has led to changed living habits, as exemplified in a much stricter application of the female dress code. Many people are now well established in exile, with jobs or private enterprises, naturally

---

[33] Pierre Centlivres and Micheline Centlivres-Demont, *Afghanistan: Case Study* (UNCHR), Geneva 1992, Kerry M. Connor, 'Rationales for the Movement of Refugees to Peshawar', in G. M. Farr and J. G. Merrian (eds), *Afghan Resistance: The Politics of Survival*, Lahore 1988, pp. 151–190, and Aristide Zolberg, Astri Suhrke and Sergio Aguayo, *Escape from Violence: Conflict and the Refugee Crisis in the Developing World*, New York 1989, pp. 150–155.

[34] Pierre Centlivres and Micheline Centlivres-Demont, op. cit., p. 12.

[35] Aristide Zolberg et al., op. cit.

affecting the will to return.[36]

Exiled groups continue to be involved in politics. Soon after the communist coup of April 1978, the communists targeted political adversaries, particularly among the intelligentsia. A number of these people left before the Soviet invasion. With living conditions inside the country becoming increasingly difficult throughout the war, the bulk of the educated élite left the country. Many of them did not settle in neighbouring Pakistan or Iran but went on to Western countries. In fact, those who were politically active, but critical of the major resistance parties, were targeted also in their first country of exile. There are at least two important results of the intelligentsia's escape. First, the general 'brain drain' effect; it is by now a common saying that there are more Afghan medical doctors in Germany than there are in Afghanistan. The same goes for all other educated groups, with crucial competence for reconstruction and development being lost. Second, the exiles often appear to be less willing to compromise than people within the country. That is worrisome, because exiles appear to maintain substantial influence within Afghanistan, and so far they have also constituted a key resource for the U.N. in its attempts to mediate in the conflict, as well as in the transition administrations that the U.N. has proposed.

5.3. Return

The exile experience affects not only the willingness of refugees to return but also their adaptation if and when they return. In spite of the massive repatriation that has already taken place, particularly in the summer of 1992, we know next to nothing about how the experiences in foreign countries affected the process of resettlement in Afghanistan.

Refugees who repatriate may have stayed away for more than a decade. Their home communities have changed, and there is considerable room for dispute. A classical conflict issue is landownership. In some places radical political groups have simply redistributed large landholdings and destroyed all archives.[37] In other places internally displaced people have simply accommodated themselves on 'no-man's land'. Similarly, repatriation may

---

[36] Hanne Christensen and Wolf Scott, *Survey of the Social and Economic Conditions of the Afghan Refugees in Pakistan* (UNRISD [United Nations Research Institute for Social Development] Report no. 88:1), Geneva 1988.

[37] Michael Knowles, op. cit., p. 31.

be accompanied by conflicts over leadership. Some of the returnees belong to traditionally dominant families, while the new local leaders may have a totally different background. This is already a problem; in several areas traditional leadership has been re-established at the cost of wartime leadership.

Interesting ideas were presented by Bernt Glatzer in a comparative sketch of two regions where repatriation has been, respectively, massive and limited.[38] The author relates this difference to the maintenance of pre-war social structures in the area of origin, reflected in a low conflict level, hence good security. Further, he finds that return is facilitated by stability of pre-war social organization during the years in exile. Lastly, ties between people in the home and host areas seem crucial to repatriation. Glatzer's observations underline the need to focus on the role of interpersonal relations in flight and repatriation.

6. The international environment

This article has been focusing mainly on internal changes rather than external ones. This is to a large extent because the international dimension has received much more research attention than the internal one. It is also because I believe that the role of internal causes has been underestimated, and because any solution to the current crisis will have to be generated from within. It is important in itself to sensitize the Afghan and the international community to this simple fact. Nonetheless, I will sketch out a few themes relating to the international environment that I view as important to follow up.

6.1. International responsibility

The international responsibility for the Afghanistan war may seem obvious, not least when it comes to the Soviet engagement. Yet, as early as 1993, Russia refused any responsibility for the situation in Afghanistan, under the pretext of being a different state not liable for the actions of the former Soviet state. In recent years, new insights into the Soviet engagement have

---

[38] Bernt Glatzer, 'From Refugee to Resident: Effects of Aid on Repatriation', in E. Eide and T. Skaufjord (eds), *From Aid During Times of War to Aid for Reconstruction and Development*, Norwegian Afghanistan Committee, Peshawar 1992, pp. 161–170.

been gained; for example, it has become clear that the 1978 coup was indigenous and that the 1979 invasion was a very divided decision within the Soviet leadership.[39] A closer look at the U.S. role might be equally interesting. There are strong indications that dominant forces in the U.S. administration were motivated by the wish to let the Soviets 'bleed' in Afghanistan, confronting the cold-war adversary with relatively little risk for the USA. As a matter of fact, invitations to negotiate a settlement, first by Andropov in 1983, then by Gorbachev in 1985, were neglected by the Americans.[40] With an international settlement at this stage, things would have looked different; it was in 1985 that the USA stepped up its arms supplies, the same year that Soviet warfare intensified. There might well be a strong ethical case for a more extensive international engagement in solving the Afghan conflict, but this case is not easily made when serious investigative research is almost absent.[41]

6.2. *Regional actors*

A common denominator in policy-oriented articles on Afghanistan is the call for regional disengagement. The conflicting engagements by neighbouring countries are well established and have been an aspect of the Afghan war since its inception. Yet, it is much more difficult to establish the extent to which neighbouring states influence processes in any decisive manner.

The situation in Afghanistan demonstrates the conflicting interests of the states in the region. However, there have been attempts to build regional cooperative institutions, such as the Economic Cooperation Organization (ECO), with the membership of Turkey, Iran, Pakistan, Afghanistan and the new Central Asian states. Needless to say, ECO has not yet been very successful. However, strengthening regional security cooperation is as much

---

[39] G. M. Kornienko, 'The Afghan Endeavour: Perplexities of the Military Incursion and Withdrawal', *Journal of South Asian and Middle Eastern Studies* 17:2 (1994), pp. 2–17, and Odd Arne Westad, 'The Foreign Policy Archives of Russia'.

[40] Diego Cordovez and Selig S. Harrison, op. cit., and Barnett R. Rubin, *The Search for Peace in Afghanistan*.

[41] Recently, the argument for international responsibility has been emphatically made by Amnesty International (*Afghanistan: International Responsibility for Human Rights Disaster*, London 1995). However, the Amnesty report has a weak empirical base for its claims, actualizing the question about how to secure a better dialogue between researchers and policy-makers including international humanitarian organizations.

a normative project as a political and economic one, and with the near absence of debate on the issue, progress is not likely. It is important that major efforts are invested in exploring the resources for and constraints on enhancing regional cooperation, preferably by researchers within the region.[42]

When debating regional influence, it must also be emphasized that the borders are less clear-cut than in developed states with strong state capacities. For example, many of those living in the border areas of Pakistan/Afghanistan, and the nomads in particular, have never paid much attention to this division line, a fact that has also made the registration of refugees problematic. In a parallel vein, several of the movements might have political, financial and military backing from neighbouring countries, support not endorsed by the governments. A number of movements in Pakistan, Iran and the Gulf states have backed their preferred groups in Afghanistan, groups that they might regard as extensions of their own international movements, rather than as independent recipients in a foreign country. Much political analysis of foreign involvement fails to account for this, presupposing that each country involved has a consistent policy. Clearly, the opposite is true, but disentangling the dynamics of external support to the adversaries in Afghanistan is no simple task.

6.3. *International humanitarian aid*

While the international research interest in Afghanistan withered with the onset of war, a number of international humanitarian organizations became interested, ranging from the U.N. to small European solidarity initiatives set up exclusively for the Afghan cause. To begin with, aid was aimed solely at the refugees in Pakistan. Throughout the late 1980s, more and more agencies started to operate in Afghanistan, and from 1992 aid was intentionally redistributed to Afghanistan in order to encourage refugee return. Much of the aid was politically motivated, as when the United States redirected its aid programme to the Afghan Interim Government from 1989 in order to strengthen its legitimacy.[43] More recently, people in

---

[42] See Rahim M. Elham (ed.), *The Impact of Nascent Soviet Changes on Central Asia and the Region,* WUFA Journal of Afghan Affairs, Special Issue, 7:2 (1992), for a number of contributions by researchers from the region.

[43] This is interesting, given that the USA did not officially recognize this government, despite having been heavily involved in its establishment.

the aid community have become interested in the conflict-driving effects of aid and the potential to design aid projects in such a way as to foster conflict resolution rather than feed the fire.[44] Further investigation of the way aid interacts with conflict should be prioritized. Given the current situation in Afghanistan, it is much more realistic to build peace by starting out with local, small-scale undertakings than by continuing to concentrate on the top-level leadership, a strategy that has failed for more than a decade.

It has become a common assumption in the aid community that refugee aid 'clientelizes' its recipients, ultimately becoming in itself an obstacle to repatriation. The designed cutback in aid by international agencies, as well as the 'U.N. repatriation package' to encourage refugee return, have been based on this assumption. For many of the refugees, education and health services in exile were better than what they had been used to at home. On the other hand, the aid community itself should also be made subject to research. For example, the clientelization argument has an important function in legitimizing aid cuts and should be made subject to closer scrutiny.

As is familiar from other places, the establishment of international organizations has the effect of legitimizing domestic challenging forces. This has been particularly true in the past decade with ethnic discrimination becoming so prominent on the international agenda. The international presence helps to legitimize domestic challenging forces, whether based on religion or ethnicity.

7. Concluding remarks

If an effort to contribute to a long-term solution in Afghanistan is to succeed, one needs to acknowledge the limitations of research. In itself, research is not the answer; there is a need for a broader collaborative effort, engaging people involved in policy-making both at various levels and in different contexts. Their contributions are essential but can be secured only by an invitation to comment on the research agenda.

The erosion of Afghan academic capacity is a problem. Nonetheless, an

---

[44] See Mary B. Anderson, *Do No Harm: Supporting Local Capacities for Peace through Aid* (Collaborative for Development Action), Cambridge (Mass.) 1996. This general booklet is to be followed by a larger book, in which Afghanistan will constitute one of twelve case studies.

enhanced international engagement would need to pay attention to the need of training a new generation of Afghan academics, even though this would often mean starting at a relatively basic level. It is possible to find talented, committed people in Afghanistan who deserve to be given the opportunity. Nor should the possibility of bringing back exiled Afghan academics be ruled out. In any case, I am inclined to argue that unless one secures a comprehensive Afghan involvement, the whole exercise remains futile.

Biographical Notes on the Contributors

Per-Arne Berglie
Per-Arne Berglie is Professor of Comparative Religion at Stockholm University. He has done extensive fieldwork in South-East Asia and the eastern parts of Central Asia and has published works on Buddhism, Shamanism and the epic traditions of the Mongols.

Johan Elverskog
Johan Elverskog is a Ph.D. Candidate in the Department of Eurasian Studies at Indiana University. He has published articles on the early history of Buddhism in Inner Asia and most recently the book *Uygur Buddhist Literature.* Currently he is a Resident Fellow at the Interdisciplinary Humanities Center, University of California, Santa Barbara.

Joakim Enwall
Joakim Enwall has a Ph.D. in Sinology from the Institute of Oriental Languages, Stockholm University. His doctoral thesis was on the Miao written language. At present he is on leave from his research project on minority languages in Sinkiang serving as First Secretary for cultural and scholarly affairs at the Embassy of Sweden in Peking.

Vivan Franzén
Vivan Franzén is a Ph.D. Candidate of Linguistics at the University of Lund. She has been a research assistant in a project on the phonology and phonetics of Modern Mongolian. Her thesis work will be devoted to language typology applied to Rumanian.

Kristian Berg Harpviken
Kristian Berg Harpviken is a Ph.D. Candidate and Research Fellow at the Department of Sociology and Human Geography, Oslo University. His main research interests are political mobilization, migration, conflict solution and arms control, with the focus on Afghanistan and southern Africa. He was Project Coordinator and Director of the Norwegian Afghanistan Committee in Peshawar, 1990–1992 and a research fellow at the International Peace Research Institute, Oslo, 1995–1997.

Susanne Juhl
Susanne Juhl is a Ph.D. Candidate and Assistant Lecturer in Classical Chinese at the Department of East Asian Studies of the Aarhus University. She is at present engaged in historical and archaeological research on Northwest China and Central Asia in the Early Mediaeval Period.

BIOGRAPHICAL NOTES ON THE CONTRIBUTORS

Mirja Juntunen
Mirja Juntunen is a Ph.D. Candidate of Indology as well as lecturer of Sanskrit and Hindi and editor-in-chief of publications at the Institute of Oriental Languages, Stockholm. Her Ph.D. work has been devoted to the textual and cartographical sources of the town plan of Jaipur. With insights in language development and sociolinguistic processes in India acquired through repeated field trips, especially to the northern parts of the country, she is now conducting research on writing systems of Indian origin in Central Asia.

Marianne Øhlers
Marianne Øhlers has an M.A. in Social Sciences and History from the universities of Roskilde and Copenhagen. During the last few years she has focused her research on nation-building and potential ethnic conflicts in Kazakstan. During the autumn term of 1993 Marianne Øhlers was a guest student at the Kazak Academy of Science in Almaty, and in the spring of 1995 she carried out fieldwork in Kazakstan.

Bo Petersson
Bo Petersson has a Ph.D. in Political Science and is at present a lecturer at the Lund University. He was formerly a research fellow at the Institute of Eastern European Studies, Uppsala, and he has had an appointment at the Swedish Ministry of Foreign Affairs. Bo Petersson has published works on Russia and post-Soviet Central Asia.

Staffan Rosén
Staffan Rosén is Professor of Korean at the Institute of Oriental Languages of the Stockholm University. He is at present engaged in a research project on the role of Korea in the Silk Road system, and he is the editor of a series of books on *Manuscripts and Block Prints from Central Asia in the Sven Hedin Collection* to be published by the Sven Hedin Foundation.

Birgit N. Schlyter
Birgit N. Schlyter is Associate Professor and Head of Forum for Central Asian Studies at the Stockholm University. She is a lecturer of Turkish, Uzbek and Central Asian Linguistics. Previously she has published works on modern Turkish and is at present conducting research on language development and language policies in the Central Asian region. Dr. Schlyter is a member of the board of the European Society for Central Asian Studies (ESCAS) as well as board member and editor-in-chief at the Swedish Research Institute in Istanbul.

BIOGRAPHICAL NOTES ON THE CONTRIBUTORS

John Schoeberlein
John Schoeberlein received his Ph.D. in Social Anthropology from Harvard University. He is Director of the Harvard University Forum for Central Asian Studies, which he was instrumental in founding in 1993. His research focuses on questions of identity and community organization among the Islamic peoples of Central Asia and neighbouring regions.

Jan-Olof Svantesson
Jan-Olof Svantesson is Associate Professor of Linguistics at the Lund University, where he is responsible for a research project on Mongolian phonology and phonetics and another project on language typology.

Maria Magdolna Tatár
Maria Magdolna Tatár is a lecturer of Mongolian at the Institute of East European and Oriental Studies of Oslo University. She has carried out extensive fieldwork in Mongolia and published a large number of papers on language, religion and culture in this Turko-Mongolic part of the Central Asian region.